Benjamin Fish Austin

The Methodist Episcopal Church Pulpit

A Volume of Sermons. Vol. 1

Benjamin Fish Austin

The Methodist Episcopal Church Pulpit
A Volume of Sermons. Vol. 1

ISBN/EAN: 9783337085896

Printed in Europe, USA, Canada, Australia, Japan

Cover: Foto ©Lupo / pixelio.de

More available books at **www.hansebooks.com**

REV. ALBERT CARMAN, D.D.,

Bishop of the M. E. Church in Canada.

REV. J. R. JAQUES, D.D., PH. D.

President of Albert University, Belleville, Ont.

THE
Methodist Episcopal Church Pulpit;

A VOLUME OF SERMONS,

BY THE MEMBERS OF THE

NIAGARA, ONTARIO, AND BAY QUINTÉ

CONFERENCES

OF THE

M. E. CHURCH IN CANADA.

VOLUME I.

EDITED BY THE

REV. B. F. AUSTIN, B.A.

TORONTO:
HUNTER, ROSE AND COMPANY.
MDCCCLXXIX.

Entered according to Act of the Parliament of Canada, in the year one thousand eight hundred and seventy-nine, by Rev. B. F. AUSTIN, B.A., in the office of the Minister of Agriculture.

PRINTED AND BOUND
BY
HUNTER, ROSE & CO.,

PREFACE.

NO book is esteemed orthodox without an introduction. Hence painful as the work of preparing one may be to the writer, and tedious as its reading may appear to the reader, the task is generally heroically performed by each as a part of that tacit and almost universal obedience men yield to custom. Most preface writers feel it incumbent upon them to introduce their works in a tone of apology. Accordingly, the average preface begins with an argument carefully elaborated to prove that the work it introduces is one absolutely needed by the public—that its place in the temple of literature is either unfilled or unworthily filled—and then ends with a meek apology to its readers for troubling them and the world with so tame and imperfect a production.

If any apology be needed for the publication of the present volume of sermons it will be amply sufficient to recall the commission of the men whose productions grace its pages :—" Go ye into all the world and preach the Gospel unto every creature." Is there any limitation here expressed or implied to the *viva voce* method of preaching ? The primitive Gospel preacher was a herald of glad tidings, and though limited in his methods by the necessities of his age, there can be no reasonable doubt that, had he possessed the multiplied discoveries of the present day, he would have utilized the printing press and all useful inventions in the promulgation of Gospel truth as quite in keeping with the terms of his commission. The burning zeal of Paul, and the whole-souled earnestness of Peter would have captured and utilized every invention of their age for reaching the public mind and heart with the saving truths of the Gospel. Why should an apology be made for a published any more than a spoken sermon ?

The men whose productions are here introduced to the reader are men called of God and set apart by the Church for the proclamation of Gospel Truth. They are, without exception, men who have made themselves heard and felt in this country and in the church of their choice. A part of these discourses are given *verbatim* as delivered by their respective preachers on various occasions. The rest were written amidst press of ministerial or official duties, and if the critical reader should here and there discover traces of hurried preparation, this fact must be a sufficient excuse. All the sermons are furnished by request, and the writer regrets that press of business and illness prevented four other ministers, who were invited to contribute a sermon each, from complying. As to the origin of the book, a single word is sufficient. It has long been felt that a volume similar to the present, giving the sermons of some of the representative men of the various Conferences, would be hailed with great interest by the M. E. Church membership and ministry, that such a volume would tend to raise the tone of pulpit effort, that it would form a small yet worthy contribution to the native literature of that body, that it would be treasured as a lasting memento by the admiring friends and spiritual children of the men whose names it bore long after their voices were hushed in the stillness of the grave. Accordingly a Committee of Publication was formed and a proposal made through the *C. C. Advocate* asking for a guaranteed sale sufficient to meet the cost of publication, and promising a donation of all the profits of the enterprise to the benevolent funds of the Church. The proposal failing, the writer as a member of the original Committee, concluded to go on with the publication upon his own responsibility, and upon promises of co-operation in the sale of the work, has already pledged nearly five hundred dollars toward the various enterprises of the Church.

The reader of this volume will find a pleasing variety in subjects and style of treatment, and can scarcely fail to happen upon some discourse suited to his peculiar taste or spiritual condition. If he believes with a modern author that "the history of the world is fast losing itself in the history of the Christian Church," and that the world's hope is somehow bound up in the destiny of the "stone cut out of the mountain without hands," he cannot fail to be interested in the clear and convincing exposition of "The Church of God." If he is striving to learn the one secret source of strength and nobility in human character, he will find it in "Strength through Faith." If the eyes of his understanding have been opened to perceive spiritual things, he will survey with unmingled satisfaction "The Wealth of True Believers." The revelation of God's character given by "The Later Prophet" must enrich the mind and heart of every reader. If any doubt should exist in the reader's mind as to the nature of scriptural confession, he will find a clear and convincing statement of that doctrine in "The Confession of Sin."

If the dreaded sleep of the Enchanted Ground of which the immortal Dreamer speaks, should have overcome any of the pilgrim readers of this book, the sermon on "Self-Examination" will quicken their steps toward the celestial City.

PREFACE.

All Christians will study with profit the elements of "Genuine Church Prosperity," and linger with mournful pleasure in contemplation of "Calvary" and rejoice in "Certainty in Christ and Christianity." The careless sinner will find in the sermons on "The Profit of Godliness" and "Sinners Admonished," thoughts worthy of deep consideration and admonitions worthy of acceptance. The earnest Christian will find the only true source of spiritual enjoyment and abundant usefulness in "Abiding in Christ," and be inspired to a lofty type of Christian life by "Paul's Experience and Prospects." All ministerial readers will be specially and profitably interested in "The Gospel Ministry" and in "Winning Souls." The student of "the Central doctrine of the Christian system" will find rich thought upon his favourite theme in the sermons on "The Atonement" and "Man and the Daysman." All lovers of clear and cogent argument will delight in the wholesale demolition of sceptical objections which is contained in the sermon on "David's Choice." Whether the reader has been in the habit of rendering to God the praise due to His name or not, he will be led by reading the "Praise of God" to admit that "it is a good thing to give thanks unto the Lord." If the dark clouds of trouble and sorrow have thrown their shadows over any reader's pathway, "Divine Companionship" will cast a cheerful ray amid the gloom, and afford real consolation to the pilgrim passing "through the valley of the shadow of death."

A clear and faithful presentation of "Salvation by Grace" through faith — the summary of apostolic preaching and the distinctive doctrine of the Reformation—appropriately closes the volume.

If the present volume meets sufficient encouragement, a second will be issued early in 1880.

B. F. AUSTIN.

PRESCOTT, May 1st, 1879.

THE METHODIST EPISCOPAL CHURCH PULPIT.

THE CHURCH OF GOD.

By Rev. Albert Carman, D.D.,
Bishop of the M. E. Church in Canada.

"These things write I unto thee, hoping to come unto thee shortly: but if I tarry long that thou mayest know how thou oughtest to behave thyself in the House of God, which is the Church of the Living God, the Pillar and Ground of the Truth."—1st Tim. iii., 14, 15.

ONE of the main difficulties we have in promoting the welfare of man on earth is in keeping societies and organizations to their central ideas. Every society has a central idea; and for the most part the central ideas of our societies and organizations partake of the character of goodness and benevolence. For, bad as men are, there are not many that associate for what is acknowledged among themselves as wrong, and crime, and sin. The greatest transgressors attempt to cast over their deeds some coloring of virtue, and to justify to themselves, at least, the violence and harm of their acts. Men do not combine to murder for the pleasure of murdering, or to steal for the sake of stealing, but they steal and murder for some ulterior end; anything, they say, to get their bread, to seize on wealth, or to repress or overthrow some opposing power. In Holy Scripture it is set down as the last depth of depravity and apostasy when men not only do wrong but take pleasure in them that do it. Surely they are far gone and diabolical when they glory in profanity and obscenity, for the violence and the vileness thereof; and when they gloat over murder and rapine, and find their chief pleasure in the murderer and the robber. Here is a frightful ruin, such a rioting companionship of evil doers—this is hell itself.

But, ordinarily, it is not so with human organizations. The prompting is to do good and get good, and men associate with this aim. In fact, this is the only safe and lasting basis of association. Sin segregates, separates, disintegrates. Its envies, jealousies, ambitions, lusts, prides, violences, guilts, suspicions, accusations, slanders and recriminations, must rend intelligent beings asunder, and snap the ties that hold us in comfort and peace. There can be there no confidence, tender affection, respect and love—society's mild and mighty bonds. Yet Christianity does not leave us so far alienated that we wish one another no good. It is a uniting, organizing energy, and under its impulses we associate for mutual benefit. We feel and acknowledge the brotherhood of man, and seek its blessings. But sin pushes in its diverting and disintegrating forces, and herein arises our trouble. Who will say, in the present constitution of things, it is not well to have Temperance Societies? And yet what true friend of temperance has not mourned in seeing Temperance Associations converted into Glee Clubs and Dancing Schools? "Rescue the Perishing" is the grand central idea. Yet hundreds associate in the organization so named that never once feel the noble impulse or do the brotherly act. Is it any wonder that it is well nigh impracticable to keep to the central idea; that, notwithstanding the devotion of the few self-denying and courageous labourers, the institution gradually slides off into a debating school or a focus of social entertainments? Oddfellowship or Masonic fraternity may have a good central life. The cultivation and direction of beneficence, brotherly sympathy, and certain mutual aid, are noble objects; but it is sad to see good fellowship degenerate into dissipation and extravagance. The defence of Protestants and the maintenance of their principles are aims worthy of the association of the noblest minds; but it is grievous to see Orange Lodges mere partisan clubs, formed and kept together to serve the party purposes of some political leader. And so throughout the range of human association. A society starts well enough, is a necessity of its times and circumstances; but likely, before long, designing men will find means to subvert its principles, pervert its energies, or divert its influence and power to their own ends.

Can it, then, be wondered at that in this same world, among these same men, with the same affections and desires, the Church of God should share, to some extent at least, the same disaster, and encounter the same difficulties in the prosecution of its work? Can it be a matter of surprise that proud, ambitious, revengeful, covetous, crafty, selfish men, sometimes creeping in unawares, should do their utmost to employ even the Church of the Blessed Christ for their own base purposes—to use even this institution of the Lord God, Almighty, for their personal ends? And how often alas! we find it even so. To many a merchant the Church is a good place to get customers; to the candidate in elections it is a good place to get votes; to the stylish it is a good place for display, and to the curious a good place to see and hear; to the sociable, it is a pleasant place to meet a friend ; to the young man it affords the best opportunity to obtain a wife ; to the young woman, a husband. And so men weigh and estimate the Church of God. To them it is worth just as much as the chance it affords for the gratification of some desire of the flesh or the mind. If it will do that, it is of some use, worthy of some attention ; if not that, then none whatever. Men flip the Church, the Church which Jesus purchased with His own blood, at their finger's ends, and toss it over their shoulders as of no account to them; they have no obligation to the Church of God. They are not members of the Church. They are nothing to the Church ; the Church is nothing to them. It is nothing to them, except it can be used for their selfish ends. Now we do not say that the Church of the living God, in its visible organizations is not a good place to get votes or to obtain customers ; we do not say it is not a good place for the young man to seek a wife, or the young woman to be found of him that becometh a husband. Were I a tradesman or a merchant, I would rather have the custom of Christian men than of any other under these heavens. Were I a politician, I would rather have the votes of Christian men than of any other in the land. With them I would rather be in the minority, than with the roughs, the godless and infidels, the blasphemous, drunken and vicious, in the majority. Elected to stay at home, I should call my election won, when the people of God, the sober and virtuous were my supporters, rather than elected to serve the rowdies of the land, and ultimately the wreckers of the State. Were I seeking a wife, where should I rather go, than among the devoted women in the House of the Lord? Yea, in the House of the Lord, and among the people of God, find I my portion, the full supply of all my temporal wants. The Church of God in covenant provides all that, and much more. But, alas, alas! for the man that can see nought but his temporal necessity, or feel nought but his vain desire; and then can imagine that the Church of Christ is to be the sport of his fancies or the tool of his machinations.

There is likely no subject of human thought, there is certainly none so often spoken of, concerning which there are so many misapprehensions, so varied and untenable views, as concerning the Church of Christ. Whether from the blindness of the mind through sin, from insufficient examination, from the multiform prejudices of education, or from the conceits of self-righteousness, nearly every man that claims to have given the matter any attention, has his own theory upon it—making the Church of God this kind of organization or that, or none at all, likely to tally with the mould of his opinion, or the manner of his life. The sincere inquirer upon this subject will, of course, go to the Word of God and be governed by it. There is scarcely any other source of information, and this is certainly the ultimate Court of Appeal. God alone can tell us the origin, nature, and end of His Church. We may imagine, speculate, and build; but all our theories and plans must stand or fall by the Inspired Word, and upon this subject the Bible is explicit. We need not be lost amid doubts and uncertainties. The Holy Spirit instructs us as to the character of the building of God, and enables us to clear away the misconceptions of men as well as to ascertain the idea of the Lord Jehovah, the central idea of the Church: and our first business is with the misconceptions of men. It is important to clear them away. We shall show, therefore, what the Church is *not*, though so thought to be by many men; and, in the second place, what the Church of God is, as portrayed in the Word of God.

In the first place, then, the Church of God is not a *voluntary human organization*. No two men, or two hundred, or two millions, ever came together, and personally, or by deputies, organized the Church of God. No man, no set of men, ever adopted its constitution, or established its laws. It arose not by the will or wisdom of man, but by the will, wisdom, and power of God. Its foundations are in eternity—in the nature, covenants, and decrees of the Eternal God; its constitution is His Revealed Will and Word; its laws are the utterances of His mouth. Men may, at their pleasure, organize a Temperance Society, a Masonic, or an Orange Lodge; they may prescribe, change, or annul the conditions of membership; they may institute or annihilate at will. But not so with the Church of the Living God. They cannot alter its conditions of membership one jot or tittle. They can add nothing to its constitution and laws; they cannot take the least thing away. No Pope, Council, Conference or Synod can interfere here. Be it remembered, we are speaking of the Church of God: not of the Church of England or the Church of Rome; not of the Church of the Presbyterians, or the Church of the Methodists. We speak of the Church of God, the Church of Christ; that Church to which a man must belong to be saved, to enter heaven. It is the kingdom of God, the kingdom of heaven. The Lord God, Sovereign Ruler, with authority indisputably supreme prescribes, and commands; it is ours to accept and obey. And we may well rejoice this is so. No pope or king, or council or cabinet, can interfere with the terms of human salvation. Our membership in the Church of Christ is between our souls and ourselves on the one hand, and the Living God on the other. God in Christ presents the terms of salvation; we, through Christ, accept, and so become members of His living body. The provisions and terms are of God; ours is acceptance or rejection. Accepting, we are saved; we are members of the Church; which is not founded or perpetuated by the will or ordinance of man, but by the mind and will of God. It is not a *voluntary* human organization.

Nor, on the other hand, is it a *compulsory* human institution. It is of no civil or political origin. No king, or court, or council, decreed or established it. It does not subsist by Act of Congress or Parliament. In this land we have fully learned this truth, and realize and practice it. Forever have we decreed the separation of Church and State; the extinction or the subordination of neither, but their political and ecclesiastical separation; and hence the independence freedom, purity, safety, and efficiency of both. And this decree of the outer and legal separation, is but the recognition of their nearer and mutual interdependence. Because I am a Christian man my civil obligations are not the less, nor, even because I am of the clergy, a Christian minister. Let the same laws govern me and the same courts try me. If I cheat, handle me as another man; if I murder, let me be hanged as any fellow in crime. We have no clerical tribunals with easy verdicts and special favors for clergymen, as was insisted upon in the days of priestly domination; nor, on the other hand, do we allow civil disabilities to be imposed upon men because they are Christians and clergymen. A free Church in a free State is the motto of this land adopted by our fathers, the glory by them achieved; and may it ever so remain. For it is in this happy relationship alone that the State in its political arrangements and measures feels the spiritual energy of the Church ; and that the Church, the Christian people, in their enterprises, and their rights of conscience and worship, enjoy the watchful care of the State This gives truth a fair field. Mighty, it must prevail, in its own intrinsic might, without Pope or King. In a true liberty, under the true light, philosophic error and religious heresy dig their own graves : putrefactions, they lie side by side in the charnel house of history, curiosities of an age when an Emperor must kiss a Pope's toe, or when a maddened people, making common havoc of tribunal, altar, and throne, cut down the symbols of godly reverence and religious worship, impersonate human pride, tyranny and ambition, and then enthrone the monster, and call it Reason. So the Church of Christ was not founded by the State, nor is it corporately, in any sense to be controlled by it. No King or Parliament gave it its charter, or enacted its laws. Nor has king or parliament any right to touch its fundamental principles and institutes, to add a jot to its constitutions or statutes, or to take a tittle from them. They are the ordinances of Heaven, the laws of the Great God to the sons of men. They are the enactments of the sovereign authority of the universe, the appointment of Him by whom kings rule and princes decree justice. They are the statutes that kings themselves must regard and parliaments obey. The King of kings and Lord of lords hath established the terms on which men are to enter His Church, become the subjects of His sway and kingdom, enjoy the provisions of His mercy and grace ; and herein is a sphere that no earthly potentate or authority can invade. Which thing is the everlasting and inviolable safety of the people of God. Which thing is their perpetual shield and defence. Whence also we can understand when men are oppressed for the truth's sake, what is meant by their appeal to a higher law. Whence also we can see how an Elijah rebukes Ahab ; how Daniel conquers Darius and his lions ; how Shadrach, Meshach and Abednego could defy Nebuchadnezzar and his sevenfold hot furnaces ; and how Peter and John, in the face of the gnashing Sanhedrim, could maintain, "Whether it be right in the sight of God to hearken unto you more than unto God, judge ye, for we cannot but speak the things which we have seen and heard." It was the clear apprehension of this sublime truth that the King of kings is the Head of all authority and power, and mightier than the combination of princes, that strengthened Luther to stand unmoved at Worms, Ridley and Latimer amid the persecutions of Mary of England, and Knox before the opposition of Mary of Scotland. The Church of God, verily, is not the creation of human kings, nor is its defence the armies of the terrible and the mighty.

Nor, again, is the Church of the living God a development, a secondary organization, the outgrowth of some preceding institution. In social and civil affairs we have such secondary or developed organizations—for example, our parliamentary system, our trial by jury, our banking and postal arrangements. These are things of development and growth. They spring out of simpler antecedent economies, and improve as to their doctrines and practices as the centuries roll on. The venerable Saxon Witanagemote and the solid central throne of William the Norman took nearly a millenium to coalesce into the Constitutional Parliament and Responsible Government of these times ! Through a hundred phases our courts have assumed their present form, and yet we change their procedure and jurisdiction from year to year. Our parliaments and courts, and even our denominational peculiarities are derived economies. But the Church of Christ is not an economy or an institution derived from any other. Of institutions it acknowledges no parent or antecedent of which it is the offspring or the offshoot. It is the immediate plantation, so far as men are concerned, the original structure of Almighty God. "Ye are God's husbandry: ye are God's building." God and the first pair driven from Eden, with Christ in promise and prospect, made a Church, the house of the Lord. In the call of the Abrahamic family it took organic form in human sight. Its principles were the same, its privileges the same, and its obligations the same as govern and beautify the house of the Lord to-day. There were the same essentials to salvation, the same holy joys in its possession, and the same inspiring hopes in its beatific visions. It has been justification by faith, faith proved by works, works rewarded in glory from the beginning. There is nothing new in genuine religion. We are to seek out the old paths and continue in them. Repentance toward God, and faith toward our Lord Jesus Christ, is the gospel for all ages. Novelties or improvements in the constitution or laws of the Church of Christ are errors. In science, in politics, and in arts, there are properly and necessarily improvements. Increasing knowledge brings changes, inversions, and revolutions. Old theories are modified or exploded, and new ones take their place. But the Church, as to her doctrines and aims, remains unchanged. God gave her light and her law at the start. It is yet the old story. "Abraham believed God, and it was counted unto him for righteousness." Yet, as to Abel, and Enoch, and David, and Daniel, it is the covenanting faith, that begins in repentance and is perfected in holy living. The Church is not an outgrowth, a result of education, a creature of temporal circumstances; not a development of any combination of social or civil forces; but it is a primitive and positive institution of the living God.

Nor is the Church of Christ a mere ecclesiastical arrangement held together by external clamps and priestly appointments—an invention of haughty and ambitious men, a scheme of ceremonial distinctions and lofty pretensions, an earth-born aristocracy with a hell-born pride. It is not a body of men aggregated by external forces, by hereditary descent, prejudice, education, or popular sentiment, and fastened together by outside bands, and straps, and chains, after the manner of arbitrary ordinances and hierarchical impositions. The Church of God, the Church of God, the Church of God are we, cry many. "Stand aside, for I am holier than thou," is the utterance of some people that have parcelled themselves out snugly, and elected themselves complacently to be the Church of God. Alas, what a strife of tongues has this spirit engendered among even Christians, so called! What a by-word and hissing, what a scorn and derision has it made the Church in the world! To hear some talk, you would imagine that the great God had given their small portion of His people, if indeed His they be, a monopoly of the divine blessings for our human race. You would think that the infinite ocean of divine love and mercy could reach us only through their beautiful little tubes. In their hands are all the fixtures and the connections. You must have their ordinances, and must have them administered by their pastorate or priesthood, pompously and blasphemously so styled, in order to be saved. And so the Church is to them a petty, close corporation, under human direction, able, by certain rites, to admit any one to eternal felicity; by denying these certain rites to any one to cast him out into eternal wretchedness. What wonder that men of sense and courage burst the bonds of such a superstition, and repudiate so groundless claims! What wonder that unthinking multitudes, men of superficial mind, or even men of profound mind, that give no definite or persistent attention to those subjects, rush to the conclusion, that the Church has no authority, no divine organization or sanction, no claim on their heart, life or obedience; that there is no Church, that what is so called is only a scheme of designing and selfish men for sinister and selfish ends! Under the impulse of a wicked heart, it does not take such men long to say, "There is no religion: there is no God." It does not take them long to say that priestly assumption, tyranny and profligacy, perfectly antipodal as they are to Christ's humility, purity and love, justify the blankest infidelity and most hideous vice. But all this is frightful misapprehension, and willing blindness and sin. They ought to see that if the vine bears vile grapes there is a life in it that can be made to produce generous clusters. They ought to see through pompous assumptions and external bonds to hidden energies and inner spirit and power. Many of them claim to be philosophers, and that is the work of a genuine philosophy. These outer ceremonies and hierarchical foundations and limitations neither bound nor constitute the Church of God. It is not the creation of crowned and sceptred pope, or mitred bishop, or hooded monk, or gowned ecclesiastic, or sprinkling priest, or immersing minister. It is not a thing of outer bond and fastening, of ceremonial and ritual, of mere order and ordinance. What it is the Bible tells us, and we shall see.

Again there are, even bearing the Christian name, that, because they apprehend clearly the hollowness of the pretence that the Church of God is a matter of ceremonial, of apostolical succession and hierarchical order, are disposed to affirm that the Church of Christ has no organization whatever, no bond of cement or union; that every man is a church unto himself; the Church, so called, is a heap of sand, every member a separate and independent particle, without any laws of succession, co-operation, ordination or subordination; that all have equal rights to the same offices, equal duties in any sphere where personal inclination may call them to live and labour, equal authority in deciding and declaring what doctrines are biblical and according to the mind of the Eternal Spirit, and equal claim to the deference and support of the disciples of Christ. There is no divinely called and qualified ministry of God with their claims upon the people; no co-operation and connexional pastorate with their guardianship of one another, and their accountability to one another, for their manner of life and the compliance of their teaching with the Word of God. There are no flocks with their shepherds, no churches with their ministers, no people with their appointed and responsible instructors. There needs no understanding for missionary enterprise and for schools; no body must direct and appoint that the Gospel be spread abroad. Nobody is called to rule, because no one is willing to obey. If a man were forced to choose between such a segregation, anarchy, confusion and irresponsibleness as this, on the one hand, and papal domination and assumption on the other, verily the latter were a thousand times preferable. There is no tyranny like that of a mob; there is no disorder like that in which every one makes his own law, frames his own doctrine, and acts his own pleasure. Better the majestic organization of Rome, with all its corruptions, than the rout and rabble of church-wrecking Plymouth Brethrenism, with its more terrific disasters. But, thank God, we are not compelled to choose between these rigid external organizers on the one hand, and these repudiators of all organization and order on the other. The Church of God is neither an immense reservoir, hooped, riveted and chained together, into which the multitudes are to be driven and "sacramented" to glory; nor is it a heap of sand, drifting and unsettled particles, to be driven here and there by every wind and wave. Our appeal is to the Bible, the Word of God. The Church of God is an organism, a living organism, with parts and their offices, members and their functions; distinct constituents, with distinct duties and positive responsibilities, and yet a united, symmetrical, beautiful, and glorious whole, perfect in its harmony and grace, radiant in its splendours, and irresistible in its power.

If we would know the true nature and character of the Church of God, we must learn the mind of God, its great Founder and Architect, concerning it. And if we would learn this mind of God, we must look into the written Word. Here we shall find the divine representations regarding it. Christ himself speaks of His Church under this instructive figure, "I am the true vine, my Father is the husbandman. Abide in me and I in you. As the branch cannot bear fruit of itself except it abide in the vine, no more can ye except ye abide in me. I am the vine; ye are the branches. He that abides in me and I in him the same bringeth forth much fruit. For without me ye can do nothing." Where is there organization if not here? Where order, law, succession, if not in the vine, in its growth, spread and fruitage? Paul the Apostle represents the Church of God under another figure, which figure he handles as a fact: "For as the body is one and hath many members, and all the members of that one body, being many, are one body; so also is Christ. For by one spirit are we all baptised into one body, whether we be Jews or Gentiles, whether we be bond or free; and have been all made to drink into one spirit. For the body is not one member, but many. If the foot shall say, because I am not the hand, I am not of the body, is it therefore not of the body? . . . But now are they many members, yet but one body. . . . Ye are the the body of Christ and members in particular." . . And He is before all things and by Him all things consist. And He is the head of the body, the Church : who is the beginning, the first-born from the dead; that in all things he might have the pre-eminence." "And given Him to be the Head over all things to the Church, which is His body, the fulness of Him that filleth all in all." "There is one body and one spirit even as ye are called in one hope of your calling; one Lord, one faith, one baptism; one God and Father of all who is above all, and through all, and in you all. . . And He gave some apostles, and some prophets, and some evangelists, and some pastors and teachers; for the perfecting of the Saints, for the work of the ministry, for the edifying of the body of Christ: till we all come in the unity of the faith and of the knowledge of the Son of God unto a perfect man, unto the measure of the stature of the fulness of Christ. . . Speaking the truth in love may grow up in Him in all things which is the Head even Christ; from whom the whole body fitly joined together, and compacted by that which every joint supplieth, according to the effectual working in the measure of every part, maketh increase of the body unto the edifying of itself in love." Who will say that in all these passages the Holy Spirit did not teach, and Paul did not believe, that in the Church of Christ there is unity, symmetry, beauty, order, law of growth, succession, energy, power? Who dares say the Church of God is without organization, rule, authority; that it is a heap of sand, a promiscuous aggregation of particles, an agglomeration of ill-jointed and perfectly co-ordinate pieces and portions, each supreme in itself, and coming together for accommodation; no one to direct and no one to obey, no principle of government and no spirit of obedience? If men will reject the high assumptions that the Church of God is a papal hierarchy or priestly consolidation and tyranny, held together by civil force or ecclesiastical ordinance, by the external bands and chains of canon and decrees of councils, of ritual, Sacrament and ceremony, let them not fly to the opposite extreme of repudiating the unity, symmetry, and beauty of the Church of Christ, its laws and rules of order, its succession and principles of growth, its authorities and governments, its subjects and obedience, its members of greater and less importance and comeliness, and yet the adaptation and indispensableness of each to all and all to each. The Church is the body and Christ the head; the members of the Church are the branches and Christ the vine. Where find we unity, grace, strength, loveliness, if not in the fruitful vine or healthful human body? These are living organisms, not forced together and held together from without, but growing up from within. The internal life-force is their bond and cement of union. It is the life-force that gathers in the material of growth, assimilates it and holds it together. And to this the Apostle plainly refers in passages already quoted: "Speaking the truth *in love* may grow up into Him in all things which is the head even Christ." "Maketh increase of the body unto the edifying of itself *in love*." "If a man love me," said Christ, " he will keep my words, and my Father will love him, and we will come unto him and make our abode with him." Under the inspiration of this idea of the love-united body of Christ. Charles Wesley writes :—

> "Hence may all our actions flow,
> Love the proof that Christ we know;
> Mutual love the token be,
> Lord, that we belong to Thee;
> Love, Thine image, love impart,
> Stamp it now on every heart;
> Only love to us be given,
> Lord, we ask no other heaven."

Under still another representation both the Apostle to the Jews and the Apostle to the Gentiles enforce the doctrine that the Church is a living organism, a spiritual temple, perfect in its unity, symmetry, beauty, perpetuity, security, and glory. "The Lord is gracious," says Peter, "to whom coming as unto a living stone, disallowed indeed of men, but chosen of God and precious, ye also as lively stones are built up a spiritual house, a holy priesthood, to offer up spiritual sacrifices acceptable to God by Jesus Christ. . . . . Unto you therefore who believe He is precious." To the same effect Paul declares to the Corinthians: "Ye are God's husbandry; ye are God's building." "Know ye not that ye are the temple of the Holy Ghost?" and to the Ephesians, "Now therefore ye are no more strangers and foreigners, but fellow citizens with the saints and of the household of God, and are built upon the foundation of the apostles and prophets, Jesus Christ himself being the Chief Corner Stone; in whom all the building fitly framed together groweth unto an holy temple in the Lord, in whom ye also are builded together for a habitation of God through the Spirit." What more direct language could be employed to display the divine idea that the Church is by no means a heterogeneous mixture, but a homogeneous structure, a

B

spiritual organization, a living organism; a body, a vine, a living temple, of divers parts, branches, members, each in its place and for its office, and yet combined into one harmonious whole? What plainer instructions could be given as to the life principles of this organism, the bands of the body, the cement of the temple, believing, loving, obeying; so united to Christ and to one another?

It will be observed that all along we have not spoken of the Methodist Church, or the Presbyterian Church, or the Roman Catholic, or the Anglican Church, but of the Church of the living God, that Church to which every man must belong in order to be saved. Out of this Church of God, the Church of Christ, no human being ever has been saved, can be saved, or will be saved. If any one could establish, as some claim, that the Roman Church, or the Anglican Church, is exclusively the Church of God, holding and exercising alone to itself all the high prerogatives and powers of the Church of God, he might well justify to himself and to the world the vain assumption that salvation for men is to be found within the pale of his communion alone. When men declare that their organization is wholly and exclusively the Church of God, it is only logical that they rush on to the conclusions that their ceremonies alone convey the saving efficacy of divine grace, and that they themselves sit in the seat of God, and exercise His kingly prerogative to pardon sin and exalt to glory. There can be no question, since the vital principles of true Church life are faith, love and obedience, a justification begun and perpetuated, that there are members of the Church of God in all the so-called Churches of earth, the denominations of Christians that hold the truth; and for the same reason there can be as little question that there are members of all the human organizations that are by no means members of the Church of God. In this Church of God alone, this spiritual body of Christ, is salvation from sin, death, and hell found. But let it be borne in mind that every human being born upon earth is *once* a member of the Church of God. Are you, dear hearer, now a member of the Church of Christ? Are you justified, saved? You are, unless you have revolted from God, rejected Christ, chosen self and sin, preferred darkness to light, because your tendencies and deeds are evil. You were once saved. Every man is saved once at least. Let us try our theology. We believe, had we died in infancy, we would have been saved. We believe that all that die in infancy are saved. Any other view would dishonour Christ. They are His in the covenant of universal redemption. Infants were made members of the Jewish Church, the ancient visible Church of God. And most Christians believe that, under covenant obligations, they by baptism, are admitted into the Christian Church, the visible body of Christ, being thereto entitled because they are in a justified relation to God, being the purchase of His blood, and till revolt and voluntary separation, members of His invisible body. No question, every human being is once justified, and so far saved; justified that on the divine sovereign act, he may receive the regeneration, if God, by sovereign decree, remove him from time before moral probation actually begins, or that he may receive the regeneration on the condition of his own act of faith if he is permitted to live into the responsibilities of an actual moral probation. Christ is declared to be the Saviour of all men, especially of them that believe. There is a universal redemption. Whether there is universal and ultimate salvation, depends on the choice and ways of men. All men are once saved; once members of Christ's body, the Church. It is the bounden duty of every man to be a member of the Church of Christ. He must be a member of that Church, accepting all that that membership means, if he would be saved from sin, and live forever with God in Heaven. We do not say he must be a Romanist, a Methodist, an Anglican, or a Baptist; but we do say he must be a member of the Church of Christ, to be saved. And if he is genuinely a member of Christ's body, he will soon and easily find somewhere a visible relationship with some of Christ's people on the earth. The spirit of love, the life of the Church, will unite him to some Christian communion, and keep him in it, alive and active. It were matter of amusement, were it not so serious in import, to hear people speak of their relations to the Church of God, and to see them in practice bandy the Church about to any or all of a thousand whims and devices. Ask a man to meet the claims of his relations to God, the obligations that arise from a membership in Christ that every one ought to have, has had, and must have, and keep, to be saved, and listen to his reply: "Why, I'm not a member of the Church! What's your Church to me? I was never a member of the Church. The Church has no claims on me. I don't owe the Church anything. Let the members of the Church meet its claims? I don't confess any." Suppose a man should speak so of a family or country, what would we say of him? "Why, I am not a member of a family. Family, home, has no claims on me, never had any claims. I've no obligations to country. I don't owe country anything. Country is nothing to me." If a man so repudiate family, home, wedlock, we would be very apt to wonder whence he came, and perhaps ask, "How came he here?" If country is nothing to a man, we are prone to inquire what he is doing, how he came into his present relations, and whither he is tending. A man that is loose at both ends, and has no bond of connection, point of support or pivot of action anywhere, needs watching. "Family nothing to me; country nothing to me; Church nothing to me?" Look out for the man; he can just as righteously say one as the other. God instituted originally three great societies, and set the first man in them all—in Church, and family, and State; and in this order, too—first Church, then family, then State; so that if any man fill his obligations in these three divine institutions, he will be a round, full, complete man, not needing the aid of human organizations or the stilts of a thousand and one voluntary associations to perfect his character, secure his happiness, and save his soul. The man that discharges all the duties incumbent on him in the Church, in the family and in the State, needs but few additions. And his duties in the Church are primordial, fundamental, universal, underlying all others, and pervading all others. Adam had them—his duties to God, religious duties—when he stood alone in Eden. Then God gave him Eve, and the duties of the household were superadded. These were enlarged with Cain, Abel, and their descendants. The extending household was the germinating State. The old Patriarchs stood, Prophet, Priest and King. Every man is born into the family, or ought to be; every man is born into the State; and every man is born into the Church. And it is about as sensible to repudiate the one as the other. It were safer—indeed it were more rational—to repudiate the State and the family than to repudiate the Church of God. Ah! what a revolt is this! We will not have this man Christ Jesus to reign over us! Here is the open rebellion of the soul against the God of Heaven; the rejection of the authority, the despising of the love and blessing of the Sovereign Lord. Born in the Church, justified, under the covenant of redemption, embracing offered mercy, accepting purchased and covenanted provisions, we might by obedience remain ever in the Church; in the Church find regeneration, sanctification, glory. But, alas, who does it? That which is born of the flesh, is flesh. The carnal mind is emnity against God. We revolt more and more, and reject the counsel of God against ourselves. No wonder the cry of the compassionate Lord is, Return! Return! why will ye die! Come unto Me all ye ends of the earth, and be ye saved. Whosoever will, let him come. In our rebellion, we make ourselves children of wrath, even as others. We go astray from our youth, committing sin. Brought into probation, some more, some less, revolt from God, and choose out their own way. Surely the regeneration is universally needed; and if parents were more sensible of their obligations, and more faithful to their duties, it were oftener found before their offspring had wandered from them, from the Church, and from God, into sin and into the world. Every one here should be a member of the Church of God, and if he is not, it is because he has forsaken his Lord, and rebelled against his God. It is our primal duty to be members of the Church of Christ.

Moreover, it is in this Church of Christ, visible and invisible, that we obtain our highest dignities, grandest privileges, brightest honours, and richest rewards. To have the love of the family is of priceless worth; to enjoy the rights of citizenship, and the emoluments and dignities of the state, is exalted opportunity; but to possess the love and peace of God in the soul, to be assured that God is our Father and we are His children; sons of God, and if sons, then heirs, heirs of God, and joint heirs with Christ; to be raised from sin, and guilt and wretchedness to be kings and priests unto God: to be assured that all things are ours, whether Paul, or Apollos, or Cephas, or the world, or life, or death, or things present, or things to come; all are ours; and we are Christ's, and Christ is God's, is to be brought into the possession of peace, riches and honour, safer, vaster and brighter than family with its wealth of affection, or state with its splendours of rank, can yield. Earth and sense and time have nothing to compare with the heritage of the people of God. The Church of God is a spiritual household, with new, sweeter, purer, richer, ever-abiding loves. It is a spiritual kingdom with new, higher, brighter, eternally resplendant dignities and glories. The kingdoms of the earth fall, the crowns fade, the glories depart, but here are kingdoms and crowns and ineffable glories through endless ages for the humble, faithful ones that believe, love, and obey God.

> "The faithful of each clime and age
> The glorious Church compose:
> Built on a rock with idle rage
> The threatening tempest blows.
> Fear not; though hostile bands alarm
> Thy God is thy defence,
> And weak and powerless every arm
> Against Omnipotence."

Perhaps, then, we have reached something of an understanding of the Bible idea of the Church of God: not a voluntary human organization; not a law-made or compulsory human organization, a creature of Act of Parliament; not an ecclesiastical establishment, set up by the wisdom and power of man, to arrogate to itself the excellency and efficacy of religion: not a mere educational system, or a political, social or financial economy, to be accommodated to the caprices of

-men, and adapted to their purposes; not the outgrowth, offshoot, or development of any other economy, either natural or accidental; but a primitive, positive, and fundamental institution of the Great God for the moral and religious good, the spiritual salvation of man: a living organization, of which God's own dear Son is the central life; a vineyard where Christ is the vine, believers are the branches, and holy living, good tempers, and good deeds are the rich clusters of grapes: a safe fold, in which Christ the Lord is the good Shepherd, and humble, believing, obedient souls are the sheep of His pasture: a living temple of which Christ is the Chief Corner Stone, and believers in Him, accepting Him in covenant bonds, are living stones: a body, of which Christ our God is the head, and believers in Him are the members of His body, his flesh, and his bones Surely here is life, and a principle of life. Here is unity, and a bond of union. Here is organization, and an organizing, consolidating force. Here are symmetry and beauty, and a mould and pattern after which they are fashioned. Here is a resplendent glory, a radiance outbeaming from the inner shrine, the central light and life. Here are the holy nuptials of the eternal covenant, the marriage supper of the Lamb. For Christ loved the Church, and gave himself for it, that he might sanctify and cleanse it with the washing of water by the word; that He might present it to Himself a glorious Church, not having spot or wrinkle or any such thing, but that it should be holy and without blemish.

"*These things* write I unto thee," saith the Apostle, "that thou mayest know how thou oughtest to behave thyself in the House of God, which is the Church of the living God, the pillar and the ground of the truth." What things? From the context, it is evident that *the things* meant by the Apostle are the provisions and plans of the organization and government of the visible Church of Christ. He is delivering his scheme of church government, and his counsel with regard to it. Timothy has supervision, is Bishop of the Church at Ephesus, that church to whose elders the Apostle gave the solemn charge: "Take heed therefore unto yourselves, and to all the flock over which the Holy Ghost hath made you overseers, to feed the Church of God which He hath purchased with His own blood." By Paul's request and appointment, he is there to keep the Church from fables and false doctrines, to preserve it from contentions and worldliness and to excite it to godliness and holy living. Very likely the divine organization that possessed the vigorous interior life of which we have been speaking would have also an external order and beauty. God the Creator that puts symmetry and grace, ornament and loveliness on the vine, the oak, the human form, that same God, the Redeemer, could not in any probability leave the Church a mass of confusion, a heap of malformations and deformities. Within and without, Zion is to be the perfection of beauty, and we have in Paul's "*these things*" at least recommended the Apostolic idea of the exterior plan and arrangement of the government of the Church of God: and that, too, in the face of all the Church's work, though it were but in embryo and at the beginning: all the Church's work of extension; raising up a ministry and multiplying the membership, avoidance of false doctrines, and preserving the purity of the true doctrines; spreading her principles, consolidating her conquests, planting her institutions, and revolutionizing a wicked world with the teachings and practice of righteousness and holiness. If an army needs organization in its campaigns in an enemy's country shall not the Church of Christ require organization in its conflicts in a revolted earth? If a great leader would leave his experience and advice to his followers, is it to be supposed that the Christian Church is left without a hint as to its line of organization and form of government. But everything in its own order. There is one glory of the sun and another glory of the moon. One star differeth from another star in glory. Yet they are all stars. When we are considering Christ the central light and life of the Church, the great doctrines of the law, atonement and grace, sin, guilt, pardon, peace, holiness, happiness, and heaven, the question of Church polity is comparatively insignificant, and sinks almost out of sight. Before Christ and the tremendous issues of sin and salvation, hell and heaven, it appears puerile and almost wicked to wrangle about polities and dispute about forms. To cast in a polity or a ritual between a sinking soul and a rescuing Jesus is a folly, yea, a crime. It is an inversion of the divine order, a turning inside out, and outside in the divine plan. Nevertheless, there are polities and forms, and they have their place, and are of immense importance. In their rank and grade they are utterly indispensable. Before men and their schemes and devices, their rejection of rule and authority, their inventions of new and strange doctrines, their raging lusts and irregularity of life and conduct, their sluggishness to-day and impetuosity to-morrow, a salutary system, a wise polity, is of unspeakable, yea, of inestimable value. Amid the wars and currents of conflicting interest, selfish designs, opposing opinions, contending ambitions, upstart views, flashing novelties; amid the darkness of ignorance and the false, misleading lights of human philosophy, the impulses of curiosity and the disappointments of speculation, what would the Church of Christ do, what any more than the empire could it do, without a regular economy, a settled government? For several reasons, this is as necessary in Church as in State. The forms and functions of government, the exercise of authority and submission thereto, are requisite in matters ecclesiastical as well as in political affairs. Order, law, justice, freedom, life, security, liberty, happiness are the things to be obtained, the substance to be possessed, and in comparison with them any form of government is a trivial matter. When these are enjoyed, what more do we want? When they are in jeopardy, why wrangle about modes and external arrangements? Nevertheless, who can doubt, who dares dispute, that the very forms of government have very much to do with the liberties of the people? very much to do with the preservation and operation of the principles of genuine freedom? British Constitutional Monarchy has matured and kept a freedom of the people harmonized with sovereign and central authority that Russian Absolutism or French Democracy knows nothing of. When it is a war of polities and economies the form of government is a matter of immense importance. In spiritual and ecclesiastical concerns, when the struggle lies between the inner doctrines, the essential life, on the one hand, and external economies on the other, the true man knows quickly where is the preponderance, and on which side to be found. He stands for the way, the truth, the life, the great salvation, amid all forms, against all forms. But when it is a struggle of economy against economy, of polity against polity, then form of government, church polity, becomes a matter of immense importance. For, perhaps, as in national affairs, polity will help purity, solidity, safety, growth, genuine prosperity. And if a polity is either preferentially or decisively stated in the sacred Scriptures, it will likely be taken as warranted and sanctioned by godly men. In the Jewish dispensation, the modes of government and forms of service and administration, were laid down definitely enough, and by positive command. If in the Christian era, because the inner life is of vastly greater importance than the exterior mode, so positive commands as to government are not given, it is not that the government is of less importance, but the soul, the life, the salvation, of so much greater value. And when even the outlines of a plan of Church government are given by an inspired apostle, we may conclude that the government is indispensable, and that the plan recommended is the choice of the Spirit of God. In this letter to Timothy Paul clearly delivers to a Bishop or Overseer the rules and directions for a Bishop, and as definitely lays down instructions for the Deacons, a distinct and probationary rank, and, as is apparent from this and other portions of scripture, even a distinct order. This twofold order appears to have been ever in view, though not insisted upon or magnified; as the Apostles as well as our Lord Christ ever kept in sight, as of primal importance, the central life and power of godliness. Sometimes they are spoken of as bishops and deacons, sometimes as elders and deacons, and sometimes as elder and younger; but with a constant recognition of the probationary gradation with authority as becoming on the one hand, and submission as becoming on the other. It was this Scriptural economy sanctioned by the Apostles, and confirmed by the primitive Church, that Mr Wesley, after much prayer and investigation, decidedly preferred for the societies which in the providence of God were raised up by him. It was this for which he made all possible provision in England, which he recommended to the societies in America for their due organization into a church, which was loyally adopted by them at the Christmas Conference of 1784, and which is maintained intact in the Methodist Episcopal Church to this day. On solid conviction, and under solemn compact, it was this that the Methodist Episcopal Church in Canada, set off by its own request from the Methodist Episcopal Church in 1828, resolved and determined to maintain. And it is this that the Methodist Episcopal Church in Canada retains to this day. And in the light of Scripture and in the light of history and experience, we trust it will be maintained to the end, or, at all events, till something much better has been found and proved. Our Episcopal Methodism affords us an economy, not shifting and changing with every conference, but giving us steadiness of government, continuity of policy yet elasticity of measures, like unto the Parliamentary Monarchy of England, thereby upholding authority to the preservation of the uprightness of our character, and the purity of our doctrines, and at the same time granting the largest freedom of action, and urging outward in every direction our enterprises of evangelism. And herein are vindicated and demonstrated its true ecclesiastical succession and genuine divine mission, having those high and holy signatures of the text; the house of God, which is the church of the living God, the pillar and ground of the truth. It comes forth a recent and tender, yet vigorous and fruitful branch of the living vine, perhaps we may be permitted in reverence to say, a divine rebuke to the lofty assumptions of sacerdotalism and hierarchy on the one hand, and to the disintegrating and individualizing tenets, to the disregard of ecclesiastical succession and order, and to the levelling of all rule and authority inculcated by many so called religious teachers on the other. With no high claims to exclude other Christians, and no low, base aims to lead a rabble or rush with a rout; with steady policy for God, and steady polity for man, it rejoices in the fraternity of the Churches, and strives together with all Christians for the coming of Christ's kingdom, the salvation of the human race from sin and hell.

It is worthy of notice that the Apostle affirms the Church of God to be the Pillar and Ground *of the Truth.* "To this end was I born," said our Lord, "and for this cause came I into the world that I should bear witness unto the *Truth.* Every one that is of the truth heareth my voice." To which, after the manner of the Greek Sophists, and the Sophists of every age, Pilate replied, "What is truth?" Christ said again, "I am the way, the truth and the life." "Christ our Saviour is the Truth, and the Church is the Pillar and Ground of the Truth." The Truth subsists in Christ from the beginning; whence the Church, His body, may well to men be represented and realized as the Ground and Pillar of the Truth. The Eternal God is the centre, source and substance of Truth; Truth of all kinds and in all its departments. To Him Truth is but one, and in Him it subsists. Christ, His adorable Son, is the brightness of His glory and the express image of His person. He is before all things, and by Him all things consist. By Him, the Eternal Word, were all things made, and without Him was not anything made that was made. The Lord God possessed Him, the Eternal Wisdom, in the beginning of His way, before the works of old. When there were no depths, no fountains abounding with water, was he brought forth; before the mountains were settled, before the hills, while as yet he had not made the earth, nor the fields, nor the highest part of the dust of the world. When the Almighty Creator prepared the heavens, the Eternal Wisdom, the Eternal Word, the Adorable Son, the Head of the Church, affirms He was there. " When He set a compass upon the face of the depths; when He established the clouds above; when He strengthened the fountains of the deep; when He gave to the sea His decree that the waters should not pass His commandment; when He appointed the foundations of the earth, then I was by Him as one brought up with Him, and I was daily His delight, rejoicing always before Him; rejoicing in the habitable part of the earth; and my delights were with the sons of men." The great work of creation proceeds from the divine energy, under the divine eye, and according to the principles of truth in the divine constitution and nature. Hence it is that science has a foothold among men; an inquiry after, a knowledge of, the divine ideas and plans in the glorious universe. Hence it is that there is an astronomy for the heavens; a geology, botany, zoology, chemistry, physiology and psychology for the earth; a biology, mathematics, metaphysics and ethics for the wide sweep of infinity. Truth, all truth, is in the God Man; His very substance, like fibre in the iron, or grain in the wood, His outbeaming intelligence and splendour shining forth naturally—aye, with a deeper nature than the light of the sun. All truth is in Him, and there is none without, outside of, above, or beyond Him; and they mistake terribly, they see but a very, very little way who divorce truth from truth, or truth from God. They are stupid and ignorant teachers, blind guides, that set truth clashing on truth, or warring against God, its source. Better might they drive back the waters to quench the fountains of the rivers, or dash back the light to darken or extinguish the sun. Depraved, yea, diabolic natures, might delight in such a work, were it possible; none others could. The obedient and pious welcome the light, the truth, the effluence of Deity. The light of science, the knowledge of the laws and principles of nature, the knowledge of the energies and ways of Jehovah, let it ever beam on us with richer and richer beneficence and with greater and greater glory. Let it show us more and more of the wisdom of the Eternal, and more and more of His vast resources for the happiness of His creatures. The intelligent Christian man must alway rejoice in the increase and spread of genuine scientific truth. But likely this is not the specific truth of which the Apostle speaks; not the truth found by scientific investigation; but the truth disclosed by Divine Revelation; not the truth pertaining to external nature, or to the intellectual laws that govern man in his relation to external nature, but the truth pertaining to man's most interior nature—to his affections, tempers, desires and sentiments, his heart and soul; when he is not in cold contact with matter, but in living communion of spirit with spirit, the spirit of man with the Spirit of God. This is moral truth; the truth adapted to man as a moral being; it is religious truth, spiritual truth, that truth of which the Church of the Living God is emphatically and exclusively the Pillar and the Ground. All truth is in our Lord, but it is only when the truth is soul-touching, soul-reviving, soul-cleansing, soul-saving, that it pertains specially to His Church, and brings the health of what He calls His body—His flesh and His bones. Other truths, scientific truths, are not less truth than these. They inform, strengthen, develop, cultivate; but the salvation of God is a matter of deliverance from guilt and sin. A man does not merely need to know, but he needs to be rescued. He does not need merely the comprehension of a general law, but he needs, as well, the apprehension and application of a specific power. The truth of God for the salvation of men has in itself a life and power. It does not lead a man very directly or mightily to God to know that the sun is 95,000,000 of miles distant, or that water is composed, as chemists say, of hydrogen and oxygen. The rules of grammar and the multiplication table are sound enough for the eternal ages; but they never converted a sinner to God, or raised a lost soul from sin to righteousness. A man must know himself, his guilt, his wretchedness, his helplessness; and then he must know God, His love and power to save, and Christ in the efficacy of His atonement; he must know, and believe, and trust farther outward than he knows, and because of what he knows of the character of the great God, and of his own character before Him; then does he come to know that for which he trusted, the peace, purity, and joy of the great salvation; and he trusts outward again and again, according to the provisions and covenants of the God of eternal truth. It is this saving, life-imparting truth with which the Church is entrusted, this knowledge of ourselves, and knowledge of God and His salvation. The schools have their place, philosophers have their place; but they give us not, nor are they commissioned to keep for us this truth of God. It is found in the Church, the true Church, and that alone. The Church of Christ is the ground of the truth. The salvation of men cometh by revelation from God, and mediation with God through Jesus Christ. No pretensions here can be too high or exclusive. Again, we say, there is no other name given among men whereby we can be saved. This by no means sanctions the uncharitableness or exclusiveness and haughty assumptions of sects, but it asserts the position and vindicates the character of the Church of God.

c

We scarcely dare trespass to say further that in these characteristics indicated by the Apostle, we have the demonstration of what people or peoples are in Heaven registered as the Church of God. What is said of this matter among proud, vain and contentious men, does not make so much difference. The Apostle says the Church is the pillar and the ground of the Truth: the ground to keep it, and the pillar to hold it up in the sight of the world. As Christ does in the vine, so does the true Church in every one of its branches; it holds and declares the Truth. By this judgment of inspiration let jarring sects stand or fall. The truth of God,—the truth of God as given in His Word, the Church must hold. It is a solemn trust; the most solemn, sacred, and important trust on earth, to hold pure and incorruptible the Word of eternal life. Here is no place for the theories of men, for the prejudices of sects, or the dogmas and speculations of schools. We dare not allow these clear waters of grace and salvation to be tinged or coloured by systems, however venerable; or other religions, however ancient or honoured of man. We dare not allow the healthful air of Heaven and eternal life to be impregnated with the poisonous vapours from the world's disease and death, the corruptions of ages of alienation from God. We dare not allow the bright beam of divine revelation to be dimmed by the mists of false philosophies, or broken and blurred by the traditions of men and the customs and doctrines of fallible and erring Fathers. The truth of God,—the truth of God as in divine revelation, the true Church must hold, must keep against all corruptions and variations through all the centuries. And this saving truth the true Church must declare, must hold up everywhere in the face and sight of men. The Church that does this, keeps and displays, holds, preaches, obeys, and practises the truth of God, the Word of God, is a true

Church of Christ; and none other is. Not any pomp of ceremony; not any sumptuousness of ritual; not any regularity of orders; not any venerableness of canons or institutes; not any learning or power of councils or synods; not any wealth, influence, rank, or respectability of membership, can be a substitute for these characteristics of the Church of Christ. If we would be His people, we must love His law and proclaim it; we must accept His salvation, and in His own Spirit display it. Having these, we have all. What could I ask for my own beloved Zion more than this? Wealth? Nay. Worldly honour? Nay. Costly ritual? Nay. The Learning of the Schools? Nay. The favour of princes? Nay, nay. None of them, nor all of them, can constitute and keep us the Church of God. None of them, nor all of them, can give us the power of the primitive Christians and of the early labourers and people of our Methodism. It was the truth of God, attended by the Holy Ghost, that made them a people. If we are to make full proof of our ministry we must declare with fidelity the Word of God, and in prayer, seek its application by the Eternal Spirit to the hearts and consciences of men. It is the fearful doctrines of depravity, sin, guilt, death, hell and judgment, and the glorious doctrines of repentance, faith, pardon, regeneration, sanctification, resurrection, and eternal glory and felicity, that are still our hope, and the hope of the world. To be such a people, proclaiming and practising such doctrines, and to have the sanction, indwelling, and aid of the Eternal Spirit, the God of Truth, in that proclamation and practice, is more than all else beside that earth has to give. And Heaven itself has nothing better to bestow than such grace and aid in the conflicts of time and their joys and rewards in the felicities of eternity. Then all things are ours, for we are Christ's, and Christ is God's.

STRENGTH THROUGH FAITH.

By Rev. J. R. Jaques, D.D., Ph.D.

Delivered before Albert University—Charter Day, 1877.

Who through Faith * * * * out of weakness were made strong.—
Hebrews, xi. 34.

THE desire to be strong—to have power—is universal, instinctive and quenchless. Few have lived long without the uttered or un-uttered wish—" Oh, that I were strong." This desire is implanted in human nature as an original impulse, and no false philosophy or fanaticism can torture it out of the mind.

The child, just so soon as it faintly comprehends what strength is and does, covets it as a precious gift. No sane mind can despise power or strength, nor be pleased with conscious weakness. To gratify this inborn desire for power or strength, good men will toil, and strive, and study, and plan, and suffer, and wearily wait, and patiently watch ; while, for the same object, bad men will dare, and plot, and plunder, and struggle, steal, wage war, and defy danger or death.

To be strong is the inner meaning and ultimate aim of true education. Not to gain knowledge of facts, valuable as such knowledge is, does the intelligent student enter upon his long course of study, preparatory and collegiate. Knowledge is the means—not the end; the end is to be strong. Sir William Hamilton expressly declares that knowledge, so far from being education, is but the instrument of education; and we may add, an instrument that may possibly be used without achieving the end in view. Education, correctly speaking, is the process of developing strength, physical, mental, and moral. As there may be vast knowledge with little education, so there may be comparatively little knowledge but great education. Knowledge is to the mind what food is to the body. As there may be great gormandizing with little gain in strength of body, so there may be great memorizing of knowledge with little gain in strength of mind.

A man's education consists not in the abundance of the things he learns, but in making himself strong in reason, strong in memory, strong in imagination, strong in noble impulse, strong in will, strong in the invincible resolve to be and do the right.

Strength as an object of laudable ambition, it would seem, scarcely needs defending in this presence on the ground of promoting usefulness. But while the contrary doctrine seems to be growing in some quarters in Church and State, it were high treason to truth to leave unsaid the great fact that Providence does not use weak minds for great deeds. But does not God choose and use the weak sometimes to confound the mighty? Yes, *sometimes*. But not often. And where the weak are chosen, it is only the weak in worldly wealth, rank, and policy, not men weak in essential manhood. Whatever enthusiasts and indolent persons may think, God is not wont to use weaklings and fools for His great and gracious enterprises.

Moreover, the very genius of Christianity requires and provides that a man be strong. The exhortation of the Apostle, "Quit you like men, be strong!" like a bugle-blast, startles us out of the delusion that Christianity is to make men less manly. We know that the mild virtues of forbearance, forgiveness, sympathy, patience, and meekness, are magnified in Christianity, and especially in the "Sermon on the Mount;" but these very passive virtues imply the existence of the active virtues of which heroes are made. The Niagara Suspension Bridge, while it is so flexible as to yield to every passing breeze, is yet so strong as to bear the shock of the tempest.

The text declares that certain illustrious worthies of the Old Testament were made strong by their faith.

"33. Who through faith subdued kingdoms, wrought righteousness, obtained promises, stopped the mouths of lions.

"34. Quenched the violence of fire, escaped the edge of the sword, out of weakness were made strong."

Without metaphysically defining strength, it is enough, perhaps, to say that strength is capacity to achieve. No man can truly be said to be strong who can do nothing. Strength manifests itself merely in results or effects, and if the results of strength are wanting, the strength is wanting somewhere, however brilliant, or pretentious, or promising it may be.

Now, faith brings strength out of weakness by two methods divinely contrived—the one indirect, the other direct.

I. Faith indirectly makes the weak man Strong by uniting all his forces.

The maxim, "Union is Strength," needs not to be proved, for it finds its proof in our sovereign common sense. How many a man has thunder in him, but it is divided and scattered, so that the world never hears it in one grand peal! He has lightning in him, but it never strikes anywhere, because it all oozes off in insensible streams, and is lost by being scattered. Many a man that might be sublimely strong, is shamefully weak, because he does not cause all within him to unite in one direction. That man economises his powers who uses all his powers to some purpose and to one purpose.

While the conscience pulls one way, and pride another, selfishness another, and all the other impulses of the mind pull divergently and discordantly, what wonder that the man is weak to will and work, and win?

On the other hand, when all the faculties of the intellect, all the impulses of the heart, and all the powers of the body, to the last drop of life blood, enter into a great covenant, and unite in a purpose, one indivisible, and fixed, what wonder that that man becomes strong and unconquerable!

Now this unity of purpose, this concentration of soul, is implied in faith. Faith is at once the cause and the effect of this singleness of aim and union of all within the man.

By a law, irrepealable as the law of gravitation, "a double-minded man," a man unconsecrated to truth and God, cannot exercise faith. It is a law equally divine that the man who is thus concentrated and consecrated, shall soon be put in possession of the wand of faith. Then when faith comes, faith reacts on the soul, and gives a diviner unity of soul. And thus faith gives strength by giving union and singleness of soul, and this may change the wavering and weak into all-conquering manhood.

II. FAITH, INDIRECTLY, BRINGS STRENGTH OUT OF WEAKNESS BY GIVING QUIETNESS OF SOUL.

There is a deep philosophy in the declaration of the Prophet, " In quietness and in confidence shall be your strength."

With what unimaginable force the world moves around its axis—a thousand miles an hour and in its orbit more than a million miles a day, and yet how still, how silent! All this prodigious force is exerted with less noise than one bustling man makes in boasting of what he can do or would do, but never does.

Many a stranger was amazed when first seeing John Wesley, who, while the source and centre of the greatest movement of the century, was himself the very embodiment of quietness and serenity; himself the source of a world-wide excitement, and yet himself unexcited. The noisy man, the stormy man, the disquieted man, wastes much of his force in friction, wear and tear.

Now see the effect of faith—" Thou wilt keep him in perfect peace, whose mind is stayed on Thee, because he trusteth in Thee."

Thus faith indirectly gives strength by giving quietness, which the Prophet declares is our strength.

III. FAITH INDIRECTLY GIVES STRENGTH BY GIVING PEACE OF CONSCIENCE.

A rebuking conscience is an element of weakness. How can he be strong who has a rebellion in his breast? A chiding conscience makes cowards and weaklings of us all. While a peaceful conscience is an armour of triple brass, the strength of many a man is worn away by the lashes and scorpion-stings of conscience. How can he be strong who night and day, devoid of rest, carries his own accuser in his breast?

Now this sublime strength, faith brings by bringing peace of conscience. For, "being justified by faith, we have peace with God, through our Lord Jesus Christ."

Thus, out of weakness men are made strong, indirectly, by faith, because faith brings peace of conscience.

IV. Faith indirectly brings Strength out of Weakness, by bringing Joy.

The melancholy man is relatively a weak man. The mental and bodily powers never reach their highest results, while the man is gloomy. A man never reaches his maximum of power till he is a deeply, divinely happy man. Gloom clogs the mental faculties. This need not be proved. All know that the joyous mechanic or labourer will do more, the joyous student will study more, the joyous Christian will be more useful than the gloomy man. Melancholy paralyzes man's best powers into helplessness, while joy exhilarates man's weakest faculties into strength.

Now this great law of mind and body, being based in the very constitution of man, so far from being ignored by the Scriptures, is announced with all the force of a philosophic formula in the words of Nehemiah—"The joy of the Lord is your strength."

And now to prove the point proposed, we need but to mark the Apostolic prescription for generating joy, "That the trial of your faith being much more precious than of gold that perisheth, though it be tried with fire, might be found unto praise and honour and glory at the appearing of Jesus Christ, whom, having not seen ye love, in whom, though now ye see Him not, yet believing, ye rejoice with joy unspeakable and full of glory."—1 Pet. i. 7, 8,

This wondrous joy is brought by faith, and since joy brings strength, again faith indirectly brings strength out of weakness.

V. Faith indirectly brings Strength out of Weakness, by bringing Temperance.

Here we use temperance in the sense in which it is used in Scripture, which is universal self-control, or government over the appetites and passions of body and soul.

To be temperate, in the Scriptural sense, is to be master of our impulses, and this is a source of man's grandest power. There are great heights and depths of meaning in the maxim of Solomon—" He that ruleth his own spirit is better than he that taketh a city." And this great imperial power of temperance, faith brings into the soul. For "this is the victory that overcometh the world, even our faith."

Thus faith, indirectly, brings strength out of weakness by bringing self-control, and self-control or temperance is strength.

VI. Faith indirectly brings Strength out of Weakness, by bringing Love.

If we were asked to name a word that should embody and mean the most of power, we should instantly name the word *Love*.

Love is a power—strength. What gravitation is to the material world, so is love to the world of mind.

Love is patience, and patience is strength. Love is patience, and patience is strength in the mother who works and watches away the weary hours for some weak or wayward child, till we wonder how she lives. Love is strength in the patriot's heart, who goes to do or die for his country. Love nerves with strength all who do the great deeds of the ages. The love of fame, of glory, of learning, of the beautiful, of gold; the love of humanity, all these are the unseen forces that dig canals, construct railroads, tunnel mountains, bridge rivers, traverse oceans, rear cities, and found empires.

It is but the love of something, or of somebody either earthly or heavenly, that drives the blood and thrills the nerves, and moves the muscles of all the men and women that move the world.

It is love that drives the chariot wheels of enterprise, of science, of art, of literature, of civilization.

It is a principle or law, with its proper exceptions, that a man's strength is exactly measured by his love. Quench out of a man's heart all his loves, and you instantly reduce him from strength to weakness.

Then, in that same paralyzed soul, kindle the flames of a great, sublime, all-consuming love, and you instantly transform him into a man of might, before whom men will give way as before the march of majesty.

Give a man love, love enough of something, and his love will tear its way out in all-prevailing will and work. And if an earth-born love makes man thus mighty, what shall not that love do that is born in heaven?

Now, then, faith indirectly brings strength out of weakness, by bringing love. For, remember, love full-orbed, sunny-faced, stalwart, royal, unconquerable— love stronger than death—love, in the divine sense, never comes till ushered in by faith. Faith, then timid hope, then victorious love. "Faith worketh by love."

Thus far we have considered faith as the *indirect* source of strength.

We now proceed to consider faith as the *direct* source of human strength. And here it is necessary to premise that man's strength inheres, (1st) in body, (2nd) in intellect, (3rd) in will, (4th) in executive ability, (5th) in moral impulse, or moral heroism. In all these departments of man's being, faith brings strength.

I. Out of Weakness of Body Faith tends to bring Strength.

We will not stop to prove, by any long argument, how faith indirectly invigorates the body by bringing peace of mind, joy in the heart, and universal temperance or self-control. Faith brings a retinue of angels into the soul, that cannot stay without blessing the body as well as the soul.

This is correct philosophy, and physiology, and theology. True piety in an enlightened mind does not make men pale-faced and puny. Our Lord prays that His disciples may be sanctified and kept from the evil, but at the same time He declares that He prays not "that they should be taken out of the world."

Whence came the falsehood that a man greatly and gloriously gifted with grace is not long for this world?

Moreover, faith, doubtless, does operate immediately on the body in many cases. This physical meaning is probably the first meaning of our text. Out of weakness of body men are made strong, in many cases, by faith directly. We dare not say that Christ, on His exalted throne, is less merciful or mighty than, when on earth, He honoured faith by healing and energizing men's bodies as well as their souls.

Nearly all our Lord's miracles were for the body. And true facts and true philsosophy alike forbid us to limit the province of faith and the power of the

Almighty, by affirming that no man can, in this age, win new vitality and new vigour to his body, by faith in the Son of God.

Facts constituting an avalanche of argument might be presented to prove that Christ has not lost all His power on earth to save men's bodies, when, to further His gracious designs, men's bodies need to be rendered immortal till their work is done.

Here let it be marked and remembered, that strength of body is an important and indispensable factor in the problem of human success. When Lord Brougham was asked the secret of success, his reply was, " body! body! body!" A well-balanced, strong body is an element of power specially needed, and to be prized, by all who aspire to do life's work well, which, in many cases, is simply a question of physical endurance and capacity for patient, plodding work.

Thus Heaven has provided that, with the outflow of faith, there shall be an inflow of strength to sustain the body in its weary work and fierce fight with disease.

And thus frail constitutions have been fortified and preserved through long lives of consecrated toil for the Master.

II. BUT FAITH BRINGS A HIGHER STRENGTH OUT OF WEAKNESS, BY BRINGING INTELLECTUAL STRENGTH.

That intellectual strength is higher than bodily strength, needs no proof. It needs only to be stated to be believed. Dr. Winship, the strong man of Boston, who can lift nearly 3,000 pounds, is not to be despised in his proper sphere. But what is Dr. Winship, with his muscle, to Sir Isaac Newton, with his mind, who could weigh the world and all the ponderous planets of the solar system?

This strength of intellect men always honour and reverence, because they see in it vast possibilities, dignity, and royalty. Now, faith operates directly on the intellect (1) by intensifying attention.

For who knows not that faith in the unseen realm of Providence and grace, is a high discipline of attention?

2. Faith brings strength to the imagination by opening up a panorama of limitless beauties and glories that eye hath not seen nor ear heard. Who shall measure with chain or compass the sweet fields arrayed in living green, and rivers of delight revealed by faith?

Amid the unconfined realms of the spiritual, and beautiful, and heavenly, and immortal, imagination may spread her wings sublime, and fly and soar till, in her dizzy flight earth becomes a tiny speck in the distance, and disappears, while imagination still journeys on and on, till she would "vie with Gabriel as he sings in notes almost divine."

What are the paltry scenes of Olympus, and the divinities of all heathen mythology, compared with the grandeurs of the Christian's heaven and the Christian's God in providence and grace?

Christianity thus elevates, expands, and ennobles the God-like faculty of imagination, and the poetical instinct. Who knows not that Christian poets have filled the world with high harmonies? Christian artists have immortalized the marble with sculptured sublimities, and the canvas with heaven-born creations, "vital in every part, that cannot but by annihilation die."

3. Faith brings strength to reason.

Faith is itself an act of high ennobled reason—reason in its highest exercise. Faith comes not to dethrone reason, but to inspire, glorify, and crown with a royal diadem. He never lifts reason to her highest honour, who refuses to trust in God or exercise faith. Why should it not expand the intellect to grasp by faith the great themes of Christianity? No man can have a growing faith without a growing intellect.

Is natural science invigorating to the mind? Is the study of creation ennobling? How much more the study of the Creator!

Is the study of human language educative? How much more the study of the language of heaven!

Is the study of mathematics of earth strengthening to the mind? How much more the mathematics of the skies, and the problems of eternity!

Do you ask for facts to prove this theory? Then take your map, and see where they have no Christian faith, and mark the feebleness of mind among the masses. Then look where they have some Christian faith, even though mixed with error, and mark the increasing mental power among the masses. Then look where the purest Protestant faith has prevailed (as Prussia, Great Britain, and the United States, and Canada), and mark the stalwart minds of the people, and the triumphant march of intellect.

To confirm all this, look again at Luther's movement of the 16th century. It was simply a revival of the doctrine of "Justification by Faith," but was instantly followed by a revival of intellect all over Christendom.

But to finally settle this question, we need but to look around us to be convinced that faith is the precursor of strength in human minds. Who are controlling the education of this country, Great Britain and the United States? Christian teachers in our Christian colleges, and Christian teachers in our common schools.

But we need not look further than our own acquaintance, to see that faith brings intellectual energy to human minds. The logic of facts we witness will settle the question.

III. FAITH OUT OF WEAKNESS GIVES STRENGTH OF WILL.

Will-force is higher than mere intellect. Whatever may be the thinking power, if the will be weak and vacillating, the man is weak and worthless. For the will is closely identified with the man himself, or the human personality.

While the intellect is a kind of mechanism, a thinking machine, the will is free, sovereign, majestic, royal, allied to the divine. The will is the great point of power. The man of giant intellect, with a child's will, is still a child. But the man with a mere child's intellect, but a giant will, is already a giant.

Now, faith operates at this great source and centre of the personality, and infuses something of the Divine Omnipotence.

(*a.*) AND FIRST, MERE NATURAL FAITH GIVES STRENGTH OF WILL.

Confidence in the general course and constitution of nature, confidence or faith in natural laws, faith in moral and natural truth—mere natural faith, as distinguished from faith in Bible truth—is an element of power.

No great enterprise can be undertaken without faith in nature's laws in man and the course of Providence. A man is no more and does no more than his faith. He who believes nothing will do nothing.

To show this, it is merely necessary to remember that no man will put forth a volition unless there be a motive. No man will ever lift an arm without a motive, and that motive may be put into a proposition which becomes an object of faith.

A man never wills to do a thing unless he believes something, first, respecting the effect; secondly, respecting the process. No man wills to raise his hand without a definite belief in the universal law of causation, or the stability of Divine administration. He believes that the effect that has followed a certain cause will continue to follow that cause, and so he raises his hand by faith.

This typical volition will illustrate all that man does or can do on earth.

Faith, then, is the source of the commonest actions of life. He, then, who will believe nothing will do nothing.

Thus universal scepticism would be universal *despair* and *helplessness*.

If you would ruin a man, insinuate doubts in his mind respecting the great principles and laws of human life; insinuate doubts and scepticism respecting truth —any truth—and you pave the way for his journey down to despair and death. Scepticism paralyzes the will. One doubter chills the grandest enterprise of man, and enough doubters will kill it. Take out of a man all his faith in nature and Providence, and man, and truth, and God, and you freeze up his enthusiasm, you paralyze his will, you rob him of his manhood, and leave him in drivelling imbecility.

They who say faith has no place in the human soul, know not what they do. What is faith but belief of truth in nature or Providence, or in the soul written by the finger of God! And "knowest thou not," says Milton, "that truth is mighty, next to the Almighty?"

Would you then send a man reeling down to ruin? Then persuade him that it makes no difference whether he believes this or that or nothing. On the other hand,

D

if you would lift a man a step sky-ward, persuade him to believe some truth—even though it be a fragment of truth. It will exalt him, inspire him, and stimulate him toward better things.

This is the effect of mere natural faith that may operate on the mind of the Deist who knows not or rejects the Scripture.

But truth, in the Scriptural sense, has a still greater potency in the human soul. Faith is defined by the Apostle in this chapter as the "evidence" or conviction "of things not seen," and—

(*b.*) FAITH, AS A CONVICTION OF THINGS NOT SEEN, BRINGS STRENGTH TO THE WILL BY REVEALING GOD AS A CO-WORKER WITH MAN.

If the army, with flagging zeal and weakened numbers, is fired and filled with new strength at the sudden sight of all-conquering reinforcements or reserve force, what must have been the effect upon the discouraged young man when the prophet by prayer revealed the armies of the skies fighting on his side?

The three Hebrew children might perhaps have endured the fiery furnace alone; but what must have been the thrillings of inspired strength when they saw walking with them the form of the fourth with the mien and majesty of the Son of God? It is a great era in a man's soul-history when he sees the *form of the fourth* in the furnace of trial. The sense of Divine co-operation lifts man into strength and victory. "Moses feared not the wrath of the king." Why? Because "he endured as seeing Him that is invisible."

(*c.*) FAITH BRINGS STRENGTH TO THE WILL IMMEDIATELY BY REVEALING THE REWARDS OF THE VICTOR.

This source of strength is magnified in the Scripture and especially in this chapter. Why did Moses "refuse to be called the son of Pharaoh's daughter, choosing rather to suffer affliction with the people of God than to enjoy the pleasures of sin for a season ?"

Why was his will thus turned and touched with heroism ? "Because," it is said, "he had respect to the recompense of reward."

A man can bear the pain that comes in the path of duty when faith looks toward the immortal, and sees pleasures at God's right hand for evermore.

If poverty come in his path, he wins new strength to bear it by a look toward "the unsearchable riches of Christ."

These are called "light afflictions." And Paul knew what afflictions mean for he had felt them all. And he said, "these light afflictions, which are but for a moment, work for us a far more exceeding and eternal weight of glory."

But how can these great heart-breaking afflictions be called light? Because anything is light if you weigh it with an infinite weight in the other scale. The man of faith finds his toil light when weighed with an ocean of heavenly rest, where "not a wave of trouble shall roll across the peaceful breast." Any reproach for Christ is light when weighed against a crown of glory, honour and immortality.

IV. FAITH DIRECTLY BRINGS STRENGTH OUT OF WEAKNESS BY GIVING STRENGTH TO THE MORAL NATURE OR MORAL HEROISM.

There is a certain moral might or majesty of character higher than intellect or impulse or will-power.

If moral power were no higher than intellect, then were Satan more majestic than Milton. There is something higher than thinking power, or policy, or eloquence, or martial courage. Something higher! Alexander, called "the Great," after conquering the world, was not great enough or high enough to conquer himself and his vices, and lost the empire of his heart before he lost the empire of the world.

Lord Bacon, after launching his "Novum Organum," called "the greatest birth of time"—Lord Bacon, who from his dizzy height, saw all the fields of human philosophy, was not high enough to resist the temptations of corrupting gold, and, as says the poet,

"Shined, the wisest, brightest, meanest of mankind."

We are overawed by the majestic sweep of Demosthenes' eloquence, as he thunders against King Philip of Macedon. But Philip, by his arms, was more than a match for the eloquence of Demosthenes; but against the august manhood of Demosthenes Philip had no arms, no enginery of war.

But hear his immortal words:

"If it is demanded how then has Philip triumphed? the whole world will answer for me; by his all-conquering arms, and by his all-corrupting gold. It was not for me to combat the one or the other. I had no treasures—no soldiers, but with what I did have, I dare to assert that I conquered Philip. How? By rejecting his bribes—by resisting his corruption. When a man permits himself to be bought, his buyer may be said to triumph over him. But he who remains incorruptible, has triumphed over the corrupter. And thus, so far as it depended on Demosthenes, Athens was victorious—Athens was invincible!"

These are his words. Thus sublime as was Demosthenes, the orator and statesman, far more sublime was Demosthenes the man. For without the insignia of royalty, he was more kingly than the king, and no crown of earth could add one gleam of glory to the brow of Demosthenes, the conqueror of Philip, who was the conqueror of the nations.

Now then this grandest power of man,—which we may call moral heroism—faith brings to human souls.

"Who is he that overcometh, but he that believeth," is the challenge, shouted by the Apostle John. And then he announces the heroic energy of faith in the triumphant truth, "This is the victory that overcometh the world—even our faith!"

Put this faith deep down in a man's heart, and you have a hero, ready to do or dare, suffer or die?

This faith fits men to be martyrs? Now Paul says, "I am ready, not only to be bound, but also to die at Jerusalem for the name of the Lord Jesus."

Now Luther is ready, "I will go to Worms to meet my enemies, even if there were as many devils in the way as there are tiles on the roofs."

Yes, put this faith in the heart, and the heroic soul is ready for torture or death, anything but cowardice and sin? Bring on your engines of torture, now—rack his limbs! Tear them asunder! He is ready now!

This is the highest power of man that is merely human. But there is another power still higher than this. For

V. LASTLY FAITH BRINGS SUPERHUMAN STRENGTH TO HUMAN WEAKNESS BY BRINGING THE DIVINE IN VITAL UNION WITH THE HUMAN SOUL.

"All things are possible to him that believeth." Here our philosophy ends, we can see and say the truth, but not understand it. The Apostles, after the day of Pentecost, always speak of God as being in the Church and in believers.

When it is said that Stephen and others were "filled with the Holy Spirit," it is no fiction or mere figure. He who is full of faith is full of Divine power. We admit this is mysterious.

How the weakness of humanity can thus be exalted into intimacy and co-operation with God, we cannot fully explain.

How the electro-magnet—which is but common soft iron—by being placed in a current of electricity, becomes a powerful magnet, no man can tell. Though held in mid air, with nothing visible touching it, with no change in weight or appearance, it suddenly becomes mighty to lift great weights. The fact we see. So we see common men, when placing themselves in the current of divine power, suddenly become mighty to lift men toward God. The touch of faith is the source of all power. Men say, "where is the secret of the power of this man?" The Corinthians said of Paul that his "bodily presence was weak, and his speech contemptible."

But Paul says "when I am weak, then I am strong. I can do all things through Christ who strengtheneth me!"

Faith brings the indwelling Christ into the soul and the indwelling Christ is indwelling all-mightiness.

"All things are possible to him that believeth." Do you then aspire to do noble things? We honour you you for such aspirations. But you say you are weak. Then seize the sceptre of faith and you shall begin to conquer, and learn the miracles of meaning in our text.

And what shall I more say? for the time would fail me to tell of Gideon, and *of* Barak, and *of* Samson, and *of* Jephthah; *of* David also, and Samuel, and *of* the prophets; who through faith subdued kingdoms, wrought righteousness, obtained promises, stopped the mouths of lions, quenched the violence of fire, escaped the edge of the sword, OUT OF WEAKNESS WERE MADE STRONG."

THE WEALTH OF TRUE BELIEVERS.

By Rev. Wm. Barnett,

Of Loughboro.

But as it is written, Eye hath not seen, nor ear heard, neither have entered into the heart of man, the things which God hath prepared for them that love Him. But God hath revealed them unto us by His Spirit: for the Spirit searcheth all things, yea the deep things of God. For what man knoweth the things of a man, save the spirit of man which is in him? even so the things of God knoweth no man, but the Spirit of God. Now we have received, not the spirit of the world, but the spirit which is of God; that we might know the things that are freely given to us of God.—1 Cor. ii. 9—12.

GREAT was the excitement created by the discovery of the rich gold fields of California. Nearly all parts of the world felt that excitement, and vast numbers were smitten with "the fever." Newspapers were filled with fabulous stories respecting the immense value of the "nuggets" found and the almost unlimited quantity of the auriferous deposits. New steamship lines were organized, railroads were built, and overland routes were opened to convey the ever increasing multitudes who rushed to ensure sudden and certain fortunes at "the diggings," undaunted by the length of journey or voyage, or the difficulties met with on the way. The walls of almost every seaport town glared with blazing advertisements announcing the departure of some vessel to the "Golden Gate." Not a few "made their pile;" while thousands sank to deeper poverty, and fell into still fouler immorality and vice. Some won fortunes of varied extent, and returned home to enjoy them with their families, or squander them in reckless folly; and some became millionaires, not always honestly, but too frequently at the expense of principle, religion, and eternal life; "for what is a man profited if he gain the whole world and lose his own soul?" To far too many this great discovery proved the cause of untold misery and irremediable woe; yet out of it, perhaps, no human intellect can measure the good that shall arise.

But my text tells us of a mine vaster, deeper, richer, fuller than any, or all the mines of California can ever be. Unite the gold and silver mines known to the ancients, Havilah, Ophir and Peru; with the discoveries of modern times, they are but as the small "drop of a bucket." Were each of earth's mountains made of solid gold, the bed of every stream and the valleys through which they flow filled with the precious dust; were the earth from its crust to its core, not only pierced and penetrated with veins of silver, but changed into precious metals; while every pebble at our feet, or atom that floats in the air, were converted into gems of priceless value; were every leaf and flower that grows, the soft down and beauteous feathers of each bird that flies, with the very songs they sing, together with the varied colours that adorn and clothe the beasts of the field, rendered invaluable not simply for their rarity, beauty, harmony, and perfume, but for their intrinsic worth; were each shell-fish, or other inhabitant of the vast deep, and the innumerable drops that compose the ocean, transformed into pearls or diamonds of the first and purest water; were this whole earth with its varied contents, animate and inanimate, one great mine of inestimable price, it could not compare with the mine opened to us in the text. Were each and every star in the sky, mines also, as varied in their character and value, as they are different in their magnitude and apparent glory; could you combine them all in one, it could not compare as well with this of the text, as the sudden flashing meteor with the glorious orb of day: For "it is written," and written truly, "Eye hath not seen, nor ear heard, neither have entered into the heart of man, what God hath prepared for them that love Him."

Would you learn something of the nature, extent, and wealth of the treasures contained in this mine, read with me a few passages from God's own Word. These are presented by way of faintly illustrating, while fully proving, the truth of the first part of the text. In Col. i. 19, we read, "It pleased the Father that in Him"—in Jesus—"should all fulness dwell." *All fulness.* Do not these words speak of amplitude, completeness, perfection? Do they not indicate blessings, riches, treasures without limit, unlimited in number, excellence, and durability? This agrees well with what Paul says in 1 Cor. iii. 21-23. "For all things are yours: whether Paul, or Apollus, or Cephas, or the world, or life, or death, or things present or things to come; *all are yours,* and ye are Christ's, and Christ is God's." And with what he says again (Rom. viii. 32): "He that spared not His own Son, but delivered Him up for us all, how shall He not with Him *freely give us all things?*" Thanks be to God, says the pious believing heart, for "the unspeakable gift." Christ is that gift—heaven's most precious jewel. Nay, says Paul, Christ is the casket containing the jewel—the fountain from whence the streams do flow. That casket contains *all things;* if the casket is priceless, unspeakable, what must its contents be? What heart has ever imagined ? what tongue shall ever tell ? Christ agrees with Paul, for in Mark xi. 24., we read, and it is our Lord who says it, " What things soever ye desire, when ye pray, believe that ye receive them, and ye shall have them." Thank God for that "*What things soever.*" Is there any limit there ? None, absolutely none, but what man himself supplies by his want of capacity, desire, or faith. As though to clinch the nail, to free us from all doubt in the matter, the same apostle adds (Ephes. iii. 10), " He is able to do exceeding abundantly, above all that we ask, or think, according to the power that worketh in us."

Would you know further of these blessings, then look for " the riches of his glory " in such passages as 1 Cor. i. 30., Rom. v. 1–5, and viii. 28–39, and for " the riches of His glory " in such texts as Ephes. iii. 15–21. Want of space forbids the insertion of these precious scriptures. I will add but one more, hoping it will apply in some degree to those that read these pages. " And of His fulness have we all received, and grace for grace."—John i. 16.

Three facts are told us in the text respecting these treasures—these shall form the theme of the present discourse.

I. These treasures are PREPARED for those that love God. Who can describe the happiness in Paradise ? or who portray the bliss prepared or kept in store for him ? Who can imagine, even faintly, the wonderful capabilities of his being—his powers of body and mind ? Who can tell what he was when God blessed him, having made him in His own image, after the likeness of God Himself ? Who can conceive what he might have become, how he might have developed, to what he might have attained, or who unfold the honour and bliss attendant upon his faithfulness, and awaiting his development?

All this he forfeited by his sin; all his present joy, all his prospective glory vanished with his innocency. As we gaze upon the wreck, the ruin which sin made of and in him, we usually think only of what he then suffered, and in what wretchedness and woe he stood exposed. Even that is inconceivable and unknown except to those who suffer the eternal wrath of an eternal God—and to them also it is known only in part. But who shall measure, count, or tell the blessings lost, the honour sacrificed, the bliss and felicity forfeited. On either side of man's sin was infinity, immensity, eternity, God. Before it infinite, immeasurable, eternal good—all lost, lost, forever lost; after it unfathomable, limitless, irremediable woe to be forever endured. And yet, thank heaven, not absolutely lost is all this good; not utterly unredeemable is man from all this evil. Man himself is wholly helpless; angels looked upon the wreck in despair, but God found out a ransom. There has been a *second* Adam—the first forfeited, the second redeems; the first sacrificed, the other saves. Adam, our earthly parent, lost all; Christ, our Redeemer, restores all. Adam sacrificed himself and ruined his race by sin; Christ also sacrificed Himself, not by, but for sin and the redemption of the fallen race. O, let us "glory in the cross," for on it the atonement was made, the redemption price was paid, the propitiation was offered, the reconciliation was effected. Let us glory in the atonement, for by it all disabilities are done away, every evil is removed, and every forfeited blessing is restored. No longer does "the cherubim and the flaming sword keep the way of the tree of life" (Gen. iii. 24); the Shekinah shines forth from Calvary, Christ having received the flaming, burning, piercing sword; being "bruised for our iniquities." The gates of Paradise—not the earthly but the heavenly—are thrown wide open now, Rev. 21, 25; and man may enter and secure immortality and eternal life, for the "tree of life" is there (Rev. xxii. 2). A new and living way is opened into the holiest by the blood of Jesus" (Heb. x. 19, 20). There Christ "standeth at the right hand of God"—Stephen saw him there (Acts vii. 56). He "receives gifts for men," and distributes them even to the rebellious upon repentance (Psalm lxviii. 18). What are these gifts but the "all things" of which I have spoken—the "things prepared" of my text.

The Apostle speaks of one of these gifts in Ephes. i. 8, "In whom (the Beloved) we have redemption through His blood, the forgiveness of sins, according to the riches of His grace." But this forgiveness of sins is only one blessing of many—one blessing inclusive in its character—including, going before and securing many others. It is but one link in an endless chain, reaching from the Cross to the Throne, from regeneration to eternal life, from present possession and enjoyment to eternal prospect, promise, and fruition; each link increasing in value, glory, bliss, as the changes of time, and the long cycles of eternity roll onward.

"According to the riches of His grace." Precious words! The atonement offered by Jesus must be infinite, all-sufficient, perfect. Only once was it offered, for it was God's atonement; no more, no other, is, or can be needed. And the blessings procured thereby must correspond with the price paid for them: their value in some way must be commensurate with the cost. Surely God would not require, nor would Christ pay, too high a price. These blessings then must be infinite, all-sufficient, perfect, "according to the riches of His grace." Not according to the meagreness of our faith, but according to the fulness and completenesss of His atonement. O, that believers but understood this as they should, and would believe and enjoy as is their glorious privilege!

And these blessings are all deposited in Jesus. In Him the fulness dwells. *Dwells*, that is the word—abides, remains, continues, and will abide, remain, continue unceasingly, eternally. He is the bank, and the banker too; His vaults are ever full; you cannot exhaust the exchequer, or in the least diminish the capital. He never leaves or changes his Office, or trusts His work to dishonest clerks. No speculation or peculation here, no danger to rich or poor. Blessed is every shareholder; their stock is well insured, their dividends ever large and full. Your Bible is full of His checks, His precious unfailing promises. Brethren, why do you not draw on Him to your hearts content? Innumerable angels draw, millions of glorified saints draw, thousands of believers yet on earth are drawing now, and you are welcome to as large a draft as any. These and millions more will draw eternally; what you may take during your short day surely cannot injure Him—the want of it may injure you. Draw then—draw heavily—draw constantly; become rich indeed.

I have already said He is the fountain; are not the streams abundant? Oft we sing,

> These streams the whole creation reach,
> So plenteous is the store;
> Enough for all, enough for each,
> Enough for evermore.

Do you believe this? Why then do you not have enough? When Moses smote the rock in Horeb, the waters gushed out so plentifully that like a life-giving stream it followed Israel in all their journeyings. "And they did all drink the same spiritual drink ; for they drank of that spiritual Rock that followed them, and that Rock was Christ" (1 Cor., x. 4). And this Rock was smitten for you, and the streams of His love and grace are following you—steadily, constantly following—urging you to bathe, wash, drink. "Whosoever will, let him drink," says Jesus (Rev. xvii. 17). O, brethren, why don't you drink ? Is it the waters of Egypt that have attracted you ? Have the waters of life become insipid to you ? O, drink—drink deeply, for this is the fountain of living waters. "And whosoever shall drink of the water I shall give him, it shall be in him a well of living water springing up into everlasting life," John 4, 14. "Shall never thirst," says Jesus. Does your experience give the lie to the Saviour's words ? Then your experience is wrong. Be assured of that. Go and correct it. Do not any longer dishonour your profession, your Saviour, your God.

Again he is the Sun, the true and only source of all light, life, health, power, beauty and bliss. On the mountain top the sky is clear, the sun's rays unobscured. Beneath, the clouds gather, the storms prevail ; if not the storms and thunder clouds, there are the fogs, and mists, and smoke of earth. O, why will Christians content themselves with the damp, dark and gloomy valleys, with their fogs, miasmas, and fevers, when they might dwell in the clear sunlight, breathe the free and pure air of heaven, and "sit with Christ in heavenly places?" O, let us leave the place of foggy doubt, of gloomy fear, of peace disturbing and health-consuming sin, and "walk in the light as He is in the light," having fellowship with God, "rejoicing in hope of the glory of God."

At this point let me say, I have a great partiality for this text, "In Him dwelleth all the fulness of the Godhead bodily" (Col. ii. 19). "The fulness of the Godhead;" surely that signifies divinity, infinity, omnipotence, eternity—all the attributes of Deity—all the perfections of God. And this fulness "dwells in Him *bodily*;" that I cannot comprehend, simply because it is incomprehensible. The same that thought, reason, intelligence, mind and soul should dwell in matter; that *I* should live in this frail body, and think, speak, and act through its organs—that I cannot comprehend. But I rejoice in the fact in both cases; as regards myself, certainly, as regards Jesus, more joyously. "Bodily:" that speaks of fellow-feeling, sensibility, sympathy. He is touched with our infirmities, and pities our weaknesses. If divine, He is able to supply our wants and administer to our necessities; if human, He loves to do so. No surly, unfeeling cashier stands at the bar of His bank, no hired clerk doles out favours in His stead. No patriarch, not even Enoch; no prophet, not even the seraphic Isaiah; no apostle, not even the beloved John; no angel, not even the archangel Gabriel, is permitted to take His place. Jesus Himself, with smiling face, with loving heart, and with bountiful hand imparts His saving grace. No wonder Paul says, "Ye are complete *in Him;*" for He presents to all who love Him a complete outfit, a perfect equipment, and brings about for them a thorough accomplishment. Nothing is wanting, nothing shall be lacking. "He will give grace and glory, and no good thing will He withhold from them that walk uprightly" (Psalm lxxxiv. 11).

II. These treasures are REVEALED to them that love God.

At a glance we see these treasures, however valuable, could do us no good unless in some way we were informed respecting them. A poor man may fall heir to immense wealth, but he remains poor unless some one acquaint him with the fact.

But God reveals by the Spirit unto us. It is His purpose that His people, all His people, each one of His children should know, should experience, should enjoy. The Spirit searcheth, says the text. Does not this imply anxiety on His part to know, and that in order that He may tell and make known. And indeed more the latter than the former; for what need of the Spirit searching? Does not the eleventh verse intimate that it is natural for the Spirit to know, as it is natural for man to know his own mind? Who should know man's mind, will, and purpose better than himself? and who should know the deep things of God, the good though mysterious purposes of His heart, better than the Holy Spirit, the third person in the Trinity, who is God? Surely it is in compassion to our ignorance, and slowness of comprehension that Paul says "the Spirit searcheth." Be that as it may, it certainly implies anxiety, and that on our behalf, not on His. The lawyer searcheth the records for his client's good.

And let us thank God it is the *Spirit* that revealeth. I could not, you should not, trust even the angels, for they are finite, and fallible. But all is perfectly safe here. When Jesus speaks, or His Spirit reveals no one is led astray. He "leads us into all truth," to peace, to God, to Christ, to heaven.

"Revealed." In His written word, say the theologian and the commentator, "To *us*," says the apostle; that is, again repeats the commentator, to inspired prophets, apostles, and evangelists, for, "holy men of

God spoke as they were moved by the Holy Ghost" (2 Pet. i. 21). Hence Paul in the sixth and seventh verses of our chapter, says, "we speak wisdom among them that are perfect," "we speak the wisdom of God in a mystery, even the hidden wisdom." For this reason we are bid listen to them. For this reason we are exhorted to "search the scriptures." To all which I heartily say, Amen. And, brethren, I would earnestly exhort you to "read, mark, learn, and inwardly digest" the scriptures of truth. Let the "man of God be perfect, thoroughly furnished unto all good works, for, "all scripture is given by inspiration of God" (2 Tim. iii. 15, 16). There is light enough in the Bible to save the world. O, let it enlighten, guide, save you.

All the above is right and true, and yet it is right and true but in part. To the inspired writers was given the knowledge of "the things that belong to our peace." In their writings we have, as we have seen, descriptions of these things, testimony respecting them, promises to those who seek them, exhortations to seek, and prayer to enjoy. And that is all, positively all, we can get from them.

But is that all we have need to know? Is that all the Spirit reveals? What about the experience of the grace unfolded to our view? What about the personal knowledge of the changes pointed out as imperatively necessary, and the fact that these changes are accomplished, or accomplishing? What about the possession of the promised and the desired good? How shall we know that our experiences are spiritual, our changes spiritual, gracious and real, and the blessings we fondly hope we have received are the gifts of God? Is there no possibility of deception here? To save us from deception should not a clear and full revelation be given, directly, to each one of us by the

Spirit of God? An error here may be not only very dangerous, but absolutely irreparable. And how easy to fall into error!

To this it will be replied, Salvation is by faith—you must believe what is written, for "he that believeth hath everlasting life." Again I say, Amen. But some things are not written in the Book—could not be written there—and these are the very things about which we naturally feel the most concern and anxiety. To assume these things is positive presumption, and such assumption is not faith.

"Rejoice that your names are written in heaven"—in heaven, not on earth—in God's register above, not in the Bible below. Rejoice they could not unless they knew their names written on high; they could not know unless it was revealed to them. In the Scriptures such a fact is not found; for the Bible is not a record of family names, or a genealogy of the sons of God. How know then? That is the all-important question.

May there not be two revelations, the one outward, on the pages of the written Word; the other inward, upon the believer's heart or consciousness? What is that revelation Christ speaks of in Matt. ii. 25, as "hidden from the wise and prudent, but made known to babes?" And that given to Peter, "not by flesh and blood" as the prophets were, "but the Father in heaven" (Matt. xvi. 17). These must be inward revelations; they could not be simple scripture unfoldings; this latter is simply impossible.

There may also be two manifestations, the one physical, the other spiritual. One we have in John i. 2, and apostolic eyes looked upon and their hands handled the Word of Life, "who was manifested to take away our sins" (1 John iii. 5). The other is given in

John xiv. 21, "He that hath my commandments and keepeth them, he it is that loveth me, . . and I will love him, and will manifest myself to him." Judas understood our Lord, "Lord, how is it that Thou wilt manifest Thyself *unto us*, and *not* unto the world?" (v. 22).

The following illustration may best explain my meaning. The United States and Canada have what are sometimes called "Homestead Laws." In these laws certain lands are located, and perhaps partly described. Certain conditions are laid down and duties imposed upon settlers; who, observing the conditions and performing the duties, become entitled to the lands. These laws are truly revelations to many a poor family, pointing out and providing a possible home for them. But the man who takes a lot, builds his cabin, performs required duties, and obtains a government deed, does he not know more on the reception of that deed than the law revealed or made known to him? Is not the deed a fuller revelation and a greater security than the laws? Do not the signature and seal upon that document inspire him with greater confidence? First he knew he might have a farm, a home of his own, now he knows that farm and house *is his own*. Here are two revelations, and the latter is the best; the first is indeed comparatively worthless without the other.

Now what saith the Scripture? It teaches me that the doctrine of justification—shows me how I may be justified. But it does not tell me I *am* justified, nor *when* I obtain that grace. And yet I cannot have peace with God until I *do* receive that grace, nor until I *know* I have received it.

It shows regeneration essential to salvation, and plainly proves that to be the work of the Holy Spirit. I may be conscious of a great change. But how shall

I know the change to be wrought of God. Shall I assume it? believe it without evidence? reach the conviction by a process of reasoning, and thus base my faith upon logic? Neither course can be safe.

It proclaims pardon. And I may be penitent; how shall I know I have obtained the forgiveness of sins. It tells me salvation is obtained by faith. But how shall I know my faith is accepted? I may believe pardon, justification, salvation are for me; but how shall I know that I have and hold either the one or the other.

But one answer can be given to all this; the Spirit reveals these things *unto us*—personally and individually unto us. I here present but one example, supported by two passages of Scripture. It is the believer's privilege to be adopted into the family of God. But how shall he know he is adopted? Paul supplies a clear answer. Rom. viii. 14-17: " For as many as are led by the Spirit of God, they are the sons of God. For ye have not received the spirit of bondage again to fear; but the spirit of adoption, whereby we cry, Abba, Father. The Spirit himself beareth witness with our spirits that we are the children of God. And if children then heirs; heirs of God; joint-heirs with Christ." Gal. iv. 6 : " And because ye are sons, God hath sent forth the Spirit of His Son into your hearts, crying, Abba, Father." Three things are plainly taught in these words: 1st, The adopted sons of God receive the Spirit of God, God sending Him into their hearts: 2nd, His work there is, as the Spirit of adoption, to witness or bear testimony *to* their adoption; to cry, and enable them to cry, Abba, Father: 3rd, Thus, knowing they are adopted, and recognized as sons and heirs, they are now free from bondage and fear.

Adoption, sonship, heirship, then, are revealed inwardly to the sons of God. These are some of the things "given to us of God." Do not these include all other blessings? Or, are all these alone revealed, and all others excluded? Surely this is but an example of the ordinary method of the work of the Spirit, and all the other "deep things of God" are revealed in like manner. In adoption is certainly included regeneration; how else can they become sons?—justification, for an unpardoned sinner can scarcely be an adopted son—sanctification, for the son should bear the Father's likeness, being "holy as he is holy"—and entitlement to glory, for that is the peculiar benefit of heirship. What then can be excluded?

It is objected to this precious Bible truth, that it represents God as constantly making new revelations, and that to every newly converted soul. This is supposed to be contradictory to all apostolic teaching, that nothing can be added to what is written in the Book of God (Rev. xxii. 18), to which it is easy and sufficient to reply, no new doctrine is revealed; no new truth is invented; but the old doctrines of the Bible are brought home with saving effect to other hearts, and Christ and His Word is thus glorified. The Bible teaches that all men are sinners; still the Spirit is sent to *convince* men of sin, and many are made to feel this so keenly, it is to them tantamount to a new revelation; but it is not a new truth or doctrine. It is simply an old truth applied with new power and effect. In like manner may the same man, believing, be *convinced* of his salvation.

III. These treasures are KNOWN by those who love God.

And that for the best of all reasons, because revealed by the Spirit of God. It is thus the text puts the matter: God prepares these treasures for us, reveals them to us, and we know them to be ours, if we love and are loved as the sons of God. Let me say in the briefest possible manner, these things are known, as must be apparent to every one, in two ways: as promised *and* received, as defined and experienced, as unfolded and possessed, as prepared and imparted, as deposited in Christ *and* lavished upon us.

"You once professed religion," said a good sister lately, to a lady friend; "why do you not do so now?" "I do not know that I ever enjoyed it," was the reply given. "Then you certainly did not enjoy it, for how could you enjoy, and not know it? If you ever enjoyed, you could never forget." Thus pointedly and positively the sister replied: was she correct? Can any one be born of God, receive the witness of the Spirit, and enter upon possession of the things "eye hath not seen," and be in ignorance or doubt of his relationship, experience and enjoyment? In the nature of things this cannot be.

How different the language of apostolic Christians. Brethren, take your concordances, note down the passages in which the words "we know," used in reference to Christian experience and believers' privileges occur. Over twenty such passages I find, and some of them read thus: "WE KNOW," "*thou* art true,"—"we have passed from death unto life"—"all things work together for good"—"if our earthly house of this tabernacle be dissolved, *we have* a building above"—"that when he shall appear, we shall be like him"—"that *we* are *of* God"—"that we are *in* him"—"that we *dwell* in him"—"that he *abideth* in us." And "we know *that we know him.*" Note again those texts containing the equally strong affirmative words, "Ye know." And there is nearly an equal number. Some read in this wise: "ye know whither I go and the way ye know "—"ye know him the Spirit of truth, for he dwelleth with you, and shall be in you "—" ye know the Spirit of God "—" ye know the grace of our Lord Jesus Christ." How precious these passages, and what force they impart to the sentence in the text, " that we might know the things that are freely given to us of God."

And now, dear brethren, suffer me to press upon you the great pivotal question on which the whole matter is made to turn,

Do you love God?

Any one can distinguish the son of a wealthy and generous man from the child of the poor and stingy. See the clothing he wears, and the money he spends. Mark the comforts by which he is surrounded, and the numerous friends he has. Note how erect he holds his head, how proud his bearing, how unrestrained his carriage. The paths of learning and literature are open to him, and bright prospects spread before him. Just as easily, and in the same natural way, should we know those who love God. We should know them by the depth and breadth of their experiences; by the wealth and abundance of their enjoyments; by the grandeur and sublimity of their aspirations and anticipations; by the blissfulness of the love that God bestows; the richness of the grace the Spirit imparts; the brightness of the glory, and fulness of the honour with which Jesus lovingly crowns them. They should be rich in faith, in grace, in power, in the deep things of God—that is, if our text be true.

What shall we say, then, of those who are perpetually complaining of their poverty, their leanness, their weakness, their darkness, their doubts, their fears, &c., &c., &c., for there seems to be no end of the black list of their aggrievances. Their light does not shine; their hearts are not glad; they have no songs by day or night. To be honest, they are mistaken in their relationship, or they are shamefully abusing it; or they, in ignorance, blindness, or wilfulness, undervalue their privileges. O, do not caricature religion; do not misrepresent the grace of God; do not falsify His Word. If you love God, prove it. Give evidence to all that "Eye hath not seen, nor ear heard, neither have entered into the heart of man the things which God hath prepared for those that love him." Give proof that "Things hidden from the wise and prudent are revealed unto babes;" and though the natural man receiveth them not, the spiritual discerneth and enjoyeth them.

THE LATER PROPHET.

By Rev. C. S. Eastman

Pastor of M. E. Church, Napanee, Ontario.

"And in the midst of the seven candlesticks one like unto the Son of Man."—Rev. i. 13.

THE term, "Son of man," was the official designation of the great prophets of the ancient time ; and therefore its appropriation by the Revelator to our Blessed Lord, as He appears amid the "golden candlesticks," (the precious and radiant emblem of the Christian Church,) is designed to indicate His office as the anointed Prophet of the Gospel Age. The functions of the prophetical office were not limited to the exercise of the extraordinary gift of unveiling and announcing the events of futurity. They were also the expositors of religious truth ; the interpreters of the moral law ; the conservators of their theocratic state. They were, in a word, the divinely authorised public teachers of religion. And our Lord Jesus Christ, as the Great Prophet of the Gospel Church, retains this distinctive character ; He came expressly as a "Teacher sent from God."

And now, at once assuming that our Lord's authority as the *Supreme Teacher* of mankind is capable of unquestionable vindication and that He is therefore entitled to our most reverent and absorbing attention, it is fitting we should direct our inquiries to the *leading subjects* of His teaching. This opens before us a field of such expansive range and transcendant interest that the mind is dazzled and overborne by the magnitude of the task to which we have set ourselves. The most that can be assumed to be done within the limit of our time is to present a very compendious outline of the great germinal truths of the wondrous system He unfolded and prescribed.

It may most reasonably be presumed that our Lord, at the commencement of His ministry, had clearly present in His capacious mind a comprehensive outline of the truths He was to impart to the world. Those truths, unlike the elaborate philosophies of the sages, were not derived from laboured investigations and involved processes of reasoning, but were evolved as pure and ultimate truth from the infinite treasury of His own divine mind. His teaching therefore possessed, in the highest meaning of the term, the quality of pure originality. If we were claiming this quality for an uninspired mind we should be considered as stating his highest claim to distinction. He who announces and verifies any new fact or principle of nature; who leads the human mind into any unexplored arcana of truth, has achieved for himself an immortality of fame as an essential contributor to the intellectual wealth of the race. But in the Great Teacher of Nazareth this is the grand distinguishing characteristic; all was original, new. It does not in any degree vitiate His claim to absolute originality that some of the truths He enunciated were previously familiar to mankind. Whatever of essential truth was found embodied in the old Jewish system was of the direct inspiration of His Spirit; and if He restated them, it was because He knew them to be the very truth of God. Having come to erect upon the earth a second temple of truth whose splendour should eclipse the glory of the former, it was His right as the builder of both to appropriate to the new whatever of the ancient material remained available. Indeed it was essential to the completeness of the new structure that He should do so. Therefore, truths which the lapse of ages had seen displaced and disconnected from their true positions, as stars are said to have wandered from their primal signs, He recalled and re-established; principles which had faded and disappeared, as stars are said to have become extinct, He rekindled and re-sphered and commanded to stand fast forever. If He repeated old and familiar truths, it was only that He might release them from the base companionship of error, and associating them with His own new and wondrous revelations, lift them to their proper place as living members of the immortal body of truth.

So that even in recasting the old truths of the primitive economy and giving them more than their original freshness and force by assigning them their appropriate place in the new and more enduring system, He displayed as striking an originality as if they had then for the first time broken upon the world from His lips. But if His claim to absolute originality should seem to be thus impaired, in the view of those who do not consider His office and relations to the old forms of truth, there can possibly exist no room for such questioning in relation to that vast body of truth which He for the first time unfolded to the world. Truths grand and vital, which, for wise though inscrutable reasons had remained concealed from the world, He unveiled and set in clear and unclouded light before the astonished and delighted gaze of humanity.

One of the subjects upon which He spoke with all

the authority of His divine office as the Supreme Teacher was the *paternal and benevolent character of God*. And this subject, as having a generic comprehension, and perhaps more than any other, representing the spirit and substance of the teaching of the Great Prophet we shall select as the theme of our present contemplation.

1. Upon the *fact* of the divine existence the world had previously acquired some correct knowledge. Indeed upon that subject the protestations of nature were most energetic and constant. Upon that subject she is ceaselessly, with all her myriad voices, making nothing less than solemn affirmation and oath. But while nature may be regarded as an oracle upon the subject of God's existence, upon the most anxious subject of His *moral character* and His relations through moral government to the moral universe she gives forth no responses; she is absolutely silent, having upon that subject received no instruction.

And therefore when the Divine Prophet came, He found the world without " the knowledge of God," vainly endeavouring to pierce the impenetrable darkness that surrounded the divine character. Hear His own emphatic statement: " O Righteous Father, the world hath not known Thee." " No man knoweth the Father save the Son, and he to whomsoever the Son will reveal Him." Nor does this statement require any essential modification from the fact that God had " spoken at sundry times and in divers manners " throughout the former dispensations. Without any unjust reflection upon the old Jewish Institute, it may be very boldly affirmed that it had given even to that favoured nation but a faint and partial conception of the divine character. What must have been the views entertained of God by Solomon, who, though selected to build the temple of Jehovah, could so quickly forsake its altars for an idol's grove. How obscure must have been the views of Jonah who, though a prophet of God, essayed to flee from His presence, and pettishly charged Him with fickleness for not involving Nineveh in the destruction he had predicted. How imperfect and partial must have been the conceptions of the divine character held by that nation who believed itself to be the exclusive subject of His favours; who had suspended heaven in their imagination over Judea as a celestial preserve for their sole occupancy; and were intensely jealous lest He should admit any portion of the Gentile race within the pale of salvation. Such were the narrow limits to which Judaism had confined the illimitable benevolence of God.

And as to the Gentile world: its condition was fully described in the language of an apostle—it "knew not God." In Greece where the dialectic philosophy, the philosophy of probabilities, had achieved its proudest results—in Athens where it was enthroned—its last supreme effort was to rear an altar "to the unknown God." At Rome the asylum of deposed and fugitive gods, the Pantheon of the world, no intelligible memorial of the true God existed.

The results of the utmost efforts of uninspired philosophy were embodied in three general ideas. The first was Atheism, which maintained that the idea of a God was a figment. The second was Polytheism, which peopled the universe with an interminable multitude of deities, the patrons of almost as many vices. The third was Monotheism, which admitted the existence of one Supreme Deity, but removed His throne to a remote and awful distance and relieved him from the care and government of His creatures.

This theory which was undoubtedly the creed of the majority, maintained that having created the universe, He had retired into the infinite solitudes of an immeasurable distance therefrom; and that His happiness so fully depended upon undisturbed repose, that the character and condition of His creatures never for a moment engaged His thought. This, as some one has expressed it, was "Atheism with a God." It admitted a divine existence but left the universe bereft of His care. The vicious were left to cherish their vices without fear of His frown, and the virtuous to practice their virtues without hope of His favour, and the helpless and suffering to send up their cries vainly for relief. Could all the sufferers that ever dwelt upon the earth have sent up their cries in one infinite wail it could not pierce the supposed distance of His abode or wake one responsive throb of sympathy in His heart.

2. But how different the view of the character and conduct of God as presented by our Divine Prophet. Drawing aside the veil that conceals Him from our view, he reveals Him in His high and holy place, not in a state of silence and solitude, but as surrounded by ten thousand times ten thousand, and thousands of thousands of holy and happy beings, each with eager obedience waiting upon His word; not in the listless repose of a resolute inactivity, but as in active and vital communication with every part of His illimitable domain; not in a state of apathy to the affairs of our world, but as actually bending from His infinite height in eager and loving attention towards it, listening to every sound it utters, observing the movements of all its living inhabitants, and approving or condemning every moral action it exhibits. He magnified to the utmost our conceptions of the condescension of the Supreme

Father by representing Him as bestowing active attention on the minutest details of mundane affairs. He leads us forth into the open fields of nature and surprises us with the amazing sight of the same hand that upholds the world, painting the lily and garnishing the fields, feeding the ravens and shielding the sparrow's nest. He appeals to every drop of rain and every ray of light as evidence of His universal goodness, and having thus confirmed the fact of His paternal providence, He prepares our minds for its highest displays by enunciating the principle that the degree of Divine attention bestowed upon any object is graduated by the rank it holds in the scale of existence. If, therefore, the grass of the field and the fowls of the air share His unfailing attention, what line can measure the depth of His regard for that being created in His own image and designed for companionship with Himself; He thus throws open the vast volume of providence and assures us that to every human being is assigned a page, upon which are entered the minutest details of his history.

3. But from this aspect of the Divine benevolence the Great Prophet leads us into a higher region still. Having assured our confidence and elated our hopes by exhibiting the minuteness of His attention to our temporal wants, He has prepared our minds for the higher exhibitions of His munificence towards us as His *spiritual offspring.* Having shown us the liberality of His hand He encourages us to a nearer approach; to take a nearer view of His character; to look into His very heart. We begin to catch the holy exhilaration of the exercise, to feel our hopes rising and our expectations growing sanguine; we feel that to rise to the theme we must give wing to our imagination and urge it to its utmost flight. But who shall utter the wonders of

God's grace? Here we contemplate an aspect of the Divine benevolence, in which all the moral glories of His nature are unfolded and beam with a splendour dazzling and overwhelming even to angelic vision. The only adequate utterance ever given to that grace was one indited by the same infinite heart in which it had its birth; and though an utterance couched in human phrase, its fulness of meaning can never be grasped by human conception—"God *so* loved the world that He gave His only begotten Son that whosoever believeth on Him should not perish but have everlasting life." "*Herein is love.*" We need not presume to raise the question whether a gift of inferior value would have availed to redeem the world; enough it is for us to know that no less a gift would have realised the vast proportions of His love; He "*so* loved" us that He resolved upon a gift defying all computation; He "*so* loved" us that He would not permit it to be said that He *could* have loved us more; He "*so* loved" us that in one infinite offering He poured out the whole treasury of heaven in our behalf. "*Herein is love.*"

The blessed Teacher enhances our conception of the benevolence of God in this amazing gift by pointing out the *awful alternative* which outraged Omnipotence might have adopted. The ends of moral government would have been attained, the rectitude of the Divine administration would have been vindicated, and the moral order of the universe perfectly maintained by leaving man in the hands of justice to endure the full penalty he had incurred. There was no constraint of moral necessity impelling God to avert the descent of the stroke of justice upon a guilty race. Man was under arrest, and the moral instincts of all holy intelligences were awaiting in awful suspense until the vials of infinite wrath should be poured out upon him. And if the thunder-blast of justice had fallen and the apostate race had been swept by the consuming tempest of Divine wrath, the whole moral universe would have responded, "Righteous art Thou, O Lord, because Thou hast thus judged." Such was the alternative open to the Divine Father. But in that awful crisis of our world, when justice had already poised his bolt and the universe awaited in trembling suspense to witness its flight, mercy prevailed to unfold the scheme of man's rescue and prompted the amazing gift of the Divine Son as the world's substitute. "Herein is love." Is it wonderful that the apostles never touched this subject but they kindled into raptures with the inspiration of their theme. Conscious that their language fell beneath their conceptions, and their loftiest conceptions fell immeasurably beneath their theme, they could only exclaim in the impotence of overwhelming admiration, "*Herein is love.*" The universe is crowded with proofs of God's benevolence, but here is one that outweighs them all. Here is a depth of love that no plummet can sound; a height that no wing of imagination can scale; an expanse that no line of measurement can compass.

4. But the Divine Teacher still further enlarges our view of the benevolence of God in the gift of Christ by setting forth the *direct results* to man of His offering. "I am come," said He, "that they might have *life*" "I give unto them *eternal life.*" Sin had deprived man of a whole order or type of life, the life that springs from the soul's union with God. His moral nature was left a reeking, putrid corpse; his moral perceptions paralyzed; his affections dead, and every spiritual joy extinguished. The whole nature was so palsied and perverted by sin that it was utterly incapable of appropriating and circulating the elements

of a divine life. But God accomplishes our restoration from this death by sending His Son to assume our humanity, and by restoring its lost union to Himself, open anew in our nature the springs of a divine life. By this mysterious adjunction of our nature to His own, He lives through all the powers of the soul; the pulses of the divine heart beat again in life-giving currents through our nature. He lives as a light in our understanding, love in our affections, and a perpetual current of blessedness mingling with the stream of our consciousness. Who shall define and portray the blessedness of this life even on earth. It is more than an element of good; it is the union and essence of all blessedness. It is existence enriched by the highest positive happiness; it is life purified and exalted to the loftiest ends, and carried upwards to its utmost capabilities of enjoyment; it is the very crown of being; it is God multiplied in the hearts of His people. And this life so blessed in its inceptivity here is to be consummated and perpetuated eternally in heaven. The benevolent impulses of the divine heart could be satisfied with nothing less for man than a glorified life; a life of ever-expanding knowledge, of ever-growing purity, of ever-intensifying rapture.

5. But if our conceptions of the divine benevolence in redemption are so wonderfully exalted by the *end* therein secured to man, how immeasurably must they be intensified by the contemplation of the *means and process* by which this end is secured. The gift of eternal life to a race by whom it had been utterly forfeited was an act of benevolence in itself so vast that had it cost the Almighty but a mere volition; had it been as easy as the fiat that gave birth to light, it would have rendered His grace a theme of just amazement to the universe. But the execution of this scheme of mercy

demanded more than the simple volition that created worlds, or the uncontrolled and tranquil circulation of the omnipotent energy that sustains them. "*The Son of man must be lifted up.*" The course of justice demanded that before sin could be pardoned it must be punished, or expiated. "Without the shedding of blood there is no remission." Therefore the Son of God must submit to such conditions that justice could deal with Him as the sinner's substitute. He must take the offending nature into union with His own that He might pour out its blood and make its soul an offering for sin. Our nature was to Him a robe of suffering assumed expressly that when the crisis of our redemption came justice could find Him sacrificially attired and prepared for the altar; arrayed in a substance that justice could smite; a victim to agonize and die. To this infinite task the Father devoted His Son, and to its execution the Son eagerly consecrated Himself. Having minutely surveyed all that would be demanded of the sinner's surety; having measured with His eye the thunder-stores of wrath that should be exhausted upon Him, He pressed the entire responsibility to His heart, and eagerly descended to the scene of His toils and agonies. And if the human soul is capable of an indefinite enlargement in its capacity of happiness or pain; if the admission of the purified spirit to the raptures of heaven augments its capacity of happiness until almost an infinitude of blissful emotion is pressed into a moment's space; what must have been the measureless capacity for suffering of that soul that He took into such intimate union with His own divinity that the two natures were but one? What must have been the intensity of that exceeding sorrow when he absorbed the infinite mass of the world's guilt, and in one awful draught exhausted the mighty cup of

Omnipotent wrath? And for the key to this mystery of compassion, the Great Teacher refers us to the benevolence of God. As we stand before the cross musing upon that amazing expedient of mercy, the agonizing Sufferer, pointing upward, bids us look into the heart of the infinite Father for an explanation of the scene. He impresses upon us the sublime fact that God loved us, not in consequence of the propitiation of His Son, but that propitiation was itself the consequence of His love; it was His own adopted medium through which He could pour out upon us the ocean-fulness of His love.

Perhaps of all the wonderful declarations of the divine prophet respecting the benevolence of God in redemption none is more pregnant of meaning than that memorable utterance, "Therefore doth my Father love me because I lay down my life that I might take it again—because I lay down my life for the sheep." That is to say, " my Father loveth *you* with a love so boundless that he loveth *me* the more for dying to redeem you. He loves you so much that whatever facilitates the expression of that love is deemed to merit peculiar tokens of His divine approval. By assuming your liabilities and surrendering my life as an equivalent for you, I am setting his compassion at liberty; I am removing a restraint from His love which threatened to hold it in eternal suspense and am leaving it free to act, to flow out in saving currents towards you without the appearance of connivance at sin or the compromise of justice, and for my concurrence in this His benevolent purpose to save you, He multiplies the expression of His complaisancy to me. Although ineffably beloved of my Father from eternity He has in consequence of my 'obedience unto death' added infinite delight to infinite delight."

And how inexpressibly must it enhance our conception of the divine compassion if we remember that there is a sense in which the sufferings of Christ were the sufferings also of the Divine Father. From eternity their subsistence in the unity of the Godhead had been only short of identity itself. Nor could the circumstance of the Son's humiliation in the slightest measure have relaxed the intimacy of their mutual indwelling. The incarnate Saviour was throughout His life surrounded by an atmosphere of infinite love. Once and again the divine complaisancy overflowing itself surprised the world with the announcement, "This is my beloved Son in whom I am well pleased." Therefore it must be said that every moment of the humiliation of Christ that love was repeating its infinite sacrifice for sinners; every pang He endured in the execution of His mission was a wound inflicted upon the divine heart. Who then shall assume to tell the anguish that must have penetrated the paternal heart, as He witnessed the Son of His love, in the hour of His agony draining the cup of trembling mingled by justice. If it be true that God is in sympathetic communication with every part of the suffering universe—that as the great sensorium of the living creation He apprehends every emotion and commiserates every thrill of pain—with what exquisite anguish must His heart have been wrung when in the crisis of His agonizing task the plaintive filial appeal of the suffering victim pierced His ear—" My God, why hast Thou forsaken me." If there could have occurred a moment when the adoration of the seraphic multitudes could have been lost upon the divine attention; if there could have occurred a moment when He could have repented the infinite sacrifice He was making for sinners, surely that must have been the moment. O, what an insight does this scene give us to the compassion of God for man, that it could endure the stress, the incalculable power of that tragic appeal of His Son. It exhibits more than the sufferings of Christ; it exhibits the throes of the paternal heart. Here is a line of measurement with which we are enabled to sound to inconceivable depths only to find that His love reaches immeasurably deeper still.

6. But the Divine Prophet sets before us the breadth and compass of the benevolence of God in redemption by showing that *its benefits are for the world*. Human selfishness has developed phases that would limit and localize its benefits. The Jewish Christians, for example, would fain have made it a local and national benefit, until the unconfinable Spirit came and showed them that it was for the world. And the inheritors of their crampt and narrow spirit would also confine it to a favoured few, a chosen and predestinated party. But an attempt to imprison the air or enchain the light would be even more salutary and consonant with the divine benevolence. Shall the ordinary gifts of providence be freely chartered to the world and the stigma of exclusiveness be reserved for His grace alone. "1 am the light of the world" was Christ's announcement of Himself—a blessing as diffusive and universal as the light. The message of mercy which He brought from the Father was meant for the ear of the world— "*Whoso* hath ears to hear let him hear," and as though the world were assembled before Him and He had obtained universal audience, this is the music that broke from His lips: "God so loved the world that He gave His only begotten Son that *whosoever* believeth in Him should not perish but have everlasting life." He gave His Son to encircle the earth with an atmosphere of grace as universal as the elemental air. The messengers

of the gospel are sent to the world with a message of mercy as wide as the race and as deep as the lowest abyss of human guilt. No ambassador of God in any clime or age shall ever be subjected to the pain of looking into any human face, however deeply scarred with the gashes of crime and saying, " for you I have no invitations of grace, no proposals of reconciliation." But everywhere and to all men he is instructed to cry, " unto *you* is the word of this salvation sent.

Such my brethren is a very inadequate statement of the teaching of the later and most illustrious Prophet respecting the paternal and benevolent character of God. Shall we not do well to pause and retrace the course of thought by which we have been led. We have been taught that the Supreme Creator having, out of the impulses of His Infinite benevolence, created us and invested us with our peculiar capabilities of happiness, bends ever in loving attention from His throne towards us reaching out His hand as a provident Father to supply our wants shielding our defencelessness, and minutely superintending the events of our history. That He unfolded the richer treasures of His grace in the wondrous act of redemption, thereby lifting our guilty world from the gloomy precincts of hell into the radiance of an orbit next His throne ; that He made even our hatred subserve the purposes of His love, and evolved from the evil of our fall a greater good than could otherwise have existed ; that He adopted our nature in the person of His Son and carried it to the highest throne of the highest heavens, thus conferring upon us an honour to which an attending retinue of angels would fail to serve even as a comparison ; that the means of all this glory was the humiliation and sacrifice of His Son ; that the benefits of His redemption are designed for the whole world; and that He hath crowned these distinctions of His goodness by sending forth His Spirit into our hearts encouraging us to call Him "Abba, Father." From whatever point of view therefore we contemplate that benevolence the prospect widens and expands before us into infinitude; it amasses glory upon glory until the scene becomes too bright for human vision. O what a God! what a Father! It is as though, having collected together all the treasures of His grace; having opened up the benevolent resources of His nature, He delivered all into the hands of His Son, saying—"these, *all* these, are for man; use them all for man; distribute them all upon man, that he may know that there is no love like Mine and that he may know also that his happiness depends only upon his knowing and loving Me." Such is the knowledge of God as unfolded by the Divine Teacher.

Let us now hear His own declaration respecting the value of that knowledge and its vital relation to our happiness. "This is eternal life that they might know thee, the only true God Jesus Christ whom Thou hast sent." Knowledge of all kinds is enriching; it is the proper wealth and heritage of a rational being. But no range of secular erudition abstract from a true knowledge of God can conduct to happiness; this is the only knowledge that in itself can guide upward to unfading crowns and eternal life. The Scriptures sometimes represent the supreme happiness of heaven as consisting in the fuller vision of God, so also the whole of religion on earth consists in knowing God as Christ unveils Him. Because, first, sin originates in ignorance of God; it prevails most where God is most completely unknown or forgotten. And, because, secondly, to know

God truly is to be enamoured of His excellence ; to be attracted, softened, subdued, and by the very intensity of love transformed into His image.

And now let me ask, are we, as tractable learners in the school of Christ, humbly asking the knowledge of God ? To what purpose have we thus far attended upon His instructions ? Have our hearts been attracted and led to submission to God, or are they yet obdurate and rebellious ? Do we joyfully contemplate Him as a Father reconciled in Christ, or do we shrink from Him with guilty distrust and dread ? With what emotions do we contemplate our ultimate meeting with Him in judgment ? Do we wait with insufferable dread the awful sentence of condemnation and banishment, or do we anticipate with exultation the ineffable sentence of acquittal and reward ? To such as do know Him in the plenitude of His gracious character, suffer the word of apostolic exhortation,—" Grow in grace and in the knowledge of our Lord Jesus Christ." But it may be presumed that at the feet of some of you must be laid the charge of the apostle, "Some have not the knowledge of God, I speak this to your shame." During all your life, by the words of His anointed Prophet God has been soliciting your attention, and and presenting Himself for your admiration, and yet it must be said, " He is not in all your thoughts." You have no delight in Him ; His benevolent and gracious character has not impressed and subdued your heart. O ! what shall you answer, when at His bar it shall be said, " I sent unto you my Son, but ye have rejected His testimony to me ; ye have refused to know Me ; ye have put away from you My counsels of mercy, therefore do I now make Myself known to you in the consuming terrors of My wrath—' Depart from Me ye that work iniquity.'" O! may the blessed Spirit that "commanded the light to shine out of darkness" shine into our hearts, to give us the light of the knowledge of the glory of God in the face of Jesus Christ.

THE CONFESSION OF SIN.

By Elijah H. Pilcher, M.A., D.D.,

Of the Niagara Conference.

If we confess our sins, He is faithful and just to forgive us our sins, and to cleanse us from all unrighteousness. 1 John i. 9.

THE Christian religion is thoroughly adapted to the wants and necessities of human nature, and the more perfectly it is experienced and practised the more it purifies and exalts humanity. Indeed the principles of divine truth, as found in the Bible, appear more beautiful and fascinating the more closely and carefully they are scrutinized. As the effect of the religion of the Bible upon individuals and upon society is understood, promoting the happiness of the one and the harmony of the other, so will it be admired and approved; and the most fruitful cause of scepticism, aside from the depravity of the human heart, is the failure of professors of religion to exemplify its power to save from sin. It is true infidels in general shew a great amount of ignorance in regard to the teachings of the Bible, but yet they know enough to lead them to pronounce judgment with much accuracy on the conduct of professors. Under the influence of their depravity and the discouraging effects of the failure to exemplify the vitality of that religion, they, through their vain philosophy, attempt to set it aside. So that one of the best and most successful methods of meeting the scepticism of the present day is to exemplify the experience involved in the text I have chosen for this discourse.

Scepticism in this day of light does not arise from the lack of evidence to support the truth of Christianity, but from a depravity of heart and will, or from an inattention to the evidence given in its favour and from neglect or refusal to investigate its claims for acceptance. It is found where there is a willingness to comply with its requirements there is no lack of light. This holds good both as it regards Christianity itself and that purity of heart and life which is so beautifully described by Christ and His Apostles. Many who most cordially subscribe to the truth of the Bible, fail to enjoy its hallowing influences. They either procrastinate the time of their obedience, or do not fully understand how to perform that which is required. Whatever may be the cause of this inattention to the things of God and eternity, it has become necessary that they should have "line upon line" of instruction; hence the necessity of a living, practical ministry, having a deep experience of divine fellowship. God in mercy has provided this for the Christian Church. The work assigned the ministry is not only responsible, but difficult of accomplishment. There is so much opposition of heart to God, so much love of the world and of self, it is very hard to persuade men to humble themselves so much as to confess their wrongs. The difficulty consists not so much in producing in them a conviction of the propriety of what is proposed, as in inducing them to enter upon the performance of what they know to be right. God

THE CONFESSION OF SIN.

has held out every inducement, as in command, exhortation, and promise of advantage, to comply.

We have in our text a duty with the advantage growing out of its performance.

The first thing to be noticed is the confession of sin. All the refined and ennobled principles in our nature at once suggest that, if faults have been committed, it is proper, indeed it is just, to make a confession to the person or party injured. In accordance with this principle, the Holy Scriptures require this very thing. Many have taken a mistaken view of this matter and have supposed and felt it was degrading of them to make confession of faults or wrongs committed, and hence have persisted in wrong. But why should this be? If there is any degradation in the case, it certainly does not lie in the confession, but in the act which calls for it. When we have fallen either into error or sin, to confess it only argues that we have either grown wiser or better, and that there exists in us a purpose to improve upon the past. This, instead of degrading, exalts us in the eyes of all virtuous and good men. What more noble, what more praiseworthy than an effort to make restitution where injuries have been perpetrated! That confession in a proper way and under proper circumstance is a duty, will be readily admitted. But what those circumstances are, and how the duty is to be performed, form a very interesting subject of inquiry, and to this we now address ourselves.

1. *To whom is the confession to be made?* Evidently to the party injured or offended. It, therefore, sometimes becomes a duty to confess to men inasmuch as they are often offended. "Confess your faults one to another, and pray one for another, that ye may be healed." This, however, is a very different

thing from that made to a priest in the confessional and for a different purpose. The one is to the party concerned to obtain his absolution for the injury done him, and not for the moral guilt, but the other is to an uninterested third party who claims to have authority to cancel the moral offence. I do not conceive it necessary to confess in detail to the world offences which are unknown to all but the "all-seeing eye." It is sufficient in such cases to confess them to Him against whom they have been committed. As to a confession to a priest, it is grounded on no warrant of the Holy Scriptures and is productive of much evil. If thou hast sinned against thy neighbour, go to him, —confess your wrong, and as far as possible make him satisfaction. It may become proper,—a duty, to confess to the Church: as, when we violate our pledges to the Church and so. work an injury to the body of Christ, or wound the brethren. Every action has a moral bearing in it, which is either good or bad as it conforms to the moral, or differs from it ; for which reason there is a *moral* turpitude connected with every violation of the claims of that law, which moral turpitude none but the moral law-giver, that is, God, can forgive. Hence after all, the absolutions granted by mortals, it is necessary to confess to God and obtain pardon from him. As the Psalmist says, "Against thee, thee only, have I sinned, and done this evil in thy sight."

2. What is implied in confession of sin? 1. An acknowledgement of the fact, which is the lowest sense which can be attached to it in any place. This may be without any just appreciation of the nature of the act, as is often the case when unconverted persons are addressed on the subject of salvation, or are reproved for their wickedness. Their frequent reply is

that they know they are sinners and that we have no right to expect anything better of them. In this there does not appear to be any correct sense of the nature of their actions. The last part of the reply is decidedly erroneous, and has been too much conceded to them, that is, that we have no right to expect anything better of them. That they do not profess anything better will be granted without hesitation, but that we have no right to expect anything better of them is not true. God and society have a claim on them which never can be relinquished, that all their time and energies, physical, intellectual and moral, be directed for the glory of the one and the peace of the other. As they exist in society and form a constituent part of it, every individual of the divinely instituted social organization has a claim—an unrelinquishable claim—upon every other member, that he so live, speak and act as to promote the love and practice of virtue in its highest sense. God, as the instituter of society, cannot yield His claim. Wherever he turns his eyes, he will find staring him full in the face, written as with the finger of God, "God, society and yourself have the right to expect the avoidance of all evil and the performance of all good." God has enforced this claim by the most sacred and awful sanctions. Amidst the smoke, the quaking, the thunders and lightnings of Sinai, He has proclaimed it. What a solemn, and yet what a careless admission is made! I have thus brought to view a principle of deepest value but very much neglected, the obligation of all to maintain a holy life; and when men admit they are sinners, it is a confession that they have neglected the most sacred obligation, and it should fill them with earnest contrition. 2. It implies a deep sense of the nature and results of sin. It is an offence against God—against society—against their own highest and best interests—a rejection of all the influences of divine mercy, as well as the operations of the Holy Spirit upon their hearts. Divine mercies have crowded thick upon us—they have been distributed with a liberal hand—every hour has brought with it some new token of divine beneficence. Even the chastisements of this life are sent in love "for our profit." The Holy Spirit has taken of the things of the Father and has shown them to us—He has often (or would have done so if permitted by us) unfolded to our contemplation the brightest, most lovely and most interesting visions of the future—of the spirit land; He has impressed upon upon us that these are not visions that pass away as the fleeting shadow, but are glorious, eternal realities. Scenes the most endearing, the most transporting to the soul, have been unfolded to our view—the Spirit has spoken in the most melting, persuasive strains to our hearts, to bear us away from sin to holiness and to heaven. All these influences have been resisted, broken through, thrown off. Society, the Holy Spirit, Christ the Redeemer, God the Father, have been set at naught. This is the nature of sin. It is a resistance to all the laws of right. The effects of sin are two-fold, that is, upon society and upon the individual himself. Let us but cast our eyes abroad over the face of nature and we shall see the very elements at war with man. The earth has become one great charnel house; the dead are piled in "heaps upon heaps." Hear the groan of the sick and dying—the sighing of the widow and fatherless—every breeze is burdened with them. Hear the bitter lamentations of the bereaved and forsaken; mark the contortions of the distressed and agonized; see the palsied limbs, the wan and wasted countenances; listen to the clanking of the chains of the prisoners enduring the penalty of violated

G

law. But especially listen to the sighs of the oppressed, enslaved and down-trodden of our race. Mark the untimely deaths, by stealth and violence, the squalid poverty and the accompanying circumstances of wretchedness and distress, and cruelty in the habitations of the poor inebriates. But the heart turns away sickened and distressed. We might continue the contemplation till we should become sick of life. And what has occasioned all his? Let the great apostle to the Gentiles furnish us with the only answer: "By one man sin entered into the world, and death by sin." Again, the effects to the individual himself are terrible. Sin carries with it a sense of shame and degradation. By it communion with God has been broken off; peace banished from his bosom; pain, darkness both mental and moral, misery and despair have taken the place, and finally, if persisted in, "eternal destruction from the presence of God and the glory of his power." Who that contemplates these results in the light of the Bible, can avoid feeling? But alas! for the mass of the human race, they never stop to think, but rush madly on, "deceiving and being deceived," until they are swallowed up in the whirl-pool of destruction, and wake up only to realize that they are lost beyond the hope of recovery. They never seem to think that they are contributing to perpetuate the turbid storm of misery, degradation and death which is overflowing society and carrying away and blighting the fairest and brightest hopes of man. If ever this thought arises, it is suppressed as quickly as possible. This sense of the nature and effects of sin involves the acknowledgment of the justness of the claims of the divine law. 3. It implies here contrition or penitence. This supposes real sorrow for the acts committed, in view, both of their nature and effects. There is much worldly sorrow for sin, that is, sorrow simply because we are found out in it, or because we have to suffer for it, "which works death." But here is sorrow, not simply because of the punishment which must ensue, but because it is an offence against God and society. Where true penitence exists it is always accompanied by a desire to reform, nay more, by a fixed determination by the help of God's grace to lead a new life, "following the commandments of God, and walking in his Holy ways." However much the sinner may appear to feel and regret his former course of life—however much he may weep over his sins—however earnestly he may acknowledge the fact, if there be no determined, settled purpose by divine grace to turn away from vice and become consecrated to God and His cause, there is no true sense of either the nature of sin, or of the force of his obligation to God; and let not such think they can find acceptance with Him.

3. Confession in this text further implies faith in the atonement made by Christ. The Holy Scriptures throughout uniformly represent the sufferings and death of the Lord Jesus Christ as furnishing the only meritorious ground of our acceptance with God, and faith as the instrument by which the virtue of His death is applied. Whenever, therefore, anything is presented, which would seem to form the reason of acceptance with God, it must be construed in conformity with this principle, and as implying faith. This is the case here. Confession is named as the condition to be performed, and is the only thing specified; hence therefore, it must suppose faith, not simple credence of the atonement as a fact existing, but a trust in the provisions made.

In Romans v. 1, it is said, "Therefore, being justified by faith, we have peace with God though our

Lord Jesus Christ." Faith being that act by which we are united to Christ, always supposes all the prerequisites and concomitants to its exercise, as the greater includes the less. Whenever, then, good works are said to form the reason of our justification, either here or at the Judgment, it is so, simply, because they spring from faith in Christ, and are therefore, the outward exhibition of the inward principle of faith or trust; "so that a true and lively faith may as well be known as a tree is known by its fruits." In like manner, when confession is said to secure pardon, as in this case, it is to be understood as including faith, that the beauty and harmony of the Scriptures may not be broken.

The next thing to be considered is the effects resulting from a proper confession of sin. 1. "He is faithful and just to forgive us our sins." Forgiveness supposes the removal of the moral guilt, and also the remission of the punishment which would have ensued. Nothing less than this can be meant, otherwise no benefit would result to us. To suppose that the punishment is remitted, and at the same time that the moral guilt remains, would be an absurdity. It would be even more absurd, to suppose that the guilt should be taken away, and yet the punishment be inflicted. Forgiveness is one of the most delightful and soul-cheering doctrines, which could be presented to guilty mortals, as we are. Is it possible that all my sins may be blotted out? Oh, how thrilling the very thought of it! Such is the interest we have in it, we would have supposed that it would have met with universal applause, more, that it would have been hailed with one general shout of joy, feeling, as we do, a consciousness of sin. But, alas, for poor fallen humanity! how blind! how recreant to its best interests! man has rejected the kind offer of Heaven, and set himself at work to sweep away this only solace from the contrite heart. God is merciful. It has been affirmed by some that God cannot in any way forgive sins, and what is still more strange, it has been asserted by some who profess to believe the Bible, that God has declared He would not forgive sins. They certainly must have forgotten certain important and interesting passages in that blessed book, as the following: "In whom (that is Christ) we have redemption though his blood, the forgiveness of sins." "Thou hast forgiven the iniquity of thy people, thou hast covered all their sin.' The Lord forgiveth all thine iniquity." "Let the wicked forsake his way, and the unrighteous man his thoughts; and let him return to the Lord, and he will have mercy on him; and to our God for he will abundantly pardon." "And that repentance and remission of sins should be preached in his name among all nations." "To turn them from darkness to light, and from the power of Satan unto God, that they may receive forgiveness of sins." The text says, "He is faithful and just to forgive us our sins." Although the number might be greatly extended, these are sufficient to establish the fact of forgiveness. How delightfully refreshing these are to the weary, burdened sin-sick soul! They, who would invalidate them, would take away from us the last gleam of hope, for the law knows no mercy; and if we are left either to pay the debtor or suffer the penalty, all is lost. Thanks to a forgiving God, He has made known His mercy, and shown us how He can be just and yet forgive the penitent believer in Jesus.

What is meant by forgiveness? I think it plainly supposes that the guilt contracted is removed or taken away—the sense of it destroyed, and as a natural consequence, the punishment is remitted, or is not inflicted. Anything less than this would not meet the necessities of the guilty sinner. Anything more is certainly included in the second benefit named in the text, and hereafter to be noticed. Some have fallen into a fatal error, as I think, in regard to the doctrine of forgiveness, by running too close a parallel between the operations of physical and moral laws. It is this, that every offence or violation of law must unavoidably be punished. "For we see," say they, "that if a man thrust his hand into the fire he will be burned and suffer pain for his temerity, because he has violated a physical law. So also in other respects; hence, God has so ordered that every infraction of the moral law shall receive certain and immediate punishment." The mistake here, consists in deciding from the operations of one kind of law, that another and entirely different kind of law operates in the same way. The argument is unsound. It is true, God will not hold the transgressor guiltless, but the punishment is reserved; and, under the remedial system provided by Jesus Christ, it may be avoided as shown above. To this it has been objected that it gives a licence to sin, because the transgressor may escape. To this I would simply answer, who that has any just sense of sin or proper view of the sad, agonizing, bloody scenes of the garden and of Calvary, and thinks that it is only through the tears, the groans, the blood, the death of Christ, he can obtain a release from the punishment his guilt deserves, can feel that he has a licence to sin? Nay, he will feel that the dignity of the law is maintained, and its awful sanction fully sustained. It is only when we keep these things out of view that we can consent to sin. It is to be remembered, too, that it is only for the sins which are past we can hope for pardon. If we repeat the sin we do it at our peril.

Another theory, which is somewhat ripe in certain places, is that though the moral guilt may be removed, the punishment is retained in every case. This is attempted to be sustained in two ways: the first is the same as that above noticed, to wit, reasoning from the effects of physical to the operation of moral laws, which has been shown to be incorrect. The second is built upon the language of Nathan to David, as found in 2 Sam. xii. 12. But upon an inspection of the case, it will be found that the punishment is not retained in the same respect as that in which the guilt is said to be forgiven. Another aspect in this case is that this particular case is made to establish a universal rule, which is not admissible. On this theory, what benefit is there in pardon? Surely there is none. The culprit must as certainly die as if the pardoning power did not exist, or was not exercised. To hold out a pardon in this way would only be to tantalize the feelings and aggravate the miseries of the wretched and condemned. To illustrate: suppose a criminal to have been arraigned before a court on a charge of high crime—tried—convicted—sentence of death passed, and the day of execution appointed, but by the intervention of friends, the case has been brought before the Executive of the country, and what purported to be a pardon obtained. This now is rumoured abroad, yet the messenger has not returned—the day of execution has come—the multitude has assembled—the criminal is led out to the place of execution—is placed on the scaffold—nearly the last moment has come—the stillness of death pervades the assembly—all are standing in breathless attention and suspense, when suddenly a cry is heard, and the expected messenger exclaims a *pardon!* and presses his way through the anxious crowd and delivers into the hand of the proper officer the proclamation—he opens it and reads. After the usual introduction it proceeds thus: "From the representations in this case to me, and after due, solemn deliberation, by virtue of the authority vested in me, I freely and fully pardon him of all the guilt incurred in the matter for which he has been condemned by the court, and command all authorities to treat him according to this proclamation." At this all hearts feel the thrill of delight and are ready to burst forth in exclamations of joy. But the officer proceeds: "Nevertheless the law must have its full force, therefore I command that he be executed at the time and place appointed by the court." How suddenly the joy is turned into sorrow, and the exclamations of delight to murmurs of disappointment and sadness. They turn away in disgust and contempt for the actors in such a farce. O! how cruel to raise expectations in order to more effectually crush the wounded spirit. By this theory God is made to act in this manner with His erring, sinful yet intelligent subjects. "He is faithful and just to forgive." According to this text justice has as much to do with the pardon of the sinner as mercy. We sometimes hear it said that mercy triumphs over justice in the justification of men. This is decidedly an error. All the attributes of God perfectly harmonize in all His administrations, whether it be the punishment of the incorrigible, or the pardon of the penitent believer. " Mercy and truth are met together; righteousness and peace have kissed each other."

If it were otherwise, God would be at variance with Himself. The plan of salvation was devised through mercy, but approved and executed by justice. Being set on foot "mercy and truth are met together," or mercy and justice are combined for its accomplishment, both as it regards the act of atonement and the application of it to the believer. So now the claims of justice are as well satisfied in the justification of the penitent, believing sinner as in the damnation of the impenitent sinner.

God having made provision for pardon, is both faithful and just to fulfil when we comply with the stipulation made. According to this plan no claim of the law is compromised, but all is satisfied. This is so, wonderful and so glorious that we would not have believed had it not been attested by the clearest proofs of divine authority. These proofs are not wanting.

The second benefit is the purification of our nature. "To cleanse us from all unrighteousness." It is not sufficient to obtain simple pardon, but it is necessary that a change of moral nature should take place. This is not necessarily included in that of justification, although this expression is sometimes used to include both pardon and regeneration in the lowest or ordinary sense. The expression in the text is used as including the entire sanctification of our nature. "To cleanse from all unrighteousness" can certainly mean nothing less. This state of grace is presented in the Scriptures both as duty and privilege. It is included in this command: "Thou shalt love the Lord thy God with all thy heart, and with all thy soul, and with all thy mind." It is contained also in the following exhortation: "Be ye therefore perfect, even as your Father which is in heaven is perfect." "Follow peace with all men, and holiness, without which no man shall see the Lord." "Therefore leaving the principles of the doctrine of Christ, let us go on to perfection." It is a privilege because it affords a much nearer and more constant access to God. It casts out fear. "There is no fear in love; but perfect love casteth out fear; because fear hath torment." This state of holiness is offered to us; and the faithfulness and justice of God are pledged for its bestowment. St. Paul confirms the same thing, when, in addressing the Thessalonians, after having offered a fervent prayer for their sanctification and preservation in that state of grace, he says: "Faithful is he that calleth you, who will also do it." That is, He will sanctify and keep in that state such as trust him. O! that it were the cry of every one, "Create in me a clean heart, O God! and renew a right spirit within me."

Again—

> "My heart, thou know'st, can never rest,
> Till thou create my peace,
> Till of my Eden repossess'd,
> From every sin I cease."

Awake! awake! put on your strength. Arise! and put on your beautiful garments of full salvation from sin; "Looking for that blessed hope, and the glorious appearing of the great God and our Saviour Jesus Christ; who gave himself for us, that he might redeem us from all iniquity, and purify unto himself a peculiar people, zealous of good works." It does not enter into my design to argue at length, the practicability or possibility of obtaining this state of purity in this life; but I would earnestly and affectionately exhort all to press towards the "mark for the prize of the high calling which is of God in Christ Jesus." He, who has called you out of darkness into His marvellous light, surely is able to renovate your natures—to make you holy and keep you so. "The blood of Jesus Christ his son cleanseth us from all sin." To attain to this we must do as the text directs, confess our sin. I know many doubt whether such a state is attainable in this life. With such I do not wish to have any controversy, but would advise them to make a perfect consecration of all their powers to God, to be made as pure as He wishes them to be, and rest in the atonement for just what is designed for them, let it be much or little. Let them "prove what is that good and acceptable and perfect will of God," and they will not go amiss. If we are not willing to do this, we have reason to apprehend there is something wrong with us. Let us go to Him in humble, penitent prayer, confessing all the sin and pollution that lurk within; asking Him to shine on our darkness, to enable us to see all that is offensive to Him; and when we have seen it, to put out our complaint before Him—to cry against "the spirit unclean"—to rely on the blood of atonement and then we shall not be disappointed.

"He is able,
He is willing, doubt no more."

Let us now conclude with a few practical thoughts. The duty of confession arises:

1. From the relation existing between the offender and the offended.
2. From the divine requirement.
3. From the encouragement held out. "He that covereth his sin shall not prosper; but whoso confesseth and forsaketh them shall have mercy." Its practical influence is beneficial to ourselves and others. To ourselves, by causing a greater degree of watchfulness over our errors and actions that we do not offend. To others by softening and tranquilizing their feelings towards us, and calling into exercise the finer feelings of their natures. There is a relief in the confession of a fault, when one has been committed, and there is a sweetness—a delight in the conscious-

ness of pardon. Therefore, "confess your faults one to another, and pray one for another, that ye may be healed."

4. That confession embraced in the text, secures pardon and purification, the greatest blessings which could be conferred on mortals here, and indeed, they are preparatory to the greatest bliss that can be enjoyed hereafter. The degree of enjoyment in heaven will be in proportion to the development of our moral capacities; which itself depends on an assimilation of character to Christ, and a due and faithful exercise of the powers bestowed, for the promotion of His kingdom and glory.

We are to remember, these faults are all known to God, whether we confess them or not, and any attempt to conceal them from Him will be perfectly futile. He will call us to answer for them in the great day of judgment. How much better to confess them, and receive absolution for them now, than to meet them there uncancelled.

The God of peace and truth help us to perform our duty in this respect, and bestow on us the blessings of the new and everlasting covenant.

SELF EXAMINATION.

By Rev. Wm. Blair, B.A.,

Of Iroquois, Ont.

"Examine yourselves, whether ye be in the faith."—2 Cor. xiii. 5.

TO be in the faith is to be born again, to be a genuine Christian, to have passed from death into life, to be created anew in Christ Jesus, to walk not after the flesh but after the spirit.

To be in the faith means more than simply joining the church or making a profession of religion. It is too bad that so great a number of people in these easy going times join the various churches without being converted. They give up a few sins, graft a few habits of piety on the old nature and sit down "at ease in Zion" the rest of their days. Such people are galvanized corpses freezing all they come in contact with. No matter what their wealth or number, a church is better without them in that relation. Let such examine themselves whether they be in the faith.

There is another class of backslidden church members who keep up their old religious forms, but are destitute of the witness of the Spirit. A man ought to know as certainly that he has been born of the Spirit as that he has been born of the flesh, yet how many in all our societies lack the solid comfort of Christian assurance.

Attend the first class or fellowship meeting within your reach, listen to that old-time professor making his sad complaint as he sings his favourite stanza:—

> "'Tis a point I long to know—
> Oft it causes anxious thought—
> Do I love the Lord or no?
> Am I His or am I not?"

Did he always sing in such a doleful strain, you ask. Ah! no; the night he was converted there wasn't a richer experience or a more joyous testimony given by any of the praying people present than fell from the lips of this same man. With what unction and pathos and power he seemed to pour his very soul into those stirring melodies, that gave fittest expression to his new found love.

But all that is over, and the life that was once under high pressure for God and His cause has sunk down to the dead level of an irksome religious mechanism. Ask him now if he knows his sins forgiven and "can read his title clear to mansions in the skies." He tells you he hasn't that ecstacy of joy that he once had; is not exactly sure about his state: but is thankful that it is as well with him as it is; he enjoys a calm peace and hopes at the last to outride the storms. The same old threadbare story from year to year, as destitute of interest as of originality. The only thing that can be said in its favour, is that the leader knows what is coming, and so can have his remarks prepared beforehand; unless, indeed, as is sometimes the case, the leader himself has the same "go on, brother—be faithful, and the Lord will bless you," for each member of his class—like those patent medicine men who profess to cure all the ills that flesh is heir to with the same prescription. The trouble with the good brother whose story is so old and stale, is that he has backslidden in heart and either does not realize it, or is not honest enough to confess it and try to regain his lost ground. He is thankful "it is as well with him as it is." So he ought to be, but that may not be saying much. He enjoys "a calm peace;" so do the mouldering corpses in a graveyard; he hopes "to get to heaven by and by," but he won't unless he perfects holiness in the fear of God; he prays, yes, but not every one that says, Lord, Lord, shall enter into the kingdom of heaven. .

It is wonderful to see a man beginning the Christian life with such good prospects and bidding fair for so much usefulness, in a few years as cold and careless and worldly as the devil wants him to be, not openly and professedly irreligious perhaps, but having a name to live and yet dead. Of all the enemies to the cross terrestrial or infernal, the half-hearted Christian does most hurt to the cause of Christ. A renegade in the citadel is more to be dreaded than a thousand foes battering at the gates. Better be no light at all than a false light. Better be cold as an iceberg than lukewarm in religion, leaving the impression upon the minds of unconverted men that the soul's salvation is not a matter of very vital importance after all. This is the man above all others who needs to take to heart the admonition of the text, "Examine yourselves whether ye be in the faith."

Nor is this a description of a solitary professor here and there, unfortunately situated, or exceptionally placed, but alas, of thousands of church members the wide world over. Pronounce even the most charitable judgment upon the average Christian life, and who can shut his eyes to the fact that if conduct and conversation be any criterion the things "seen and temporal" are sought after, with far greater relish, than things "unseen and eternal." On Sunday afternoon a professedly Christian father looks out and seeing the roads blocked with snow says to his children, "I guess you hadn't better mind going to Sunday School to-day;" next morning he harnesses up his double team, ploughs through the drifts and faces a driving storm to take his children to the public school. An intelligent and respectable church member grumbles that the prayer meeting is kept up till 9 o'clock, but can stay up till midnight at a political or grange meeting without finding a particle of fault. A man who expects to get to heaven when he dies spends more money in tobacco than he gives to the cause of Christ, and wastes more time smoking it than he spends in praying for the good of his soul. Men calling themselves Christians, under a plea of hard times give up their religious paper, curtail their church subscription, and stay away from missionary meetings, but take their political paper, pay their store bills, and eat, drink and wear as much as usual. With many most solemnly pledged to all the purity and peculiarity of the Christian life, the absorbing desire seems to be entire conformity to the world; in other words, they try how little religion they can get along with, and yet be respectable church members, and not miss heaven. However it may happen to such people in the world to come, some of them do manage to get along without much religion here, and thus is even in the case of many who are by no means drones in the church. There is too little attention to the more spiritual duties and exercises of the Christian religion, such as closet devotion, self examination, meditation on God's law, self-denial, fasting, hungering and thirsting after righteousness and such like. This is sad enough.

But to make the matter still worse, some people won't hear plain preaching on the subject; they prefer a siren tongued herald, who will cry "peace, peace, where there is no peace," to a son of thunder, who lifts up his voice like a trumpet to tell them their short comings and sins. In the preacher's beat as in the physicians, there are found people who would rather take chloroform than a lively cathartic, choosing rather to shut their eyes and run the risk, than honestly and anxiously to know the worst and apply the remedy. Now likely when these people started in religion, they were really sincere, and for a time ran well, but see what they are to-day. Let us inquire why. Some likely never count the cost. As the unthinking horse rusheth into battle, so some people dash into a religious meeting, and a few weeks afterwards as quickly dash out of it again. Some say to their neighbours, "If you make a start, I will," as though they had no mind of their own, and would hinge their eternal salvation on the action of another. Too frequently those who start because others do, stop because others do. Some again take up religion as a sort of experiment—in other words they condescend to take the Lord on trial, and if everything goes to suit them they will go on, but if not they will back down. No man ever found the "pearl of great price" seeking it in that fashion.

Others make the mistake of supposing that the end of the struggle or rebellion, that results in conversion, is the end of all strife, and henceforth they fold their arms and sing " 'tis done, the great transaction's done," when instead the conflict is just begun. The process of conversion with them is the crowding and jostling that one sometimes has to go through, in order to secure his ticket at a railway station. In their subsequent Christian life they manifest the easy, self-satisfied air of a man in a sleeping-car who says, "I have my ticket now, let me sleep the rest of the way."

Others again begin the Christian life without having their minds made up to live without committing wilful sin. In a slipshod, apologetic sort of way they rhyme off the current saying that a person can't help sinning, everybody sins, everybody must sin, it is their nature just as it is for the grass to grow, or fire to burn. To blame a man for what he can't help is unjust.

If a man cannot live without committing sin, it would be unfair in either God or man to punish him for it.

"Whosoever is born of God doth not commit sin." "He shall be called Jesus, for he shall save his people from their sins." What is grace worth that is not able to keep a man from the evil that is in the world? What is an atonement worth that isn't able to present a follower of Christ faultless before the throne of His glory with exceeding joy? A salvation that proposes to save to the uttermost and yet doesn't save from commiting wilful sin, is, to say the least, a very queer salvation. Of course Christians who hold such low views of the atonement, at the time of their conversion, soon fall into condemnation, and either backslide altogether, or keep up a form of godliness long after they have lost the power. A further fatal mistake made by a good many young converts is, that some Christian duties may be neglected if others are attended to, without doing any very serious damage to the soul. Such crosses as ladies wear for ornament, or hang up to adorn their parlour walls, are easy enough to carry, but when it comes to a crushing weight upon one's shoulders that makes the sweat exude from every pore, a good many feel like saying, "I pray thee have me excused." So with some professing Christians, who never think of bearing a cross for Jesus' sake unless they feel like it, and then they think the only difference it will make in eternity will be a few stars less in their crown of rejoicing. Alas, alas, we very much fear it will make all the difference between crowns and chains, between a robe of light and a sheet of flame. It is a question for every serious Christian to consider, whether in the economy of grace a man can elect to have a starless crown. The man who says "I'm not ambitious of distinction in the celestial country—let others strive for seats of honour near the throne, I'll be content if I barely squeeze through and get the seat next the door." The professor who talks in that strain and lives accordingly is surely deceiving himself, and will soon find to his eternal disgrace that even the lowest place in heaven was too good for him.

Another fruitful source of trouble to some Christians is their neglect of the Bible. They attend church, and prayer and class meeting regularly, but do not "search the Scriptures" to any very great extent. In the main they try to live as Christians around them live, instead of taking the Bible for their guide, in matters great and small. It may be a libel and it may be the honest truth to say that a good many church members regard the Bible as a dry tedious book. To say the least, it looks bad to see a man who regards the Bible as a revelation from heaven, poring for hours over ephemeral periodicals or devouring sickly trashy novels, and once in a great while, as a sort of sop to his conscience, sitting down and falling asleep with the Bible on his knee. What better evidence is needed that the doctrine of total depravity is true! Just as the mariner carefully consults and closely follows his chart, so should every Christian use his Bible as he sails over the high seas of life.

The last occasion of spiritual declension to which we shall refer is the haste and rashness with which some Christians plunge into things, of the propriety of which they are not quite certain. Sometimes a good man finds himself in this dilemma; he would like to do a certain thing but is not quite positive that it would be right; a great many Christians do it, even some Christian ministers practise it (smoking for instance); but on the other hand, many good people condemn it, what is he to do? Give his soul the benefit of the doubt. He is not *sure* that it would be right, he is *sure* that it would be no harm not to do it. He had better not do it, lest the Spirit should be grieved by the risk he is willing to run for the sake of a mere passing gratification.

So far we have been describing Christians whose religion is at a very low ebb, and trying to suggest the probable causes: the remedy is close at hand, by self-examination and a fresh application of the blood of sprinkling. Every Christian ought to examine himself frequently to know how matters stand between his soul and God. As college students grow more and more anxious as their final examination approaches, so ought the Christian, as weeks and months and years fly past, give increasing diligence lest he fail in the terrible ordeal of the judgment. What charges this latter trial with such tremendous interest is the fact that a candidate who fails can never have a "supplemental." Meantime, the wise and safe course is to give earnest heed to the injunction of the text and examine *ourselves* before we are examined by the Judge of quick and dead, and the less we feel inclined to this duty the greater the need of setting about it.

(1.) We ought to examine ourselves in the light of past experience. Are we conscious of a steady growth in love and zeal and usefulness since the hour of conversion?

(2.) We ought to examine ourselves in the light of such lives as those of Hester Ann Rogers, Alfred Cookman, the Dairyman's Daughter, Robert Murray McCheyne, John Wesley, and others, whose names are in the Book of Life; and we ought not to compare ourselves with the low standard of the lukewarm professors around us.

(3.) We ought, above all things, to examine ourselves in the light of God's Word, which is the only rule and the sufficient rule both of our faith and practice—frequently proposing to ourselves such plain pointed questions as the following:—

(*a*.) Do my neighbours and the members of my own family get the impression from my life that with me religion is the principal thing—that everything else must bend to religion?

(*b*.) Does my inconsistent life ever give occasion to the enemies of God to blaspheme?

(*c*.) Next to my own salvation, is it the supreme passion of my life to snatch brands from the eternal burning?

(*d*.) Do I regard myself as a steward entrusted with some time and means which I am to use to the best of my ability in advancing the interest of the Redeemer's kingdom—fearing nothing so much as that the Master should be compelled to say at the last—"Thou wicked and slothful servant."

(*e*.) Do some of my neighbours, less able than myself, contribute more liberally to the institutions of the Church?

(*f*.) Do I transact all my business on the principle laid down in the Bible—"Love thy neighbour as thyself?"

(*g*.) Would I die rather than sin?

(*h.*) When duty and feeling clash, which do I generally follow ? and—

Lastly—Am I perfecting holiness in the fear of God ? Is it the earnest longing, constant cry of my heart—

> " More purity give me, more strength to o'ercome,
> More freedom from earth-stains, more longings for home,
> More fit for the Kingdom, more used would I be,
> More blessed and holy, more, Saviour, like Thee."

Should the reader, after the most rigid and prayerful examination, find himself lacking some of the essential marks of the genuine Christian, let him not despair, but turn to the 2nd chapter of Revelation, and in the 4th and 5th verses read what a backslidden professor must do to be saved:—" Nevertheless I have somewhat against thee because thou hast left thy first love. Remember therefore from whence thou art fallen and repent and do the first works, or else I will come unto thee quickly and will remove thy candlestick out of his place, except thou repent."

"Examine yourselves whether ye be in the faith." Amen.

GENUINE CHURCH PROSPERITY.

By Rev. James A. Campbell.

Of Georgetown, Ont.

"Then had the churches rest throughout all Judea and Galilee and Samaria, and were edified; and walking in the fear of the Lord, and in the comfort of the Holy Ghost, were multiplied."—Acts ix. 31.

THE *history of the Christian Church* is singularly variegated. Light and shade, cloud and sunlight, seem ever to have been assiduously and persistently contending for the preponderance and the sway. To the casual observer, the varying successes of these contestants might appear to have been the result of the capricious influence of fortune. But to the careful and intelligent student, there are manifest certain inflexible principles interwoven throughout, to whose dictation every result must be attributed—a fundamental sovereign law underlying the whole, and, upon its own just conditions, crowning with victory, glory and honour, or permitting inglorious defeat and disastrous reverse.

2. Our attention is here directed to certain *prosperous Churches*. Prosperity is always gratifying. There is a charm and attractiveness peculiar to a prosperous Church. It is delightful to be a member of such a Church. It is most exhilarating to be the pastor of it. The surrounding world admires and is willing to help

it. The more it prospers the more capable it is of prosperity. Every thing is fresh, lively, beautiful, refreshing, happy, like nature, in the full exuberance and luxuriance of spring time.

3. But *in what does genuine Church prosperity consist?* A very common and erroneous fancy is that it consists in the accumulation of whatever contributes to the increase of its social influence. Its membership is increasing; its congregation is growing; its churches are enlarging; its wealth is accumulating; its popularity is extending. If this be the correct idea, where is the Church that enjoys so great prosperity as the Church of Rome? But, doubtless, the proper view is that genuine prosperity consists in the addition and assimilation of such elements as increase its efficiency in the great work of leading men to Christ. No Church is prospering which is not increasing in power and success in saving souls, whatever may be its external growth in wealth and popularity. Indeed, it is not difficult to fancy a Church growing in numbers, in wealth, in popularity, and yet exemplifying utter and unqualified failure, rather than genuine prosperity as a Christian Church. The phrase in the text, "were multiplied," implies more than a multiplication of church buildings, more than an increase of membership and of financial ability. They "were multiplied" spiritually and morally. Their newly-acquired members were not only "added to the Church," but also united to Christ. They grew in grace and increased in moral influence, power, efficiency and usefulness. That only is genuine prosperity which proceeds upon a proper basis, and which is the legitimate result of the combination and concurrence of the natural Scriptural elements of true prosperity.

4. *The elements of true ecclesiastical prosperity* is a

most important subject of inquiry, and is worthy of most careful investigation and patient research. Those elements are clearly and concisely indicated and exemplified in the passage of Scripture under present contemplation; and all the experience, learning and intellect that might be called into requisition for the elucidation of the subject will just corroborate what is here briefly, but plainly, set forth, " Then had the churches rest throughout all Judea," etc.

I. *Scriptural edification* is the first of those elements introduced to our notice here. "The churches .... were edified."

1. This is *fundamental*. The whole Gospel system is the production of infinite intelligence, combined with absolute holiness. Its foundations are laid in justice and truth, and with utmost precision the whole superstructure corresponds with those fundamental principles, and exhibits to the most intelligent and fastidious eye an edifice unrivalled for graceful symmetry, collossal strength, gorgeous loveliness, sublime magnificence. But an intelligent knowledge of the doctrines of the Gospel, an understanding and appreciation of its principles and its requirements, are fundamental also to personal faith and godliness. This is the only substantial basis of symmetrical faith and character, and of uniform, consistent Christian practice; and as this becomes augmented there will be a corresponding approach to Scriptural Christian perfection, proportionate development of resources and exercise of energies, with attendant efficiency and success in the Church.

2. Alas for the *prevalent neglect* of the intellectual element in religion! The Romish Church, deeming it a preferable expedient to keep her people in ignorance, assumes the responsibility of prohibiting the study of the Word of God. And thousands of Protestant people

possess but a meagre conception of the sublime truths of the Gospel, of whom many are regarded as important constituents of the Church of which they are communicants. They have a slight familiarity with certain incidents of Bible history, but know comparatively little of its doctrine, and less of its spirit. How few, comparatively, there are who, with diligence and eagerness, "search the Scriptures," and carefully and patiently investigate its doctrines. The great mass of professing Christians are content with a very limited and superficial knowledge of religious truth, such as, with even ordinary observation, one would almost involuntarily and imperceptibly acquire, being a resident of a Christian community.

3. The *inevitable consequences* are but too strikingly apparent. Wherever, and in whatever degree, such neglect exists, religious privilege, enjoyment, devotion, fervour, are at a discount. Love of the world is increasing, while the deep longing and yearning for God and holiness are declining in intensity and imperativeness. Faith is diminishing, love growing faint, zeal abating, activity waning, fruit decreasing. Languor, lassitude, moral apathy and poverty of soul prevail. The social, domestic and private means of grace are either utterly neglected, or they are cold, formal, without freshness, interest or profit. There are apostacy, spiritual sleep and death within the Church; and there are disregard, thoughtlessness, carelessness and godlessness without. The vital warmth has fled from mother Church; the spiritual pulse has ceased its beating; all is cold, stiff and dead, and the world around, perishing from hunger, is crying for heavenly food.

4. *Activity is indispensable to prosperity.* This is true in a very extended sense. It is true in the natural world. Even the luxuriance and flourishing

state of a plant depends upon the activity of its vital organism in appropriating and assimilating the elements of nutrition. It is obviously true in relation to secular human business. One man fails of prosperity, even with propitious circumstances, and men say that he is too slow, too dull, he has not enough life to be prosperous. Another with no greater advantages moves along upon a high tide of prosperity, and he is said to be an active business man who will make anything prosper that he undertakes. Apply this rule to personal religious experience and the truth is exemplified overwhelmingly. That Christian who is tardy, sluggish, idle in regard to religious duty will evince but little growth in grace; will be like the stunted shrubbery upon the barren sandy plain. But he whose hands and head and heart are full of work for God, for souls, and for the Church, will thrive amazingly. He will exhibit a most luxuriant spiritual growth. He will flourish like the green bay tree or the lovely olive. The same doctrine is eminently true when applied to societies and Churches. The Church being made up of individuals, the aggregate of its individual prosperity constitutes an important item in the prosperity of the whole. But in conjunction with this there is a more general prosperity. The Church, as a whole, has its interests and its institutions, and the prosperity of these depends largely upon the activity of the Church as such. Large and various enterprizes, broad and liberal plans, are requisite to the success and prosperity of any Church. If the Church have but few and small un-undertakings, she will experience greater difficulty in maintaining and promoting these than she would more abundant, broader, more heroic undertakings. The greater Christian activity a Church practises the more capable it will be of efficient action, and the more abundant prosperity it will achieve.

5. But *faith is the mainspring of action.* Throughout the whole intellectual world action is invariably the result of faith. Even the lower animals are governed in their actions by what their instinct tells them will be to their advantage. Men are governed in secular business by their faith. Every enterprise inaugurated is based upon faith in the consummation of some desired end. The actions of every day life are performed upon the faith that beneficial results will accrue thereby. Even compulsory acts are performed from choice between two evils, the choice being based upon faith. But religious life is preeminently a life of faith. Faith is the basis of practical repentance, the condition of justification and adoption into the family of God, and the dictator of every action of subsequent religious life. It is faith that prompts to prayer, to attendance upon the means of grace, to supporting the Church to toil and sacrifice for the glory of God and the salvation of men. Consistency, rectitude, and intensity of action are dependent upon the uniformity, soundness and strength of faith. One man possesses faith with all these qualities developed in a high degree; he is a most valuable and eminently useful member of society. Another has faith, but it lacks uniformity; and his course is marked with inconsistency; to-day he is all zeal and animation, to-morrow he is careless, and indifferent. The faith of another is unsound, and an erratic, defective life is the result. The faith of yet another is weak; he undertakes nothing great, he prays but little, and but occasionally attends the means of grace. Whatever he does is done languidly, indolently; his life is fraught with weakness and

failure. Whatever the character of a man's faith it will surely stamp its impress upon the actions of his life. Churches also are characterized and governed respectively by their prevailing faith. The faith of a Church is largely that of its individual adherents; but there is a connexional faith, a correlative faith, a conventional or conjunctional faith which includes the prevailing *belief* in regard to the great essential, cardinal doctrines of revelation, *conviction* of duty in general and in detail, and *confidence* in the efficiency of the instrumentalities employed with divine influence and co-operation. This faith is the basis and the spirit of all ecclesiastical activity. This is the active, potent energy which preponderates and predominates over every minor element, prompting and guiding every enterprise and achieving every grand result and every glorious victory.

6. But *knowledge is the foundation of faith*. It is not faith itself, but the foundation of it. Faith without knowledge is a fabric without a foundation. It is, like a castle built in mid-air unsupported. It is the faith of the enthusiast, and disappointment is its inevitable doom. Enterprises of any description inaugurated and prosecuted upon faith of this character, must inevitably culminate in utter failure. But as religion transcends everything else in importance, it is especially indispensable that religious faith be securely established upon an adequate and permanent basis. Genuine faith is not a groundless or sentimental thing. Rationalists imagine that faith is essentially at variance with reason. But faith is not contrary to reason, though frequently towering far above it. It is rationally based upon knowledge as its foundation, and the uniformity, soundness, and strength of it depend chiefly upon the extent and correctness of that

knowledge. The Holy Scriptures is the great fountain of religious knowledge. It is God's only complete and perfect revelation of religious doctrine and duty. It is the only competent standard of religious faith, character and practice, and it is imperative upon all Christian people to improve every available opportunity and facility for their Scriptural edification in the things of God. Without this faith is groundless. Without it activity has neither impulse, guide nor stimulant. And without it there can be no genuine, abundant, or permanent prosperity, either to an individual or to a Church. This doctrine is authoritatively corroborated by the Word of God. Paul said to the Ephesians, "I commend you to God, and to the Word of His grace, which is able to build you up." That man is blessed whose "delight is in the law of the Lord, and in His law doth he meditate day and night." "Search the Scriptures." "Take fast hold of instruction; let her not go; keep her, for she is *thy life.*"

II. *Progressive filial piety* is the second element of Church prosperity suggested in the text, "Walking in the fear of the Lord."

1. *Progression is a normal condition of true religion.* Religion is essentially aggressive, and contains a powerful propelling element, to be destitute of which implies a want of genuine Christianity; and to be disobedient thereto is to violate a fundamental principle of its constitution; but to possess and obey will ensure eminent happiness and usefulness in time, and highest reward in eternity. Individual Christians must ever advance in knowledge, faith and love, or their tendency will be to retrogression. There is no state of Christian experience in this world void of capability of improvement. The greater proficiency achieved in

Christian life renders the greater advancement still possible. Forward is the watchword of every true Christian. Backward is death, but forward is life and happiness. The Church should ever be advancing. Napoleon's famous advance on Moscow was brilliantly prosperous; but his retreat was fraught with shocking disaster and heartrending adversity. If the Church become terrified at the foe and retreat, or if she offer a compromise, or adopt a conciliatory policy, there can be no reasonable hope of eminent prosperity in the campaign. Armed and equipped from the heavenly arsenal, with fervent, enthusiastic zeal for the glory of God, with firm reliance upon the arm of Omnipotence, every regiment, battalion, company, every officer and private, with every implement and supply, must press forward with face to the foe, if decisive victory would be achieved, and permanent prosperity assured. The Apostolic Churches were not sitting at their ease, not standing idly in the way, but "walking in the fear of the Lord."

2. *The governing principle and motive of religion* is here indicated, "the fear of the Lord." This does not imply shy distrust or servile apprehension of God. Christians do not fear God as slaves fear their master, or as oppressed, helpless subjects fear a tyrant. Their fear is that of an affectionate, dutiful son toward a kind, compassionate, loving, judicious, powerful father. Such a son will entertain a wholesome fear of offending such a father; not merely because that offence would necessitate punishment, but that it might occasion pain to one so greatly beloved. This fear implies a deep, heart-felt reverence of God, blended with a careful, loving solicitation for His uninterrupted gratification.

3. *This fear is indispensable to genuine prosperity*

of a Church or an individual. *Intelligent* exercise of its energies, *judicious* employment and development of its resources, *sagacious* improvement of offered advantages, facilities and appliances, are all important requisites to eminent prosperity in a Church; and the Holy Scriptures declare that "The fear of the Lord is the *beginning of wisdom."* Without this, whatever a person's natural intellectual endowments, whatever his educational attainments, his religious life is doomed to failure. Without this, vain will be the keen perception and profound erudition of the fathers of the Church, fruitless the combined intelligence, culture and research of ecclesiastical bodies; all is evanescent as a bubble, and must vanish as "the baseless fabric of a vision." "The fear of the Lord is the *beginning* of wisdom." It is the *foundation* of wisdom, without which all learning, knowledge and wisdom are like a house built upon the sand, or like a grand masonic arch with the key-stone wanting.

4. *"The fear of the Lord" must characterize all practical Christian life.* In their whole demeanour, Christians should act in "the fear of the Lord." They should ever entertain a vivid consciousness that the all-seeing eye of God is upon them. All contingencies should be decided in "the fear of the Lord." It should determine every purpose of life, and prescribe the manner in which every undertaking is performed. This would not only save from numerous snares, mistakes, troubles and sorrows, but also very perceptibly tend to advancement and development in knowledge, faith, spirituality and godliness. It would promote the elimination of evil excrescences and the evolution of perfection of character and life, and culminate in most distinguished prosperity. The Church should ever maintain "the fear of the Lord." In its legislation and its

administration, in all varieties of ecclesiastical labour; in its plans, its enterprises; in its songs, its prayers, its sermons; in its entire experience and practice, it should be governed by "the fear of the Lord." Without this, the blessing of the Lord cannot be rationally hoped for, and alas for the Church, if it forfeit and alienate the divine benediction. Paul may plant, and Apollos water, but God only can give "the increase." Without this, there can be nothing but failure eventually. But "walking in the fear of the Lord," the Church will be consistent in character and practice, and achieve eminent, glorious and permanent prosperity. "The fear of the Lord is a fountain of life."

III. *Abounding spiritual comfort* is the third element of Church prosperity suggested in this passage, "Walking .... in the comfort of the Holy Ghost."

1. In relation to *the felicitous element of religion*, there exist *two extreme views*, both of which are *erroneous*. One is that this is the principal part of it, that it is the *summum bonum* of religion. If so, religion must be exquisitely selfish; whereas one principal feature of genuine Scriptural religion consists in the absence of selfishness as a predominent ingredient, and the possession of a broad, noble generosity. The emotional is by no means the most important part of religion. Blossoms are not more important than fruit, nor is the fruit personally enjoyed by Christian people themselves more important than that borne for the glory of God, and distributed for the happiness and well-being of perishing humanity. If personal enjoyment be the sole object of religion, then we consume all our fruit, we have our reward in this world, and cannot consistently look for further reward in the world beyond; and to be without reward there, would imply certain alternative punishment.

I

2. *The opposite error* is that all the enjoyment of religion is reserved for the future life, with the exception of such as naturally results from the practice of virtue. But holiness of heart alone can beget holiness of life, and if the latter produce enjoyment, much more should the former. Again, true religion consists in the union of the soul with God, and it is the union and communion of the soul with God that renders heaven a place of glorious beatification, and surely the same cause would produce a similar effect in this world. The old, but not obsolete, notion of *enjoying* religion is perfectly natural and Scriptural, and the religion that consists wholly or chiefly in forms, logical principles and orthodox creeds, without any spiritual enjoyment, is but a poor, frivolous substitute for the warm, living, comforting, joyous religion of the Gospel.

3. *The source of true religious comfort* is the Holy Ghost, as our text clearly intimates. This suggests the necessity of the Holy Ghost in the Church. In early times this was deemed indispensable, the Church realizing its inefficiency without that, and the great Head of the Church prohibiting the exercise of its great commission until that was obtained, " Tarry ye in the City of Jerusalem until ye be endued with power from on high." And still the Holy Ghost is the source of true spiritual power, without which the Church is utterly impotent and disqualified for the achievement of the glorious victories and the sublime triumphs possible to it when enlightened, sanctified, vitalized and energized by the Spirit of God. But genuine religious comfort and enjoyment are no less the product of the indwelling Spirit of God, than is religious power. The comfort of religion does not all arise from the prospect of future bliss, from the consciousness of innocence, or from the uncertain hope of flattering adu-

lation. The Holy Ghost is the great Comforter. To comfort is a leading prerogative appertaining to His office. The Father hath sent Him into the world in Christ's name to comfort the people of God; and this good office He will surely perform for all who love the Lord Jesus Christ in sincerity. Joy is one important fruit of the Spirit, and it is the exalted privilege of all genuine Christians being filled with the Holy Ghost to be filled with holy joy; yea, to "rejoice with joy unspeakable and full of glory."

4. *The bearing of this element* upon religious prosperity is abundantly apparent. That Christian makes but little progress religiously who finds no enjoyment in communion with God. If he obtain no comfort from the Holy Ghost in the hour of trouble, affliction, toil and darkness; if in moments of solitude and sadness he receive no rays of light; if in the exercise of religious duty or privilege there be no thrill of pleasure or joy from the Holy Ghost, religious life will soon become insipid and intolerable. That Church cannot achieve even respectable success where spiritual comfort and enjoyment are at a discount, and where it exists in insignificant degree. The world is quite dilatory enough in embracing religion for the sake of its benefits; and if religious people are always morose, dejected, of a sad countenance; or if they find it necessary to seek enjoyment in the amusements of the world in order to supplement the enjoyment of religion which is thereby admitted to be inadequate, the world will not hasten to relinquish present pleasures for a life of sadness and melancholy, and they will be reluctant to make profession of a choice of Christ and His religion, and yet be compelled to seek required happiness in earthly sources. But Christians who find abundant comfort, happiness and joy in the service of

God will grow loving, vigorous, active, faithful. A joyous heart bringeth "a continual feast," and "doth good like a medicine." The persuasiveness and fascination which the calm, sweet, peaceful, joyous element of religion exerts upon humanity is truly magical and marvellous. It rarely fails to excite the admiration and homage of the unsaved, however erring, lost and hopeless, and to awaken an ardent longing and deep yearning to possess the priceless pearl. It seems to afford a fresh and vivid view of the sweet associations, the innocence, endearment and happiness of the long forsaken Father's home, and to display in striking contrast the chill, servility, poverty, and wretchedness of the life of sin. Like a soft, sweet, familiar song of fatherland, in a strange and distant country, it presents to the unhappy wanderer an appeal more convincing than the logic of Aristotle, more entrancing and captivating than the eloquence of Cicero, and more sweet, pathetic, and enchanting than the strains of Homer. Genuine Christian joy is a glorious personal privilege, of all Christian people, and its experience and expression are enjoined as important to the promotion of the success of the Church of God. "Let the righteous be glad; let them rejoice before God; yea, let them exceedingly rejoice." "Rejoice in the Lord always; and again I say, rejoice."

In these times, in this land, the Church possesses immense possibilities and immense responsibilities. In the times to which our text alludes the Church possessed advantages and faithfully used them. "Then had the Churches rest throughout all Judea and Galilee and Samaria, and were edified; and walking in the fear of the Lord, and in the comfort of the Holy Ghost, were multiplied." They had rest, not from Christian labour and sacrifice, but from the storms of human rage, and the fires of cruel persecution; and that they improved to their own edification and comfort, and to the diligent exercise of Christian privilege and duty. So God prospered them. They "were multiplied." Now the Church enjoys an extended period of rest from the open violence and persecutions which the enemies of Christianity have been wont to wage against it. Opportunities, advantages, and facilities for promoting the world's salvation are pre-eminently superior in this age, and gigantic enterprises are being successfully operated to the accomplishment of that great purpose. But there are dangers menacing the Church still. There is danger of the relaxation of Christian effort, danger of enervation and corruption, danger of compromising with sin and the devil, danger of subordinating Scriptural knowledge and authority to human speculations and assumptions, danger of the loss of spirituality and vitality, and danger of the substitution of forms, ceremonies and cold philosophies instead of the light, life and power of genuine religion. Any of these things would be disastrous to the Church, and calamitous to the world, retarding if not precluding the success and prosperity of the Church in the achievement of its sublime mission—the world's evangelization. In proportion as these things do prevail, they weaken the Church and impede its progress. But when the Church is thoroughly consecrated to God, when it enjoys the purifying efficacy of the blood of Christ, and the divine energy of the Holy Ghost, it will surely prosper. When the Church, enlightened by the word of divine truth, exemplifying its doctrines by a life in conformity to its teachings, filled with spiritual life, comfort and "joy in the Holy Ghost," with living earnestness, and joyous countenance beaming with holy emotion, goes forth like the sun in his strength and glory, she will prove preeminently efficient to thaw away the icy accumulations from the moral world, warm it into new and gushing life, burst the clouds of moral darkness, dispel the shroud of spiritual gloom, and present to the astonished gaze of men and angels a ransomed world, in all the glittering brilliancy, gushing vigour, charming loveliness, rapturous joyfulness, and sublimely magnificent luxuriance of a most glorious spring-tide.

"Brethren, my heart's desire and prayer to God for Israel is that they might be saved." Amen.

CALVARY.

By Rev. Geo. Abbs.

Of the Ontario Conference.

"The place which is called Calvary."—Luke xxiii. 33.

THERE appears to be a magic spell resting around some of the places and scenes with which we have been familiar. How tenaciously the affections cling to home and its associations. Thoughts of a tender father's care and a loving mother's unwearied watchfulness and heart-felt sympathy, will, in the ripe years of manhood, stir to its depths the better part of our nature and call up memories that lighten the burden of life and fill the heart with joyous emotions. Though thousands of miles intervene between the individual and the place of his birth and early home-life; and sin may have dimmed the moral vision and debased the character, thoughts of the old roof-tree, the well-worn family Bible, the hallowed hour of prayer, in which he had so frequently joined, will awaken the slumbering conscience and lead him back to his boyhood's days.

The place where a person has been led to Christ possesses peculiar attractions, and to him appears like holy ground. Though it may have been but a schoolhouse constructed of logs, or a plain church without ornament or architectural pretensions, it seems more sacred than any other place on earth, and "thither the warm affections move." The sermon under which he was awakened, the preacher who delivered the message, the brethren who pleaded with God in his behalf, the keenness of his conviction, the intolerable burden of sin and the joy that filled his soul when Christ said, "Peace, be still," can never be effaced from his mind.

Places of historic interest, marking great epochs in the lives of nations, possess the power of exciting the most lively patriotic feelings. The granting of Magna Charta by King John, rearing a barrier against the abuse of the royal prerogative, and regarded by after ages as the basis of English liberties, can never be forgotten by Englishmen, nor can Cressy and Agincourt, Trafalgar and Waterloo lose their interest while the British nation endures. And with Americans, the dark days at Valley Forge and the brighter light that dawned upon their struggle at Yorktown are incidents in their history which must ever hold a place in their memories.

So with Bible scenes and events, around which cluster consequences the most momentous and interests the most profound that men and angels can possibly contemplate; particularly those which transpired at "the place called Calvary." All other events fade into insignificance when brought into contrast with those enacted there. Let us approach with sacred awe the spot where hangs the bleeding Saviour, and with mingled feelings of wonder, penitence and love, contemplate the tragic scene.

The envy and hatred of the Jewish rulers have become so intense that they scrupled not to adopt measures to secure the arrest and death of the blessed Jesus, whose immaculate life and repeated rebukes were as barbed arrows in their consciences. In Judas, one of the disciples, who was covetous, and a thief, they found a tool suited to their purpose, and bargained to give him thirty pieces of silver for the impious act of betraying his Lord. False witnesses had been subpœnaed, but they agreed not in their testimony; the mock trial before an unjust tribunal brought to a close, resulting in the delivering up, by an unscrupulous judge, of an innocent victim to merciless foes; the cruel mocking, buffeting and scourging inflicted with an unsparing hand, when the maimed and bleeding Son of God is led away as a "lamb to the slaughter," bearing His own cross, to the place of crucifixion, where the last sad scene is enacted. Truly this was the " hour of the power of darkness."

The mode of punishment and death, to which our adorable Redeemer was condemned, was inflicted only upon the vilest criminals, robbers and murderers, providing they were slaves, hence to degrade Him to the lowest possible point, He was crucified between two thieves, as disclosed by Isaiah, "and He was numbered with the transgressors." Truly, angels may gaze with astonishment at the degradation to which the Lord of life and glory has been subjected, and nature groan,

"When Christ the mighty Maker died
For man the creature's sin."

We notice that Calvary was

I. The scene of singular phenomena. The unnatural darkness that occurred at the time of the Saviour's crucifixion, extending over all the land, from the sixth to the ninth hour, that is from twelve o'clock till three in the afternoon, was evidently a token of the divine displeasure, calculated to strike with misgiving and dismay the hearts of the wicked men who had been the instigators and perpetrators of the fearful crime. Some, who are ever striving to account for all the miraculous interpositions mentioned in the Bible on natural principles, have endeavoured to make it appear that the darkness was caused by an eclipse of the sun. But this could not be, as astronomy allows none at that time. That this darkness was not natural, is evident from the fact that it happened at the passover, which was celebrated only at the full moon, a time in which it was impossible for the sun to be eclipsed, natural eclipses occurring only at the time of the new moon. In view of these facts we are driven to the conclusion that the obscuration of the sun was not only preternatural but miraculous and indicative of God's great displeasure with those who clamoured for the Saviour's blood.

The upheaval of the trembling earth, and the rending of the granite rocks were phenomena that attended the giving up of the ghost of the Son of Man, shewing that nature sympathized with her dying Lord, that creation groaned a requiem to his departure, and was more susceptible of feeling, if the term is allowable, than were the hearts of those who scoffed at the agonies of the expiring Son of God.

The bursting tombs attested the dignity of the crucified One while His dying cry awoke to life their slumbering inhabitants, who came forth after His resurrection and undoubtedly accompanied him, as trophies of His victory over death, hell and the grave, to mansions in the skies. It is nothing to our purpose to speculate as to who these saints were who were raised from the dead; it is enough for us to know that such was the fact and it affords indubitable evidence of the Saviour's power to destroy death and " him that had the power of death."

The rending of the Temple's veil "from the top to the bottom," which occurred at His death indicated that the way into the Holy of Holies was now opened through His precious blood. The Temple was divided into two apartments by a rich curtain. The outer portion was termed the Holy Place, and the inner the Holy of Holies. Into the latter no one was permitted to enter but the High Priest, and he but once a year on the great day of Atonement. It was this veil or curtain between these two apartments which was rent in twain, signifying the abolition of the whole Mosaic ritual, the removal of the partition between Jew and Gentile, and the admission of the latter into all the gracious privileges of the glorious Gospel. Precious immunities, but how great the price at which they were purchased. This brings us to notice that

II. Calvary was the scene of unparalleled suffering.

How intense must have been the physical suffering of our blessed Lord. The crown of thorns in mockery pressing upon His sacred brow; the scourge wielded by willing hands, prompted by hating hearts, making long furrows in His back, drenched with His own gore, and the nails driven through His quivering hands and feet, transfixing them to the wood. It may not be amiss to say, that because the hands and feet are the instruments of action and motion, nature has provided them with a greater quantity of nerves than any other portions, and it follows that where they abound the sense of pain must be more acute and severe, hence the agony that results from the piercing of these members. Add to this the anguish caused by the weight of the body being suspended by the lacerated limbs; straining every muscle to its utmost tension when the cross was suddenly lowered into the place prepared for it. Could cruelty the most refined adopt better measures to intensify the pain thus inflicted upon the blessed Jesus!

But His bodily sufferings were trifling when compared with the anguish of mind He endured in the garden and upon the cross. There are times when we crave companionship and sympathy, and we do not suppose that the Saviour, in His manhood, was an exception to the rule. This He was deprived of when it was most needed to alleviate His sorrows. One disciple had basely betrayed Him, another denied Him, and all, through fear, had forsaken Him and fled, leaving Him alone in the fearful conflict with men and devils who, apparently, were holding high carnival, and about to triumph. In this extremity too, when the burden of the world's sin was pressing Him sorely, His Father hid His face, leading the suffering one to cry "My God! my God! why hast thou forsaken Me?" How true the language of the prophet when speaking of the world's Redeemer: "I have trodden the wine-press alone; and of the people there was none with me" (Isaiah lxiii. 3). Thousands of Christ's followers have been persecuted and put to the torture because of their fidelity to Him. They have endured "cruel mockings and scourgings, bonds and imprisonments; they have been stoned, sawn asunder, slain with the sword;" condemned to endure the anguish of the rack, the thumb-screw, the stake, and other tortures the most excruciating that human ingenuity could devise, or hellish malice invent. But amid all the pain thus inflicted, the mangled sufferers had the cheering presence of their God, and the strengthening influences of His abounding grace. Of these the suffering Son of God was deprived, and in His dire extremity the light of His Father's countenance was hidden from Him. Why this pain? Why the shame and degradation that were heaped upon Him? Not for His own crimes, for the unjust, time-serving Pilate, before whom He was tried, was constrained to say: "I find no fault in this man" (Luke xxiii. 4), and Isaiah declares, "neither was any deceit in His mouth" (Isaiah liii. 9). He was the embodiment of purity in thought, word and act, all that was true and good, lovely and graceful, met in Him. "For such an High Priest became us, who is holy, harmless, undignified, separate from sinners, and made higher than the heavens" (Heb. vii. 26). Thus, though spotless in life and character, He bore, uncomplainingly, what was only inflicted upon the vilest criminals.

> "Was it for crimes that I have done,
> He groaned upon the tree?
> Amazing pity, grace unknown,
> And love beyond degree."

We must remark that—

III. Calvary was the scene of the most stupendous events that ever transpired.

Around Calvary centre the brightest hopes and deepest interest of the human family. Angels, men and devils have gazed with wonder and astonishment at the strange scene that there took place, and at the influence the suffering Lamb of God has exercised upon mankind. Other events have been great, but when placed side by side with this, they appear but trifling. Kingdoms once mighty have been overthrown and scarcely a vestige remains of their ancient grandeur. Cities adorned with magnificent palaces and temples, and possessing fabulous wealth, have been destroyed, and the hooting owl now sits solitary in the place where once thronged the busy multitude. The earth furnishes abundant evidence of strange riftings and upheavals, mountains having been cleft asunder and cast into the sea, or levelled with the plain; lakes and rivers have been lost in the earth, or have appeared where formerly it was dry land. These events in the political and physical world have been productive of tremendous results. But what are earthquakes and changes in the material world? what are alterations in the boundaries of earthly kingdoms, the destruction of some cities or states and the rising up of others to fill their places? what the blotting out of a world when brought into contrast with the wondrous work wrought out on Calvary by our Emmanuel? The beauties of nature and art may fade and crumble, the prestige and power of worldly potentates be broken, and material wealth with all its glamour vanish, but the marvellous event that occurred in Judea, when the "Messiah was cut off, but not for Himself," and the effects of that glorious moral victory achieved by the Captain of our salvation, must live in the minds of all sentient beings down through the ages of eternity. It is true, that there the heel of the Mighty Conqueror was bruised, but He rose superior to all His foes and crushed the serpent's head.

The very means adoped by Satan to frustrate the grand scheme of human redemption, recoiled upon himself and became instrumental in his own overthrow. There the claims of justice were fully met and satisfied, and the promise made to the first guilty pair verified to the letter. There the ransom price was paid to the uttermost farthing, the atoning work finished, so that with the Apostle Paul, we can exultingly say: "Be it known unto you, therefore, men and brethren, that through this man is preached unto you the forgiveness of sins" (Acts xiii. 38).

In speaking of Christ's paying the price, or meeting the demands against us, we must be guarded lest a wrong impression should obtain. It may be well to ask, What debts did He pay for us? Some answer the question by saying, that He obeyed the law for us, gave in our stead and in our name that obedience which we owed thereto, so that this law cannot now demand perfect obedience of us. We regard the theology contained in this answer as very unsound and mischievous, as it confounds two things essentially different, and views the atonement in the light of a commercial transaction, which it will not bear. Did Christ pay our debts in the sense above indicated? Did He obey the moral law that we might be discharged from our obligation to do so? Did He love God and His neighbour in our stead that we might be exempt from the duty? No unprejudiced person can fail to perceive that in this sense He paid no debts for us. Had he done so it would have been redeeming us *from* God, who never can relinquish His claim to our love and obedience and not *to* God, the very object of His death, and would have been subversive of all moral government. Consequently it appears evident, and in harmony with the divine economy, that when the phrase, Christ paid our debts, is used, we must understand, not the debt of obedience and love, but the debt of penalty. This He did pay, even to the uttermost, and blotted out, with His own precious blood, the hand writing that was against us, yielding Himself, voluntarily, to the death of the cross that we might have eternal life through faith in His name.

This brings us to consider that the sufferings and death of our Lord were voluntary in their character. To take any other view would brand the Almighty with injustice and cruelty in compelling an innocent, unwilling victim to take the place of the criminal and endure the punishment his crimes deserved. To render a substitution valid, honourable and efficacious, there must be perfect voluntariness on the part of the substitute. That this qualification was possessed by our Lord Jesus Christ in an eminent degree, and that it originated in Himself, is confirmed by His own utterances. It is recorded: " Lo, I come: in the volume of the book it is written of Me, I delight to do Thy will, O my God" (Psalm xl. 7 and 8). Again: " Therefore doth My Father love me, because I lay down My life, that I might take it again. No man taketh it from Me, but I lay it down of Myself, I have power to lay it down, and I have power to take it again " (John x. 17 and 18). These passages prove that his life was not taken from Him. His death was not the result of crucifixion, for the time He was upon the cross, only a few hours, was too short to terminate the life of one in the vigour of manhood and in the enjoyment of perfect health, there being no known lesion of any of the vital organs. Again, it was no unusual thing for those who were crucified to survive two or three days, or even longer, excruciating as the torture was; and when Pilate was informed that Christ was already dead, he marvelled that He had died so soon. In view of the attendant circumstances, we are inclined to the opinion advanced by Sir James Simpson, Dr. Stroud, and others, that the death of the world's Redeemer was the result of rupture of the heart, caused by the overwhelming mental agony He endured while suffering for our sin, bearing our griefs and carrying our sorrows. According to the authorities above named, in rupture of the heart, large quantities of blood escape from the interior of the organ into the pericardium, or heart sac, which is separated into red clot and limped serum, and this corresponds with the " water and blood" which flowed from the wound made by the soldier's spear in the side of the crucified Saviour.

The sufferings and death of Christ were also vicarious.

Some tell us that He came as a teacher merely, to give us clearer views of God's requirements, our own duties to Him, to ourselves, and our fellow men, and to set us an example of obedience, shewing us how to suffer and die. Is this all that Calvary and its dreadful sufferings mean? Tell it to the penitent sinner, groaning to be delivered from his intolerable burden, and what consolation could it afford him? Place his dying Lord before him as the exponent of God's pure and holy law, with its righteous and reasonable requirements, and furnish him with no grace to keep that law, and what would the result be but despair of ever being able to meet its demands. But, beloved, we are not left to grope our way in the dark on this all-absorbing point; the Scriptures of divine truth, the only infallible guide, give us the required light. The sacred Oracles declare that Jesus "gave Himself for us." We are told that "He was wounded for *our* transgressions, He was bruised for *our* iniquities; the chastisement of *our* peace was upon Him; and with His stripes *we* are healed" (Isaiah liii. 5). "Christ hath redeemed us from the curse of the law, being made a curse for us; for it is written, Cursed is every one that hangeth on a tree" (Gal. iii. 13). "In whom we have redemption through His blood, the forgiveness of sins" (Eph. i. 7). It is unnecessary to quote further, the foregoing plainly pointing to the precious truth, that the Lord Jesus Christ became our substitute, and that through the merit of His blood we may be redeemed from sin and enjoy the full benefits of His great salvation wrought out on Calvary.

This brings us to notice, finally, that

IV. Calvary was the place of glorious triumph.

The cup of suffering was filled to the brim and though bitter the draught, the Man of Sorrows placed

K

it to His lips and drained it to the dregs. The burden of sin, too heavy for us to bear, was laid on Him and He shrank not from the crushing load. Justice with her stern demands met Him at the cross where He satisfied her claims to the full and arched over the chasm between the sin-cursed earth and eternal glory. Satan at that moment of anticipated triumph was met on his own chosen ground by the Anointed One, driven from the field of conflict and hurled from his usurped position. The dark cavern of death was entered by the mighty Conqueror, who seized the grim king of terrors in his own domains, wrenched from him the sting wherein he trusted, and lighted up with a halo of glory the tombs of all His saints. In the very agonies of death, intent only on saving men, He absolves the penitent thief and takes him as a spoil from the blood-stained battle-field of Calvary to the Paradise of God. If ever there was a period in the Saviour's history when a doubt might have been entertained of His ability to save, it was when, though innocent, He occupied the place of the vilest criminals. But even then He manifested His power by rescuing a soul from the thrall of sin and Satan. Mighty Deliverer, how great Thy suffering and deep Thy degradation, but how glorious Thy triumph and high Thy exaltation! Around the cross of Christ cluster the strangest anomalies and apparent contradictions. There we have poverty and riches, humility and majesty, insult and magnanimity, weakness and power, death and life, a dying malefactor exercising the prerogative of a God. Well may we say

> " Here the whole Deity is known,
> Nor dares the creature guess,
> Which of the glories brighter shone,
> The justice, or the grace."

Calvary is the centre of the world's hope and thence must come the power to civilize, elevate and save the nations. From the Cross alone comes the grace to convince " of sin, of righteousness and of a judgment to come, and from the same source flows the stream to wash away the stain of guilt from the penitent believer."

How inestimably precious to the heart of every saint is the place where the redeeming work was done, deliverance for his soul wrought out, the grace purchased by which he is enabled to overcome and claim a seat in heaven. While gazing by faith upon his crucified Lord, his strength grows firmer, his hopes brighter and the strong impulses of love lead him exultingly to exclaim :—

> " Death, hell and sin are now subdued ;
> All grace is now to sinners given ;
> And, lo ! I plead th' atoning blood,
> And in Thy right I claim my heaven."

But while Calvary will raise many from sin and its consequences to life and glory, others, through rejecting the salvation there provided and so freely offered, will sink to death and destruction, some of them under the very shadow of the Cross.

How terrible the consequences of deliberately refusing the gift of life so lovingly pressed upon us ! What madness for the perishing to spurn God's proffered benefits and trample under foot the blood of the everlasting covenant ! Stop, my brother, no longer turn a deaf ear to thy loving Saviour's pleadings and promptings; cease thy rebellious opposition to the strivings of His spirit and give thyself up to its teachings. Would the starving reject offered food ? The drowning spurn the means of escape ? The sick and dying turn from the kind physician and his infallible remedy? If not, then we imploringly ask, why wilt thou waste thy life, embitter thy death, and enter eternity with the character of a rejector of Christ stamped indelibly upon thy lost soul? Rather yield thyself a willing sacrifice, crying

> " I sink by dying love compelled,
> And own Thee conqueror."

THE PROFIT OF GODLINESS,

By the Rev. W. H. Graham,

P. E. of the Ottawa District, M. E. Church.

"For bodily exercise profiteth little, but godliness is profitable unto all things, having the promise of the life that now is, and that which is to come."—1 Timothy iv. 8.

THE desire for profit has a universal hold on the human family. Convince men that they can make a profit out of any enterprise however costly, or undertaking however arduous, and they will be ready to prosecute the work. Our mountains have been tunnelled; our rivers bridged; our valleys filled up; and the very bowels of the earth pierced, and forced to yield her treasures, to make profit for man. To this desire we are largely indebted for the wonderful improvements and discoveries of the present age. God, laying His hand on, and directing this property in man, makes it redound to His glory and the good of the race. The material schemes, however, of men are only profitable, frequently, as far as this life is concerned, and not always that. But we have in the text something that promises profit for both worlds, viz.: "godliness." We will consider,

I. The nature, and define the attributes or properties of this priceless pearl that our Father in heaven offers through the merits of the Son of His love to His fallen children on earth.

II. The profit of godliness.

III. The reasons why we should seek godliness.

I. THE NATURE AND ATTRIBUTES OF GODLINESS CONSIDERED AND DEFINED.

Godliness consists in a restoration to the soul of man, of the image of God, lost in the Fall; and the purification of all the faculties of his moral manhood, embracing the renewal of his fallen nature, the lifting up of his thoughts to things above, and the influencing of his will by the Spirit of God. This godliness includes that wonderful, mysterious, and yet possible transformation, spoken of by Christ in his conversation with Nicodemus—the new birth. It embraces the "new heart" and the new spirit, and the taking away of the "stony heart out of our flesh," and the giving of a "heart of flesh," as promised by Ezekiel. It is the answer to the prayer of the Psalmist, "Create in me a clean heart, O God; and renew a right spirit within me." Godliness is that new creation spoken of by the apostle, "Circumcision or uncircumcision availeth nothing, but a new creature." It embraces the witness of the Spirit, and the indwelling God. Godliness in the life consists in loving God with all the heart, mind, soul, and strength; in loving our neighbour as ourself. Godliness includes perfect and joyful obedience to God. No man can retain the favour of God, or bear His moral image, nor should he wear the livery of God unless he obey, from the heart, the precepts written in His Word. The doctrine of devils, that the godly man is relieved from the obligation of obedience to God, should find no favour in the Christian Church. Nothing else can take the place of implicit and loyal obedience to our Heavenly Father; and the man that dreams of having favour with God, and a title to eternal life, and of finally reaching a place at His right hand, and continues to live in sin, hoping that somehow the merits of Christ will cover up his iniquity, is fearfully and fatally deceived, and perhaps will only be awakened by the fearful malediction, "Depart, ye cursed, into everlasting fire, prepared for the devil and his angels." In the midst of Plymouthism and Antinomian doctrines of that kind, we cannot too strongly urge the important truth, that the only road to heaven is the narrow way of holiness of life, and heart. Godliness in the life consists in a holy and loyal attachment to the ordinances and person of Christ—such loyalty as was exhibited by Joseph, in the midst of his terrible temptation, when he cried out, "How shall I do this great wickedness, and sin against God;" or such loyalty as was exhibited by the three Hebrew children, when they declared to the mighty Nebuchadnezzar, right in view of the fiery furnace, and in prospect of being speedily cast therein, "Be it known unto thee, O King, that we will not serve thy gods, nor worship thy golden image which thou hast set up;" or such loyalty to the ordinances of God as was exhibited by Daniel, in the face of the inexorable, unchangeable edict of his much beloved monarch, that none should offer any petition to any God or man but himself, when he bowed down three times a day, and poured forth his supplications for himself and his country, heeding little the storm that was gathering around him, knowing and feeling only the importance of the duty of the hour, simply doing right and leaving the result to God.

Such loyalty to the person of Christ as was exhibited by the aged Polycarp who, when he was commanded on the penalty of immediate death to touch the incense with fire, that they might report he had offered incense to the emperor and cursed Christ, cried out, "Eighty and six years have I lived, many years have I known Christ. He never did me wrong, how can I deny Him? my Redeemer and King. Lead me forth to the wild beasts or the fire; I cannot, I will not deny my Redeemer, my Lord." Such attachment to Christ and His cause as made the apostle cry out "the love of Christ constraineth us," to seek after the lost, lift up the fallen and preach the Gospel to every creature, so that some might be won from a life of sin, from the doom of the damned, to a life of holiness, to the eternal rest of heaven. This godliness possessed by men has in all ages filled them with such a burning desire for the glory of God and the salvation of their fellows that they have gone forth to every land, bearing the message of peace, not counting their lives dear unto them, if thereby they might glorify God, spread the knowledge of the Redeemer, plant the standard of the cross, and lead men to believe on the only name given under heaven or among men whereby they must be saved. This godliness includes the practice of not only the heroic virtues of religion, but the proper performance of the every day duties of life. The godly man will be led by his godliness to the constant abnegation of self and obedience to the declaration of the apostle, "Look not every man on his own things but, every man also on the things of others." Perhaps there is no virtue harder to practise than is found in carrying out the Golden Rule, "Whatsoever ye would that other men should do to you, do ye even so to them." And this embraces the very thoughts of our hearts. Who would desire that others would think meanly of them? Perhaps without cause. Hatred of our fellows is entirely contrary to godliness. Our words also should be kind and godlike, our actions loving and merciful like unto the Master's. How much we need the sweetening influence of the love of Christ, and the baptism of His spirit, so that in all we think or say or do we may bear His image from day to day. Godliness in life includes perfect, fair dealing in all our transactions. The bankruptcies that are practised by professed christians are a disgrace to the Church. Large liabilities and no assets—and yet a man be a child of God—perfectly preposterous. Men professing godliness sometimes resort to sharp practices to obtain for goods of any kind more than their real value, and pride themselves on their sharpness. They say we are very clever,—God writes them down thieves. An old lady was questioned by her minister on Monday to see how much of the sermon delivered on the Sabbath evening before was retained, she had forgotten the text and could not remember the divisions nor principal heads. The minister complaining, said, "You might as well not have heard it," She answered, "No, sir, no, sir! I remembered enough to burn my half bushel, for it was too small; to throw away my yard-stick, for it was too short; to have my weights made right for they were too light; and with the blessing of God to commence this morning to lead an honest life." What a turning over there would be in our towns and villages among our business men, if the Sunday sermons took such an effect? What a seeking out among our rural population there would be for the persons who had been cheated in buying spavined horses for sound ones upon the word of somebody whom they took to be "honest." In a word, godliness consists in being and living like unto God's only begotten Son on the earth, and walking before him in newness of life.

II. THE PROFIT OF GODLINESS.

Godliness is profitable for a man's material interest and worldly advancement. It may cost to be godly! The institutions of the Church are supported and its chief burdens borne, and its toils endured by the godly, and yet it costs, even in money, much more to be a sinner than a saint. The saints of this Dominion pay, say a million of dollars per year for the support of the christian ministry, and say nine millions more in interest and other expenses connected with the Christian church, while the liquor bill of the ungodly for this Dominion is, say seventy-five millions (75,000,000) of dollars. Tobacco costs the smokers about eight millions of dollars per year, or two dollars per capita tax for the Dominion. Other things being equal, by his industry, frugality and temperance, the godly man prospers better than his neighbour who spends his substance in riotous living. Godliness is profitable for domestic peace and home happiness. Where godliness dwells there will be no divorces. The well-regulated godly house is the best earthly type of heaven. Godliness is profitable for mental illumination and intellectual development. When Cæsar invaded Great Britain he found a people so degraded that he declared they were unfit for slaves. Some years after several females were sold in the market place in Rome, and a christian inquiring who they were was told they were Angles. Give them, said he, the love of Christ and it will make them angels. The Anglo-Saxon race have been illumined and lifted up by the mighty lever of the grace of God. Our noble Queen reigns over two hundred and fifty millions of the human race. The security of her throne, the attachment to her person, the love of her subjects, is largely secured by the purity of her character, which is the result of her godly training. Everywhere, in every age, the declaration of the word holds good, "Righteousness exalteth a nation," &c.

Godliness is profitable for a man's inward peace: "as I live, saith the Lord, there is no peace to the wicked." " But great peace have they that love Thy law, and nothing shall offend them." When the clouds of sin and darkness that have hidden so long the smile of our Father above, and shut out from our souls the warming rays of the Sun of righteousness, and all misconceptions of God and His nature have been driven away by the mighty breathings of God's eternal spirit, and there comes down upon our hearts the sweet consciousness of His eternal, unchangeable love, and Christ whispers to the throbbing, hoping heart, "Peace, be still," and we sink into the everlasting arms of the Infinite, and feel that we have now no will but God's, and all our being is permeated with divine grace, then we exultingly exclaim, " I waited patiently for the Lord, and He inclined unto me and heard my cry, and took me up also out of an horrible pit and miry clay, and set my feet upon a rock, and established my goings, and put a new song in my mouth, even praises unto our God." They are strangers to peace who are strangers to godliness.

This godliness is profitable for the world to come. "'Tis not all of life to live nor all of death to die." The other life is measured by the cycles of an endless eternity. Man must and will live for ever. Upon his moral and spiritual state here depends man's eternal interests. On the one hand the godly man is an heir of God and a joint heir with Jesus Christ of all the vast worlds which Christ has created and is now the owner.

Whatever glory Christ has with the Father, whatever honours of judgeship over all the races which God has made, will the godly man share. While

> The highest place that heaven affords
> Is to our Jesus given;
> The King of kings, and Lord of lords,
> He reigns o'er earth and heaven,

yet strange as it may appear the humblest child of God is bone of His bone, flesh of His flesh, united to Him by an indissoluble tie, and a king and priest to God he reigns with Him forever.

The profit of godliness consists in the exchange of the spotted robes of man's own righteousness for the pure robe of righteousness of the saints. In the exchange of the wicked, proud, deceitful old heart, disgusting to angels, abhorrent to God, the laughing stock of devils, and the plague of the owner, for a heart pure and holy, a soul unstained with sin, a conscience clear as the sunlight, a body touched by God's omnipotent power, changed into the likeness of Christ's glorious body, and a seat at the right hand of the eternal Father forever.

III. Reasons Why we Should Seek Godliness.

(*a*) We would urge men to seek godliness because of their immortality. Our being is an endless one. We must live forever. Our souls run parallel with God, and never can die. How insane, what fearful madness it is to live without God and without Christ in the world, in danger every day of death, that must be death eternal, if we are unsaved.

(*b*). By the love of the Infinite, our names were written on His hands. We found a lodgment in His heart when it burst asunder on Calvary's cross. And even now His heart of burning pity is moved with deep sympathy for our fallen state. He knocks at the door of our hearts. The Infinite seeks permission to enter and dwell in the soul He has himself created and redeemed by His most precious blood.

(*c*). If we would be of any great use to our race and make the world better because we have lived in it, and leave foot prints in the sands of time that will be perfectly safe for others to walk in, and by our example bless humanity, we must seek and obtain this godliness.

(*d*) If we would escape the penalty of sin, the doom of the damned, the flames of an endless hell, the company of devils and damned ghosts, of murderers and harlots, of the mean and the sordid, the lawless and degraded, the wicked and abominable of all countries and ages forever, we must repent and seek godliness. If we would have a home with the redeemed, a seat at God's right hand, a palm of victory, an heirship with Christ, a crown of glory, and eternal happiness, we must seek and obtain this godliness.

ABIDING IN CHRIST.

By the Rev. R. E. Lund,

Of Campbellford, Ont.

"Abide in me and I in you. As the branch cannot bear fruit of itself, except it abide in the vine; no more can ye, except ye abide in me."—John xv. 4.

TWO principal thoughts demand our attention in the text:—

What is it to abide in Christ; and what fruit comes of this spiritual union?

That every branch shall bear fruit, is the will and design of the Husbandman. Without fruit they are wholly valueless to Him—they cumber and dishonour the Vine. That every branch shall bear fruit of good quality and in reasonable quantity is clearly the divine purpose.

The true and only condition of fruit-bearing is here strongly marked; "the branch cannot bear fruit of itself; . . . no more can ye." To bear fruit unto holiness, ye must abide in the true Vine.

I. First we are to inquire, What is it to abide in Christ and what is necessary thereto?

1. We must first be *in* Christ; for man cannot possibly *abide*—either in body or spirit, where he has never been.

(1) Inspired history teaches that the whole human family are descended from one common parent—the first Adam. We were every one born of him, after his transgression and consequent separation in spirit from God; after the curse had fallen upon him and after his expulsion from the Paradise of liberty and life.

(2) We every one inherit the nature of this sinning and separated parent. As our nature grows and our personal character forms and developes, we present, each in his own way, an unmistakable likeness to the parent; every branch bearing the fruit of the wild vine —the sour grapes.

(3) We are, therefore, by nature and natural generation not *in* and of the " true Vine," but in and of the wild; not of the second Adam but of the first, and not *in* Christ. And though every branch of this wild vine has come into being under the gloriously full and unlimited Covenant of Grace in Christ Jesus, we have every one so used and abused our personal right and power of choice as moral agents, that " All we, like sheep, have gone astray; we have turned every one to his own way," the way of sin and death.

(4) The question of interest just here, is necessarily this:—How shall we, who are *natural*, and by the election of our own wills, *fruitful* branches of this wild vine, become *living* branches of the true Vine—Christ Jesus the Lord?

Very many, when pressed with this anxious thought, have made answer to their conscience and to God, thus: "I will do better." "I see the past has been wrong; I will henceforth try to do right." This is a radical error, and fatal, at least, in two principal points. It first assumes that a *corrupt* tree *can* bring forth *good* fruit; while our Lord has declared (Matt. vii. 18) that it *cannot*. It next assumes that there is no need nor necessity, in order to our safety and salvation for time or eternity, for a vital union between our spirits and the Lord Christ—between the branch and the Vine Than which, nothing can be further from the light of reason and the truth of God. Others there are who say, " I will wait. I hope, by a strict course of mental and moral discipline, to overcome my nature and become changed, and thus be accepted of Christ." Here, too, are terrible and fatal errors. Can the corrupt branch of a corrupt tree change and transform itself and its nature to goodness? Can a branch of the wild vine become one with the true vine by culture and growth? Is this not reversing every established law, whether in nature or in grace? To ask these questions is but to answer them. How then can man—sinning and sinful man (Rom. iii. 23)—whose heart is deceitful above all things, and desperately wicked (Jer. xvii. 9)—whose carnal mind is enmity against God; for it is not subject to the law of God, neither indeed can be (Rom. viii. 7), by the power of his own volitions become a new creature with a pure heart, a loving mind and an obedione will, in all things conformed to the will of God? It is not of the will of the flesh, nor of the will of man, but of God (John i. 13).

(5) The Scriptural answer to this grave question is clearly this: The branch must be broken off the *wild vine* and grafted in the *true Vine* (Rom. xi. 17-24). We must be severed and separated in spirit from the *old* or first Adam and united in spirit to the *new* or second Adam—the Lord from heaven. Our life " in the flesh" must become death, and we made alive from the dead through Jesus Christ our Lord. These thoughts will aid us in the interpretation and understanding of our Lord's teaching to that man of the Pharisees who came by night to Him (John iii. 1-21) :.

"Except a man be born again (or from above) he cannot see the Kingdom of God. . . . Marvel not that I said unto thee, ye must be born again."

For this wonderful transformation we sinners are prepared by our "repentance toward God"—a repentance (literally a turning) that comes from seeing and believing the truth that God has spoken about us and our sins—about *me* and *my sins*. To the possession of this we are brought by "believing in the Lord Jesus Christ"—a believing that sees the truth about Jesus the Christ; that further sees through the light of the truth, the God-man—the Christ Jesus whom the Father has given to all other sinners and *me*, and that with a full heart receives Him, and all that He is and all that He did and does, as *all my own*. "As many as received Him to them gave He power to become the sons of God, even to them that believe on His name, which were born not of blood, nor of the will of the flesh, nor of the will of man, but of God" (John i. 12, 13).

2. To abide in Christ means not only that the believer be truly "grafted in" and united to Him. It implies and requires a permanent and growing union.

(1) That the soul so "born of the spirit" shall be settled, fixed and established, shall be "rooted and grounded in love," dwelling in love and made perfect in love.

(2) That there shall be growth, development and perfection. It necessarily involves a "going on to perfection," "perfecting holiness in the fear of God," "pressing towards the mark for the prize of the high calling of God in Christ Jesus," "till we are come in the unity of the faith and of the knowledge of the Son of God, unto a perfect man, unto the measure of the stature of the fulness of Christ."

L

3. This *abiding* seems conditioned upon two things, on the part of the believer in Christ.

(1) The complete and continued consecration of our whole being, "a living sacrifice, holy, acceptable unto God" (Rom. xii. 1). *All* I have, *all* I am, and *all* my possibilities, a *whole* and *abiding* burnt-offering to God.

(2) Then full and unwavering faith in the *written* promise of our faithful covenant-keeping God, "I will receive you." We shall then fully prove that He *does* receive us and make us *all* His own.

> "Saviour, to Thee my soul looks up,
> My present Saviour Thou!
> In all the confidence of hope,
> I claim the blessing now.
>
> 'Tis done; Thou dost this moment save—
> With full salvation bless;
> Redemption through Thy blood I have,
> And spotless love and peace."

II. We are next to inquire what are the fruits of this union—this abiding in Christ?

1. The first of these is *life*—spiritual or eternal life —(1 John v. 11, 12). The branch *in* the vine, lives *by* the vine. The vine sends its own life-current through it. As Adam's sin separated him from God, cut him off from the fountain of life and caused his immediate death, so our union with God in Christ Jesus places our spirits in direct connection with the same divine life and we live, because Christ liveth in us.

2. We are new creatures.

"Therefore if any man be *in* Christ he is a new creature; old things are passed away; behold all things are become new" (2. Cor. v. 17). The heart lately "deceitful and wicked," now a new and clean heart. The carnal mind become spiritual. The tree being made good the fruit is also good—fruit unto holiness—fruits of the spirit; love ever flowing upward to God and outward to all men.

3. Freedom from all condemnation:

"There is therefore now no condemnation to them which are *in* Christ Jesus . . ." (Rom. viii. 1). No condemnation on account of all our sins (1 Peter ii. 24.) None because of the absence of works of righteousness (Rom. x. 4), and none on account of our character. With an abiding consecration and faith we have the abiding merit and power of His most precious blood that cleanses us from all sin (1 John i. 7). And, abiding in Christ, no condemnation at the Judgment seat. "For who shall lay anything to the charge of God's elect? It is God that justifieth. Who is he that condemneth" (Rom. viii. 33)?

4. Christ abides in us. "Abide *in* me and *I in* you." Though absent yet divinely and sweetly present! "If a man love me he will keep my words, and my Father will love him, and *we* will come unto him and make our abode with him (John xiv. 23). He comes in to feast with us and we with Him (Rev. iii. 20). Oh, glorious Guest! Oh, glorious feast!

5. Salvation from all sin:

From the dominion and power of sin and from indwelling sin. "Whosoever is born of God doth not commit sin; for his seed remaineth in him, and he cannot sin, because he is born of God" (1 John iii. 9). "Whosoever abideth in Him sinneth not" (verse 6).

6. Power divine—the power of the Holy Ghost abiding on us. Not power to work miracles, cure diseases or the like, but

(1) Power with God (John xv. 7) to ask and receive of Him; to prevail with Him Jacob-like (Gen. xxxii. 28); such power as rested upon the spirit of Enoch, Noah,

Abraham, Joseph, Moses, Elijah, Daniel, David, and the Apostles, and that illustrious line extending down to modern times, and of whom the world was not worthy, and by which they lived and walked in God.

(2) Power over the world, over the Devil and over self! Our whole life a song of praise and a shout of victory through the blood of the Lamb.

7. Meetness for all the will of God. "Vessels unto honour, sanctified, and meet for the Master's use and prepared unto every good work" (2 Tim. ii. 21). God can then *trust* us and *use* us.

8. A glorious eternity with Him.

Now are we the sons of God. Then we shall see Him as He is. We shall be like Him—in body and spirit, sinless, spotless, faultless before the Father and the holy angels. We shall be with Him where He is. We shall share His glory for ever and ever, for "we are heirs of God and joint-heirs with Christ; if so be that we suffer with Him, that we may be also glorified together." Amen.

DAVID'S CHOICE.

By Rev. I. B. Aylsworth, M.A., LL.D., P.E.,

Napanee District.

2 Samuel xxiv. 14.—"And David said unto Gad, I am in a great strait; let us fall now into the hands of the Lord; for his mercies are great; and let me not fall into the hand of man."

IN the first verse of this chapter we read, "And again the anger of the Lord was kindled against Israel, and he moved David against them to say, Go, number Israel and Judah." In Chronicles xxi. 1, where this same event is recorded it reads, "And Satan stood up against Israel, and invoked David to number Israel." Putting the two statements together we would infer that Satan induced David to number Israel, and the anger of the Lord was kindled in consequence thereof.

David was in a great strait, not, I apprehend, that he had any difficulty to decide whether he should fall into the hands of the Lord or into the hands of man; for he knew that the tender mercies of the wicked is cruelty. He knew that man could let loose the dogs of war, but he could not stop them. He knew that war inflamed the worst passions of men, and made them tenfold more like fiends of hell than they otherwise would be. David had had an experience with men and knew something of the unrelenting cruelty of man, and therefore he said, let us not fall into the hands of man.

For Gad, David's seer, had been sent to offer David three things: either three years' famine; or three months' war; or three days' pestilence. To choose war would be to fall into the hands of man; pestilence and famine are from the Lord. Two evils were from the Lord and one from man. His strait then was to decide between pestilence or famine, and David very wisely decides to let God himself choose, for His mercies are great. And, therefore, God sent the pestilence, for this was the more merciful of the two. Famine is a lingering death of torture; literally the same as being burnt up from within. So Moses says they "shall be burnt with hunger;" and modern chemistry proves this statement to be scientifically true. And when we reflect that in India and the East during the last year seven millions have starved to death, how thankful should we be in this highly favoured land that we have all things and abound. When I read the accounts it cuts me to the quick. Only think of whole families being three days, five days, without food. Father, mother and childen crying in vain for bread, until they perish in heaps. Those whose barns and cellars never fail can scarcely realize such terrible facts. On the other hand, pestilence is a sudden death, and perhaps as many would perish in three days by pestilence as in three years by famine, yet the suffering to the victim would be very much less, although the annoyance and inconvenience to the living would be much more.

What was the precise nature of the sin of David on this occasion the record does not inform us, and, for want of time, I shall not speculate; sufficient for us to know that he did sin, and he knew he sinned, and confessed that he had sinned and that he had done very foolishly. Every time a man sins he does a foolish thing, and every time he is awakened to a sense of his sin he feels that he has acted the fool. "What fruit had ye in those things whereof ye are now ashamed?" Job and the chief captains of the hosts knew David was infatuated and determined to sin. They tried to dissuade him, but the king's word prevailed and Job proceeded to number the people and gave up the sum thereof, which was one million three hundred thousand men that drew the sword; equal to any of the most powerful nations of Europe at the present time. It is possible that the people, perhaps the younger portion of the nation, importuned David to number Israel; for the anger of the Lord was kindled against Israel; and the punishment fell on the people until David exclaimed, "Lo, I have sinned, and I have done wickedly, but these poor sheep, what have they done?"

Although we do not know just in what David's sin consisted, yet from the fact that so great a penalty was inflicted for one sin, we may learn some valuable lessons.

1. We may be sure of this, that God reads the heart and detects sin there, and hates it in its beginnings. We see the outward manifestation of disease, in the sunken eye, the hectic flush and the emaciated body; but the physician can detect it in the blood. We see the outward displays of sin, in profanity, lying and lewdness, and we hate it; but God sees the moral virus as it rankles in the thoughts of the heart and ripens into purposes and deeds of evil. Therefore, as Shakespeare aptly advises,

> "We must resist beginnings, whatsoever is ill,
> Though it appear light, and of little moment.
> Think of it thus—that what it is augmented
> Would run to sharp and strong extremities;
> Deem of it, therefore, as a serpent's egg,
> Which, hatched, would, as its kind, grow mischievous;
> Then crush it in the shell."

2. We may learn also that those who are favoured with great advantages in this life are under greater obligations to walk circumspectly, "To whom much is given, of them shall much be required." David had been a long time in the service of God, and he must have known the importance and necessity of obeying God in heart and life. His sin might have been a piece of selfishness in simply going on his own responsibility, not waiting to know the mind of God. Ungodly men may live on and follow their own devices, not heeding the will or purpose of God; but their time is coming. A Christian professes to be led by the Spirit of God, and it is offensive to God for them to enter upon any important enterprise without knowing that God wills it. It may appear a small thing, unworthy of notice to the unregenerated, but in the eyes of God it is the beginning of rebellion. It was apparently a small failure in Moses that shortened his days and kept him out of the promised land; but Moses had been so long in the service of God, and had sustained such intimate relations with Him, that he should have known better. This apparently small sin was in itself more aggravating than some outrageous crime of an ordinary sinner. It is significant to notice how exceedingly careful David was in the future to follow the mind of God. He would not offer a sacrifice that cost him nothing, and he " could not go before to enquire of God, for he was afraid because of the sword of the angel of the Lord." (Verses 24 and 30.) Christians are sometimes betrayed into the fatal delusion that they can indulge in the same frailties as worldlings without serious consequences. But the vows of God are upon us; we claim to be converted, we must let our light shine, we must shun the very appearance of evil. For if the light

that is in *thee* be darkness, how great is that darkness.

3. We see also how low a person can fall when once he lets go his integrity. David descended to crimes darker and more treacherous than can be found anywhere else in the annals of history, especially in the matter of Uriah the Hittite. It was not the publicans and harlots who crucified Jesus, but the Scribes and Pharisees, of whom it was said, "ye compass sea and land to make one proselyte, and when he is made, ye make him two-fold more the child of hell than ye are yourselves." The Corinthian Christians harboured a criminal among them who was guilty of a crime for which the Gentiles had no name.

4. We see what a great calamity came from apparently so trivial a circumstance. Seventy thousand people lost their lives in a few hours for one sin of one man. The little unpleasantness in the case of Henry Ward Beecher has done more harm to virtue and purity than one hundred Brigham Youngs could do. Of David in the matter of Uriah the Hittite, it was said he had caused the enemies of God to blaspheme. And they do to this day.

5. And if such severe judgments fall upon a praying man for his sins and shortcomings, what will become of the finally impenitent? "If the righteous are scarcely saved where shall the ungodly and the sinner appear?" "Thou standest by faith. Be not high-minded but fear; if God spared not the natural branches, take heed lest he spare not thee."

The enemies of our holy Christianity attempt to make capital out of this whole affair, against the Bible and against the God of the Bible. This case they attack as one of the weak points in the inspired volume. They say it is a hard, cruel thing that seventy thousand innocent people should be cut down for one sin of another man.

But our first business is to settle whether it is true. "This is a hard saying, who can bear it," some said to Jesus. But the first question is not whether it is hard, but is it true. Your hand is fractured, you send for the physician, he says your arm must come off; it is hard, but is it true? You send for the quack, he says bind it up and save it. It pleases you, you keep your arm, and lose your life with your arm. Who is your friend? the flatterer or the one that told you the truth? It is the truth, although it may be a hard truth, that will make you free, if you obey it. The remedy may be severe, but desperate diseases require desperate remedies. There are some hard things indeed, in this Bible, but sin is a hard disease, and the Bible contains its remedy.

The record of the case under consideration bears the appearance of truthfulness upon the very face of it. It does not read like myth. We are endowed with a literary sense, and we can tell a cunningly devised fable from straight history. When we read Homer or Virgil we know it is mythology. When we read Thucydides or Livy we know it is history. We can discriminate between the myth and the real history of Britain or Rome. An imaginary history cannot be as true to life as real history. We have not the slightest reason to doubt the old Testament record, but an hundred-fold more reason to believe it than any other history. This case of David is recorded in two places, and the trivial discrepancies that may be detected show it is not a cunningly devised story, or its author would have been cunning enough to make everything perfectly harmonize. Well now, if this Bible is true, it will take care of itself, and needs not that any one should apologize for it.

And if this Bible is true, and this is a true report in this case, then the God of the Bible must be the true God. If these seventy thousand men fell in a few hours, they must have fallen by an invisible hand, and that invisible power must be God; and if the God of this Bible is the true God, then He will take care of Himself and needs not that anyone shall apologize for Him. And if God is true and the Bible is true, and both will take care of themselves, the next consistent act is for you and me to take care of ourselves. Many people make a pretext to neglect God out of the very reasons why they should serve and fear Him. The one who had received the one pound in the Gospel came "saying Lord, behold here is thy pound, which I kept laid up in a napkin, for I feared thee because thou art an austere man: thou takest up that thou laidest not down, and reapest that thou didst not sow. And he said unto him, out of thine own mouth I will condemn thee, for thou knewest that I was an austere man, taking up that I laid not down, and reaping that I did not sow. Wherefore then gavest thou not my money into the bank, that at my coming I might have required my own with usury."

To illustrate: the teacher says to the idle scholar: " Now I have borne with you three months and you have not applied yourself. I have coaxed and bribed you and all in vain; I have exhausted every expedient, and now if you come again without knowing your lesson I will punish you. The boy comes up the very next time and has not studied. "Why did you not study?" "Well, you said you would flog me if I did not study, and therefore I would not." The very reason why he should have studied he urges as a reason why he did not. Men know that there are hard things in the Bible, and that is proof positive that they know something about the Bible. They have enough knowledge to induce them to act. They know something at least about God; if they have never heard more than that there is a God, they have at least heard that much. So that they are not absolutely ignorant. If they have heard of the severity of God, they must also have heard of the goodness of God; for all along the the ages the two great facts are joined and equally apparent, and no one could know of the one without knowing the other. Out of men's own mouths therefore they will be condemned; and at the judgment every mouth shall be stopped.

The objectors, however, have the most serious trouble with King David himself. Splendid specimen of a christian, they say. One lately said in the public prints, "David is a fit companion only for harlots and murderers, and yet the Bible calls him a man after God's own heart." So far as the Bible is concerned, it is sufficient to say that because it has reported all the sins and weaknesses of its characters, it so far differs from all human productions. If a human mind had invented this story about David's life and character, and with the evident intention of describing a true servant of God, he never could have ventured to put in an account of so many of his sins. In all cases the Bible tells the truth and nothing but the truth, and therefore " it is truth."

Now concerning David, before he is judged, condemned and banished, we must know and consider all the facts in the case. "Doth our law judge a man before it hear him, and know what he doeth?" They tell of a Dutch judge, who, after hearing the prosecution, refused to hear the defence "for fear he should change his mind." Many refuse to hear anything about David but his sins lest they should change their minds. But God is at least more merciful and just than man, and He will hear both sides of the case.

1. Before we dispose of David we must put his *repentance* along with his sin. As soon as he reflects, even before the seer came to him, we find him confessing that he had sinned greatly, and had done foolishly. If a christian at any time steps aside in the least he gets no mercy from men. "There," they say, "there's your loud professor. He's an abominable hypocrite, and that's what most of them are." And so their tongues run. But hold, before you decide that man's fate and send him on to hell without judge or jury, you must follow him home; and go, stand by the door of his closet, and listen to the bitter anguish of his soul as he reviews his day's transactions and pours out his complaint unto God, and asks God to forgive him his sins, and heal all his back-slidings, and if possible, counteract the evil of his example and restore unto him once again the joys of salvation. And God, whose mercies are very great, does have mercy upon him; for a humble, broken and a contrite heart, O God, Thou wilt not despise, but Thou wilt forgive iniquity, transgression and sin. Thus, while man condemns him, God forgives him. Man sends him to hell, God takes him to heaven. Then "let us now fall into the hands of the Lord, for his mercies are great, but let us not fall into the hands of man."

That's all very well, you say; that makes it easy to get to heaven. Sin one day and repent the next. "A man may come to your meeting on Sunday and make a great ado, and loud profession, but follow him out into the streets and into his business, a Sunday christian and a week-day devil. Is that your gospel?" Not exactly. If you know any such man, don't spare him. But that is not David. We are discussing his case now. You will notice in his case that he never repeated the same crime. One case of Uriah the Hittite was enough for a life time. After the sin of numbering Israel, you will notice how carefully David moves. And these little facts are strong evidences in favour of the truthfulness of the whole narrative. David is like a man who has fallen on very slippery ice, and hurt himself considerably; and with careful step, a little bent forward, he starts for the shore.

2. In the second place, with David's sin we must consider David's *prayer*. Hitherto he had had an experience with God. He had learned that God could and would hear prayer; that He would hear the prayer of a sinner, and even of a back-slider. In answer to prayer he had already been taken up out of the horrible pit and the miry clay. Heretofore God had blotted out his iniquities according to the multitude of His tender mercies. And whether he had trials, afflictions or sins, he had learned to take them all to God in prayer. The true christian, whose heart is right, may be tempted and may fall, but he has learned the way back to God and the throne, and starts without delay. A few years ago a man was turned out of the church for an attempted crime that no decent man would be guilty of. He came over to a neighbour's the next day for advice and sympathy, and was told to get back into the same church again, just as soon as he could. Said the neighbour, "if you throw a wolf out of a sheep pen, he will make for the woods; but throw a lamb out and he will bleat around the pen and want to get in again. Now, wolf or lamb, run or stay." The honest hearted Christian will get back to God again as

soon as possible. To whom should we go when foot-sore and weary; when heart-sick and lashed by a guilty conscience, but unto God, who alone can forgive and shield and comfort and save. When the great whale is struck by the sword fish, he dives to the bottom of the ocean, where the water is so heavy it will crush the brains out of the more tender-headed enemy. A short time ago the submarine cable refused to communicate. They discovered the damaged place, and found the cable broken and a whale covered with parasites, and wound up in one end of it. He had been scraping himself on the floor of the sea to liberate himself, and coming in contact with the cable, broke it, and lost his life. The Christian flies back into the bosom of God and there abides until the storm is over-past.

> What a friend we have in Jesus,
>   All our sins and griefs to bear!
> What a privilege to carry
>   Everything to God in prayer!

3. We must add to David's sin, his *affliction*. Many are the afflictions of the righteous, and David was a man who had his share of them. A gentleman heard a beautiful singer on her first appearance in public. She had splendid natural and acquired endowments; but he said she just lacked one thing. Some one should marry her, and then desert her and break her heart, and then she could sing with a tenderness and pathos which would melt an audience to tears. It is the bruising of the rose that causes it to shed forth an aroma and sweetness an hundred fold more than it otherwise could. Of Jesus it is said He was *bruised* for our offences. It was this bruising which enabled the chief among ten thousand, to become the author of eternal glory and salvation to as many as be-

lieve on Him. Dr. Ives said he never could fully sympathise with the hereafter until death entered his own household. Some one thinks that every preacher is better qualified to weep with those that weep after he himself has been afflicted. I well know what the loss of a tender three year old daughter—an only child, means. It is a bitter experience; but "out of the eater comes forth meat, and out of the strong comes forth sweetness." David had a more varied experience than any other man of whom we have any knowledge, either in sacred or profane history. At one time we see him seated upon the proudest throne of earth, swaying a peaceful and happy sceptre over a numerous and powerful people. At another time we find him hiding in dens and in caves and skulking like a coward and an outlaw before his enemies and pursuers. Again we see him seated in his sanctum composing and writing some of the rarest poetic strains which ever came from the pen or mind of man. Then we follow him again a captive prisoner in the hands of his enemies, the heathen kings, feigning madness, frothing at the mouth, biting at the wall, and playing the rôle of a drivelling idiot, to save his life. At one time David is the most popular man living; the observed of all observers. Men, women and children vie with each other to shout his praises. "Saul has slain his thousands, but David his tens of thousands." After this we find him submitting to the curses and revilings of a "dead dog," saying, let him curse, "it may be the Lord will look on my affliction, and that the Lord will requite me good for his cursing this day." David was bruised, but the bruising refined and perfected him, for these light afflictions will work out for us a far more exceeding and eternal weight of glory.

4. We must also contemplate with David's sin, his

punishment. The punishments he received in this life were partly as a natural consequence of his crime, and partly the direct judgments of God. All punishment partakes, more or less, of the same elements. If the child disobeys and burns his hand in the fire, the suffering is the natural consequence of his sin, and he merits an additional chastisement for his disobedience. If a man continues to pour adulterated liquors into his stomach, the natural penalty is an inflamed stomach, a diseased liver, poisoned blood, nervous paralysis, and an unnatural appetite for more poison. The rebellion of Absalom followed, as a natural result, from the crime against Uriah the Hittite. After debauching his wife he sends for him to come home a few days on the pretence of particular regard for him, but really with the expectation of concealing his crime. Failing in this, he makes him drunk. This failing, he puts his death warrant in his hand and sends him back to die. A more treacherous and scandalous transaction it is difficult to conceive. David thought to keep the whole matter a secret, but failed. His sin found him. He was startled as was Moses when he exclaimed, "this thing is known." Afterward his son Solomon was enabled to write the proverb, "He that walketh uprightly walketh safely, but he that perverteth his way shall be known." To be known as guilty of such crimes, was punishment enough for any man who had any regard for his character. These base and cruel crimes were whispered from family to family, from tribe to tribe, from man to man and woman to woman, and everybody lost faith in the king. And because everybody lost faith in the king, Absalom was enabled to steal the hearts of the people. Absalom never could have stolen their hearts away from King David, if David had never been guilty of such terrible crimes.

Another result of these crimes was that David became a slave to Joab, the chief captain; for Joab was of necessity into the guilty secret. After this Joab ruled and David was slave. David tried to get rid of him, and failed. At one time he did put Amasa in his place, but Joab quietly walked up to Amasa and killed him, and took his place again and kept it until David's death. And when Solomon his son came to rule in his room and stead, he dismissed Joab and put another in his place.

The lessons from these facts are very plain. A man becomes morally weak in proportion as he loses his moral character, and very often a man becomes a slave to his own servant, or wife, or neighbour. A few months ago a gentlemen threatened to dismiss his hired man, but the man told him to do so if he dared, and he would publish his crimes in the papers. John was not dismissed. I visited a member once at his home, and when he did not please his wife, she ordered him to stop his mouth, or she would expose him. He became silent immediately. He that walketh uprightly walketh safely.

5. There is one thing more must be mentioned in David's case, and that is, his *perseverance*. He never let go his hold on God. Often his foot had well nigh slipped, but he righted again and took a fresh start. Success does not consist in never falling, but in getting up every time you fall. It is by patient continuance in well doing that men secure glory, honour and immortality. We begin the christian life as babes in Christ, and grow until we can endure strong meat. A great many people expect that as soon as one starts in the christian life he will be a perfect christian. It is as unreasonable and impossible as for a child to be a perfect man. You give the babe a thirty years'

struggle, first, under the tender watchfulness of a mother's love, and a father's kindness; struggling through various diseases and accidents, steadily meeting and conquering the hard knocks and obstacles that are in his path, nay, until he arrives at years of maturity and becomes a full grown man. But as soon as one becomes a babe in Christ, you demand perfection. You will give a blacksmith five years to perfect his trade; you give a doctor ten years of practice after his five years' study, before you expect a skilled physician; you give a student twenty years' hard study before you expect much of a scholar. After forty years' schooling, Paul could say, "I have *learned* in whatsoever state I am therewith to be content." But because a man does not come up to your idea of perfection as soon as he starts for heaven, you lose faith in him, and pronounce him a fraud. The father is trying to learn the year old child to walk. The child takes a step and falls, and is hurt, and cries. Does the father whip him, or scold him, or lose faith in his ever walking? No; he stands him on his feet again, encourages him, helps him, until finally he can stand, and walk, and run. So God, whose mercies are great, gives us another chance, helps us up, encourages us, has faith in us, gives us a chance to grow, gain strength and develop. This is Paul's meaning, when he says, "we are not under the law but under grace." The infinite mercy of God is manifested in the glorious gospel of Christ, that if any man sin we have an advocate with the Father, even Jesus Christ, the righteous; and therefore it is better to fall into the hands of God, and not into the hands of man. Man never could exercise the patience and long suffering and kind forbearance that God can. "But God, who is rich in mercy, for his great love wherewith he loved us, even when we were dead in sins, hath quickened us together with Christ (by grace ye are saved)," and "if when we were enemies we were reconciled to God by the death of his Son, much more, being reconciled, we shall be saved by his life." Now the great mercy of God is not manifested to encourage us to fall into sin, but it is manifested to encourage us to get up every time we do fall. And the grace of God gives us a chance to repent and reform, and profit by the lessons even of our own sad experiences. A great many serious persons are misled by the hope that when they start in the christian life their trials are over, when in fact they have just commenced. Because they meet with difficulties, and are assailed with temptations, they conclude that God has never blessed them. Because the remains of carnality and the motions of sin discover themselves in their hearts, they too hastily conclude they never were converted, and give up in despair. All this is wrong, and of the Devil. He first tempts a convert, and then turns around and whispers, you would not be tempted thus if your conversion was genuine, but he is a liar and the father of lies.

Our progress may be slow in the christian graces, but we must let patience have her perfect work. The student may not see much progress the first day at school, but one year or five years will tell, especially if he compares his progress with those who do not persevere. Jacob and Esau started out from the same home, at the same time, and under the same favourable circumstances. In seventy years one is known as a profane person, the other a fine old christian patriarch. The reason of this vast difference is, the one prayed and the other neglected to pray. The man who leads a praying life will get better and better, and nearer to God. The man who neglects to pray will generally soon begin to swear, and while he lives will get worse and worse. We see history repeating itself all around—brothers and sisters, members of the same household, diverging, part toward heaven, and the rest toward hell. And if the good in this life get better, and the bad get worse, the same thing will hold in the world to come. The good will get nearer the Throne and nearer to God, while the bad will eternally plunge deeper into outer darkness. This is the great gulf fixed, which can never be passed. If the good and the bad are eternally diverging, what becomes of the vain hope that some time in the endless ages they will all come together, and all will be saved? All reason and scripture are against it.

But you say, look at your text. God's mercies are great. And if He will hear prayer and forgive sin here, will He not in hell? Now it is not for me to decide what God will do in the infinite ages. All we know is what is revealed. The Bible holds out no encouragement. "Thou shalt mourn at the last when thy heart and flesh fail thee. And I also will laugh at your calamity and mock when your fear cometh." The foolish virgins repented and were very sorry, but it was too late.

Although we will not decide what God will do in the great future, we may safely conclude as to what you will do. If you do not repent here, neither will you repent there. If you hear not Moses and the prophets, neither will you be persuaded, though one rose from the dead. If the Gospel cannot soften you, the punishment of hell cannot. "If they do these things in the green tree, what will they do in the dry?" If the husbandman cannot cause his tree to bear fruit in the garden with the best of care, would it bear fruit if transplanted to a barren mountain, and the mountain on fire? If the love of sin and the fear of man, which bring a snare, prevent men from repenting in this life under the grace of God, will not the same causes produce the same results under wrath in the flames of the pit? The terrible probability is that there is no second chance, or day of probation, and that now is the accepted time, and now is the day of salvation, and we had better all "fall *now* into the hands of the Lord."

Even if it could be proved that after burning a while in hell, we would be taken to heaven, it is infinitely better to go the straight way to heaven, and keep out of hell, if we can, even if it is only an hour. And since it might be a million years, yea, since it might be eternal death, the risk is too great. All reason cries out against taking such a terrible risk if it can be avoided. Wisdom warns us to fall now into the hands of God, and make our calling and election sure.

And since time is short, and death is certain, and may come upon us as a thief, you had better fall into God's merciful hands now. This very moment, you have serious impressions, but in one hour they may be gone, never to return again. Therefore, "let us fall now into the hands of the Lord, for his mercies are great; but let us not fall into the hand of man," for "if the blind lead the blind, they shall both fall into the pit."

SINNERS ADMONISHED.

By Rev. A. T. Ferguson.

Preached in Bethel M. E. Church, Winnipeg, Man., 17th Nov., 1878.

" Thus saith the Lord, Stand ye in the ways, and see, and ask for the old paths, where is the good way, and walk therein, and ye shall find rest for your souls."—Jer. vi. 16.

THE traveller over the vast prairies of our country sometimes comes to a point from which two trails diverge, one bearing to the right hand and the other to the left. The divergence may be so slight at first that it appears a matter of indifference which trail he takes. But it may make a great difference in the end.

There are just such points of divergence in the journey of life. We have reached one to-night. As we sit together in this sanctuary, a company of eternity-bound travellers, two paths are open before us, the path of life and the path of death. To the thoughtless observer it may appear a matter of little importance which path we take; but our choice to-night may decide our destiny for heaven or hell. How important it is then that we should choose the right way, and yet how liable we are to choose the wrong. Hear then the admonition of the text: " Stand ye in the ways and see, and ask for the old paths, where is the good way and walk therein, and ye shall find rest for your souls."

The first injunction of the text is, "Stand ye in the ways and see," in other words stop and think; use the intelligence that God has given you and calmly "consider your ways."

Consider your obligations to God as your Creator. He has made you for Himself. You are His property. He has absolute right to control and dispose of you. But do you recognize that right? Are you not living without any regord to His pleasure? "Will a man rob God?" indignantly asks our Maker. And yet you are deliberately robbing Him of the love of your heart and the service of your life. And can you expect to prosper in such a course of sacrilege? Does He not warn you, saying, "Woe unto him that striveth with his Maker?" Hast thou an arm like God? Can you hope to successfully resist His power? Surely not, for the eternal purpose of His will is declared, "As I live, saith the Lord, every knee shall bow to me and every tongue shall confess to God."

Consider your obligations to God as your preserver and benefactor. Has He not done you good and not evil all the days of your life? But how have you requited his unmerited kindness? A Macedonian soldier was once shipwrecked and cast upon the shore almost dead. A kind hearted countryman finding him thus, took him to his home, cared for him until he recovered, and when he departed gave him money for his journey. The rescued soldier spoke his thanks and promised to secure royal bounty for his benefactor. But when he appeared before the emperor he related the story of his own misfortunes and asked to be recompensed by the gift of the house and lands of his friends. His request was granted and he returned and drove out his former host. You inwardly exclaim, what base ingratitude! and you will feel glad when you hear that when the emperor found out the true state of the case, he not only restored the lands to their owner but caused the soldier to be branded upon the forehead " The ungrateful guest." And yet, dear fellow sinner, is not your ingratitude as base ? You have received God's gifts, and yet have robbed the giver. Has He not reason to complain of you as of rebellious Israel, "Hear, O heavens, and give ear, O earth, for the Lord hath spoken, I have nourished and brought up children, and they have rebelled against me. The ox knoweth his owner and the ass his master's crib, but Israel doth not know, my people doth not consider." One has truly said "the greatest miracle in the world is God's patience and bounty to an ungrateful world."

Consider your obligations to God as your Redeemer. You were hopelessly ruined by sin. A curse rested upon you, and it was beyond the power of man or angel to help you. But God loved you and "gave His only begotten Son " that believing in Him you "might not perish but have everlasting life." As the result of that redemption you are yet on " praying ground." Justice has been demanding your death, but the atoning blood of Jesus has been pleading for your life. You are out of hell this moment, not because you deserve to be, but because God has no pleasure in your destruction. He is " not willing that any should perish but that all should come to repentance." But how are you treating that pleading Saviour ? Are you not consenting with His murderers ? At the battle of the Alma a wounded Russian was crying piteously for water. A kind hearted English captain disregarding the fact that it was an enemy who was suffering, halted to relieve him. But as the noble captain ran forward to join his regiment, the wretch whom he had befriended, fired, and shot his benefactor. O sinner ! every day you live in sin you are guilty of similar treachery. You are piercing afresh the heart that bled for you. You are adding thorns to the crown that lacerated the brow of your most devoted friend. Will you not consider? Perhaps you have not thought of it in this way. It may be that partially through ignorance you have done it. But I set it before you to-night. I call upon you to consider. "Stand ye in the ways and see." You have been going wrong, but it is not too late to get right. Thank God for that; it might have been otherwise.

The text admonishes us, in the second place, to inquire, "Ask for the old paths." Consideration begets inquiry. As soon as the prodigal in the parable realized his condition he began to look about for relief. And as soon as a man is fully alive to the fact of his perishing state, because of sin, the question arises in his mind, what shall I do? Is there no way of escape? When, under the preaching of the apostles on the day of Pentecost the Jews were convinced of the murder of their Messiah, they said with great earnestness, "Men and brethren, what shall we do?" Oh that such a spirit of inquiry might take possession of you all to-night!

As we consult this blessed Guide Book we find that there is an old path, a good way, a way beaten with the feet of myriads of pilgrims who by it have passed up to the heavenly Zion "with songs and everlasting joy upon their heads." It is "called a way of holiness" for "the unclean shall not pass over it." The way of salvation is pre-eminently a "way of holiness." Whatever other qualification the traveller may lack he must be holy, for "without holiness no man shall see the Lord." "Know ye not that the unrighteous shall not inherit the kingdom of God." Heaven is a holy place, and "there shall in no wise enter into it anything that defileth, neither whatsoever worketh abomination or maketh a lie." You must part with your sins if you would "see the King in His beauty and behold the land that is afar off." There can be no compromise on this point. The language of the Apostle Paul is very explicit in reference to this. "Now the works of the flesh are manifest, which are these, adultery, fornication, uncleanness, lasciviousness, idolatry, witchcraft, hatred, variance, emulations, wrath, strife, seditions, heresies, envyings, murders, drunkenness, revellings and such like; of the which I tell you before, as I have also told you in time past, that they which do such things shall not inherit the kingdom of God." "Alas," says one, "I know that 'the path of life' is 'a way of holiness' and I am perfecly conscious of my sinfulness. But how can I enter this way? How can I overcome the evil that is within me and around me?" I answer, through faith in the Lord Jesus Christ. The divine promise is, "If we confess our sins He is faithful and just to forgive us our sins and to cleanse us from all unrighteousness." He here promises forgiveness—that is, the removal of your condemnation, and cleansing, that is, the removal of the sinful disposition. This is what you need—a divine regeneration through faith in the atoning blood of Christ. This is what is spoken of in the prophecy of Ezekiel where we read, "A new heart will I give you and a new spirit will I put within you. And I will take away the stony heart out of your flesh and I will give you an heart of flesh, and I will put My spirit within you and cause you to walk in My statutes, and ye shall keep My judgments and do them." Then your duty and your interest is to come to Christ directly, seeking forgiveness for your past sins and His renewing and sanctifying power upon your heart. This is the "old path," the only "good way."

But the text not only exhorts to consideration and inquiry, it requires obedience. "Walk therein." When the "good way" is known, we must "walk in it" if we would have eternal life. Knowledge of the right way alone will not save us. Right opinions, however essential to right obedience, have no saving effect without it. Christ said "If ye *know* these things, happy are ye if ye *do* them." As the compass is of no use to the mariner unless he sails by its direction, so the Scriptures are of no use to us unless we obey their instructions. If you are sick, it is not enough that you have heard of a skilful physician, or that you have full confidence in his skill. If you would be healed, you must consult him and take the medicine he administers. And so it is not enough that you have heard of Christ or that you have a general belief in His ability to save you. You must come to Him and put your case in His hands and trust Him for a present and perfect cure if you would know His saving power upon your heart. But just here you will probably find the greatest moral struggle of your life. So long as you only *intend* to seek salvation you will meet with no opposition. So long as you are content to put the matter off with a pious resolution, you will not be resisted. But when you attempt to bring yourself to a present surrender— a present acceptance of Jesus Christ as your Saviour and your King, it will cost you a struggle. The world, the flesh, and the devil will conspire to prevent such decision. But though the world may sneer and the devil rage, and the flesh shrink back, it must come to a "just now" if ever we are saved. And though it may involve a struggle, be true to your convictions, and then it will be the death struggle of the reigning power of sin within you and the birth pangs of a new and noble life. It will be like the struggle of the eagle as it breaks the chain that tethers it to earth and spreads its pinions for a loftier flight. Here is the path, "walk in it" though the gate through which you enter is a strait one. Here is the Saviour, come to Him though you have but strength to come and fall at His feet. Rest not, O rest not, I beseech you, till through grace you can sing,

> "'Tis done, the great transaction's done,
> I am my Lord's and He is mine."

The exhortation of the text closes with a gracious promise, "Ye shall find rest for your souls." The first experience of a pardoned sinner is peace, "Being justified by faith we have peace with God through our Lord Jesus Christ." The change experienced is well expressed by Isaiah, "Though Thou wast angry with me, Thine anger is turned away, and thou comfortedst me." The power of sin is broken, the curse is removed and the heaven born spirit nestles peacefully by faith upon the bosom of infinite love. Like the disciples struggling hard against contrary winds and angry waves upon the sea of Galilee, is the soul in the throes and agony of conviction; but like the same disciples sailing peacefully on a sea of glass in the great calm which the presence of Jesus brought, is the soul that has "passed from death unto life." Jesus says, "Come unto me—and I will give you rest," and thousands of witnesses are ready to testify from actual experience, that Jesus does give a rest, an inward calm, a conscious peace to the soul. Dear sinner, such a rest may be yours tonight if you will but accept of Christ heartily and trust Him fully. Oh, will you do it? Heaven, earth and hell await your answer.

THE GOSPEL MINISTRY.

By the Rev. Thomas Webster, D.D.,

of Newbury, Ont.

"Study to show thyself approved unto God, a workman that needeth not to be ashamed, rightly dividing the word of truth."—2 Timothy ii. 15.

THE Holy Scriptures present the only perfect system of rules, for the moral and religious government of mankind, that has ever been produced. No code of uninspired lawgivers can be found at all comparable with it, for, of necessity, every other scheme invented as a remedy for the ills that flesh is heir to, or to correct the evil propensities of our sinful nature is, itself, subject to the taint of human depravity; to mutation; and to consequent imperfection. "The law of the Lord," therefore, alone "is perfect." Hence the propriety of a continuous reference to it for our instruction, and of the application of its statutes and ordinances to our own daily lives.

The Gospel, made known to us in the Holy Scriptures, is both capable of benefiting the world in two grand and glorious respects, and is also designed specially for that purpose. First, in Christianizing every kindred and tongue and people in every portion of this vast globe; and secondly, in promulgating the principles of civilization, and of freedom from human oppression, as well as from the slavery of sin. And the instrumentality for carrying these designs into successful operation is the Christian ministry. How important, then, that those composing it should be themselves converted and imbued with a proper idea of the grave responsibility resting upon them.

That Paul considered it to be so, is abundantly evident from the manner in which he admitted Timothy—his son in the Gospel—into the Christian ministry, as well as from his charge to him contained in our text.

The evangelist, Luke, in his narrative of the Acts of the Apostles, gives an account of his conversion to Christianity, as well as of the conversion of his mother Eunice, and his grandmother Lois. The mother and daughter were Jewesses, and themselves well instructed in the scriptures, had taken pains to instruct Timothy as carefully as they had been, and with other devout Jews were expecting the coming of the Messiah, therefore there does not seem to have been any hesitation on their part in accepting the teaching of Paul that Christ was the very Messiah of whom the prophets wrote and spoke.

Timothy's conversion, it is supposed, took place on the occasion of Paul's first visit to Lystra. It was not until Paul's second visit that he seems to have entertained the idea of taking Timothy out into the ministry; and several years must have intervened between these two visits.

It would appear that Timothy possessed five essential qualities requisite to the successful career of a preacher of the Gospel in the apostolic times: First, he bore an unblemished moral character: Second, he had a thorough knowledge of the Holy Scriptures: Third, he was devoutly pious: Fourth, he was gifted as a speaker; and

Fifth, he had a zeal which enabled him to be steadfast in the faith, and to push forward the cause of his Divine Master, despite the most formidable opposition, hazarding even life itself, so that he might carry the banner of the cross to victory, or win the crown of martyrdom in the attempt. Few as the incidents of his life, which have been given to us are, they are sufficient to prove that he was in very deed a workman that needed not to be ashamed, and that there is no cause for wonder that he became very greatly endeared to Paul, and probably to all the other apostles and brethren. And though many centuries have passed since his life's work was done the force and influence of his saintly example is still felt in all the churches. I have said one of Timothy's qualifications for the ministry was steadfastness. He was not taken out to preach as soon as he professed conversion. The genuineness of that conversion had in a measure been proved. He had not shown a disposition to backslide because he was not pushed forward more rapidly; nor did he seem to desire to enter upon the work of the ministry as a matter of convenience. He was, says Luke, "well reported of by the brethren that were at Lystra and Iconium;" and Paul believing this report of him to be a correct one, now, on this his second visit, eagerly accepted the ready services of the youthful disciple. Duly ordained to the office and work of the ministry, he becomes for a time, the companion of the chief apostle in his travels, and when circumstances have made a separation necessary, we find the aged Paul in the fulness of his ripe experience thus charging his younger brother and friend.

And now, without further tracing Timothy's history, let us consider the text more immediately in its direct bearing upon the Church at large and upon the Christian ministry.

The subject naturally divides itself into three heads:

1st.—The qualifications of the Christian ministry.

2nd.—The work the minister of Christ is expected to perform.

3rd.—The results which may reasonably be expected from a faithful discharge of ministerial duty.

1st.—The qualifications of the Christian ministry.

There is no position in which one can be placed, of greater honour or of more responsibility than that of a minister of the Lord Jesus Christ.

Kings and potentates have their ministers of state, chosen with the utmost care, because of their supposed qualification and fitness for the position they are to fill. They are expected to transact the business committed to their care with fidelity and dispatch, and if remiss in the discharge of their duty, they are held to a strict account for their remissness. And justly so. The most momentous interest of the state are given into their keeping—sometimes the safety of thousands of citizens, or subjects, nay, even the safety of an empire itself may depend upon the prompt action, the sagacity or jugdment of a minister of state. How great then is his responsibility. With what terrible consequences is, sometimes, a single mistake fraught.

But if this is true of ministers of state, how much greater is the responsibility resting upon the ministers of Christ's kingdom. The salvation of men for time and eternity is, in a measure, dependent on faithful discharge of ministerial duty.

The world has been redeemed unto God by Christ; but He has commissioned His ministry—called by Him to the work—to carry the glad tidings of redemption, and the conditions upon which its benefits may be attained to its sin-stricken and enslaved inhabitants. Shall one so commissioned undertake the matter lightly, or be careless of the manner in which he delivers his message? Not if he fully realizes the gravity of the work devolving upon him. How solemn the charge as given by the mouth of the prophet. "Lo thou, O son of man, I have set thee a watchman unto the house of Israel; therefore, thou shalt hear the word at my mouth and warn them from me."

It is incumbent then upon the Christian minister to *study* God's word, so that he may have a clear conception of its meaning, and thus be qualified to make the meaning clear to those he is called upon to instruct. There should be no remissness, no delivery of only such parts of the message as suits the ambassador's own private feelings; no smoothing down or rounding off of the stern truths contained therein; and no denunciatory threats made which are not to be found there, nor are those which are there to be wrested from their true significance. There ought to be no tampering with God's awful, and yet merciful, message to man on the part of His messenger.

But an earthly potentate's messenger, or ambassador, is a man of reputation, and just so should a Christian minister be. It is an indispensable qualification for his admittance into the ministry, or his retention therein, that his reputation for morality is unblemished. "Be ye clean that bear the vessels of the Lord," is the positive injunction of the Scripture. Not only is the minister of Christ to keep his heart with all diligence, but he is closely to watch his words, that they may tend to the edification, and instruction of those with whom he is brought into association. While he should be the very reverse of sour or taciturn, he should also avoid light and frivolous conversation in his intercourse with the people to whom he is sent. He should study to show himself approved unto God. And if this be his study, his constant aim, he will be guilty of no action, utter no word, of which he need afterwards to be ashamed, or which will bring the cause of Christ into disrepute. It is, in short, one essential qualification of a minister that, while he is kindly and genial in manner, he be also dignified, both in the pulpit and out of it. And, here, permit me to digress a moment, and say that there is a very wide difference between true dignity and insolent arrogance, or empty conceit; between Christian friendship and unbecoming familiarity; between firmness in the discharge of ministerial duty and overbearing usurpation of authority, while pretending to administer discipline; between feeding the flock with the true bread and starving them with brilliantly-tinted husks; between folding the sheep and driving them out into the cold, or to seek shelter elsewhere. My brethren, it is important that you should mark these distinctions.

The pulpit is the principal platform from which the important message, involving the salvation of the race, is to be promulgated; it should, therefore, be sacred. In it no idle story should be told to cap a climax, or provoke a smile, even though it may remotely illustrate the subject under discussion, or the continuance of preaching, interlarded with such stories, may draw out crowds to listen, who will materially aid in the financial support of the church. Eventually such support will be found to have been bought too dearly. The Church was not designed as a place of recreation, nor the solemn service of God instituted to afford an hour's amusement to the people. To both minister and hearers that hour is fraught with momentous results. How careful, then, ought both to be.

As Methodists we lay great stress—and properly so—upon the responsibility resting upon a Christian minister, as witness the following quotation from the charge to an Elder, at the time of his ordination, taken from the Ordination Service.

"And now again we exhort you in the name of our Lord Jesus Christ, that you have in remembrance into how high a dignity and to how weighty an office ye are called: that is to say, to be messengers, watchmen, and stewards, of the Lord, to teach and to premonish, to feed, and to provide for the Lord's family, to gather the out-casts, to seek the lost, and to be ever ready to spread abroad the Gospel, the glad tidings of reconciliation with God.

"Have always therefore printed in your remembrance how great a treasure is committed to your charge. For they are the sheep of Christ, which He bought with His death, and for whom He shed His blood. The Church whom you must serve is His spouse and His body. And if it shall happen, the same Church or any member thereof, do take any hurt or hindrance by reason of your negligence, ye know the greatness of the fault, and also the horrible punishment that will ensue."

I have before remarked that the Christian minister should study the word of God so that he would clearly understand its meaning. In doing this he should give close attention to the letter of the word itself. This is of the first importance. Then he ought to avail himself of every aid that can be obtained to thoroughly understand the Scriptures. A thorough college training is a very efficent aid, and if to this can be added a sound theological course, at an accredited Biblical institute, it will be better still. Familiarity with the languages in which the Scriptures were originally written will materially aid him in coping with sceptics, and in answering the cavils or the specious arguments of the so-called Liberal Christians of the present day. All this, and much more, is implied in being *thoroughly* versed in the Scriptures. In this age, it is almost essential, if not altogether so, that a minister be well read up in the modern sciences, else he will meet many objections which he cannot answer. He should be a ready speaker, and have such a zeal for the spread of the Gospel, as will enable him to overcome every obstacle in the way of success that is not absolutely insurmountable—a zeal which will prompt him to risk even life itself, if in so doing he can save a soul from death.

But above and beyond all these qualifications, he must possess "a heart in every thought renewed;" must be himself a child of God, and have the evidence of the Holy Spirit bearing witness with his spirit that he is such. A workman so qualified will be successful, and need not fear that he will be ashamed of his work or that his Master will be ashamed of him.

We come now, in the second place, to consider the work the minister of Christ is expected to perform.

It has already been stated, that the true Christian ministry has been chosen and called by God to proclaim salvation to a sinful world, through the redemption wrought out by Christ our Saviour, and to persuade fallen man to comply with the conditions of the plan of salvation. How is this work to be performed? In various ways. By the preaching of the word; by faithful pastoral visiting; and by being "instant in season and out of season" in warning the unrighteous of the danger of continuing in sin, and urging them to repent of sin and seek forgiveness through the merits of their gracious Reedemer.

His own heart warm, and all aglow with the love of God, and imbued with a measure of the compassion which caused the Son of God to offer himself a ransom for sinners, he will, or ought to, preach a full and free salvation to all who will accept of it, on the terms laid down in the Scriptures, viz: repentance towards God, and faith in our Lord Jesus Christ. He should impress upon the minds of his hearers, that the Gospel gates have been not merely "set ajar" for the entrance of a few, but thrown wide open, that "whosoever will may come," provided they come in God's appointed way, and enter in. But while he thus proclaims this free salvation as set forth in the Saviour's own invitation, he must be equally careful to point out, that the whole tenor of the Scriptures quite as emphatically declare that the Most High will not condone, or tolerate sin, though He may bear with the sinner for a time. He should remind his congregation that the warning "The wicked shall be turned into hell, with all the nations that forget God," is as much inspired as the gracious invitation "Come unto me, all ye that labour and are heavy laden, and I will give you rest;" and that those who persist in rebellion against Him, will as certainly be punished for their rebellion, as those who repent of their sins will be pardoned.

Under the faithful preaching of the Word, there will be more or less conviction for sin. It is part of a minister's work to instruct those who are so convicted; to explain the plan of salvation; the nature of saving faith, and what is meant by the "Witness of the Spirit." He should be very explicit and clear in his explanations, using *Scriptural* terms as much as possible, and be careful not to "darken counsel with a multitude of words."

Especially, in times of revivals, is there need of very great care. Merely getting up an excitement, "running a meeting," as it is sometimes termed, for a few weeks, without properly instructing those who have been awakened and striving to *establish* them in the way, is not, in my opinion, true revival work. It is a lamentable fact, that, with many uninstructed souls brought into Church fellowship through the instrumentality of erratic preachers of this sort, the last state has been worse than the first. But, in genuine revival work, where every pains is taken to instruct the awakened in the Scriptures, and to establish the converted, such disastrous results do not, as a rule, follow.

But teachers of false doctrines creep into neighbourhoods, or churches, and attempt to overthrow the work of God; as witness the apostles of Mormonism, Unitarianism, and a host of other isms of the present day. These the minister of Christ must meet and withstand, or the work in his hand will fail, and perhaps ruin to hundreds ensue.

Is the spiritual life of the Church in any place low? It is a part of the minister's work, having that Church in his charge, to strive to arouse it to greater vitality. Are there those within its pale whose lives do not conform with their professions? it is his duty to look after, and remonstrate with them—perhaps to take stronger measures. Nothing is more detrimental to the prosperity of the cause of God, than looseness in the lives of professed Christians. It sometimes happens, that in times of revival, the minister is sorely troubled with persons of this kind, who, just then, are very zealous, and the work is greatly hindred; but the minister should be firm in endeavouring to remove these stumbling blocks out of the way of sinners, even though he be compelled to suffer reproach for so doing. If through lack of judgment, or from want of proper discernment of character, he should encourage them, it will be found, in the end, that the meetings, in which they have taken a prominent part, have been a fruitful source of evil instead of good as was designed.

No minister should be guilty of religious charlatanism, nor should he allow it to go unexposed in others, for by it the unconverted are staggered when contrasting the conduct of the average religious charlatans with that of men of only strictly moral habits.

Lecturing is a work in which a minister may often engage with good effect, provided he does not in consequence neglect his pulpit ministrations.

But preaching and lecturing and attending special meetings do not cover the whole ground of ministerial labour. Pastoral visiting is as necessary to the well-being of the flock as preaching. The minister must come in personal contact with his people, — must associate freely with them. There are careless ones to be admonished, doubting, timid ones to be encouraged, and delinquents to be reasoned with and warned. All this can only properly be attended to by pastoral visiting. In this connection might be mentioned the visiting of the sick and destitute. The Sunday school, prayer meetings, and other social means of grace should also engage the pastor's care.

And here it may not be amiss to say a word or two to the official boards of every congregation or charge. If it is the duty of the minister to attend to every part of his work, it is no less incumbent on his official members to see to it that he is sustained financially, not harassed with the thought of how he shall make both ends meet when pay day comes. When the minister and charge co-operate thus with each other in harmony, and in Christian effort for the salvation of souls, and the upbuilding of the Church, success is almost certain to crown their labours.

In brief, then, the workman is to "rightly divide the word of truth;" is properly to supervise and manage the work given into his charge; and see that no incompetent or injudicious person wrests it from his control. He is carefully and prayerfully to watch over his flock; and to "feed the lambs." And he should remember that for the faithful discharge of his duty he will have to render an account at the Day of Judgment.

This being an abstract of the work which the Christian minister is expected to perform, how careful then should the Conferences be to select the proper men to carry it on to a successful conclusion.

Thirdly.—What then are the results which may reasonably be expected from a faithful discharge of ministerial duty?

When the truth, in righteousness, is proclaimed it might reasonably be expected that conviction for sin would immediately seize upon the consciences of the unconverted; but this is not always, nor, indeed, often the case; still the workman ought not to be discouraged because he does not immediately reap the fruit of his labours. His work is, in a measure, not unlike that of the agriculturist. Before the husbandman puts in his seed many days of weary toil are spent by him in preparing uncongenial soil for the reception of the seed. And after the seed is sown, time is required for its germination, then for its healty continuous growth, and finally its perfect maturity. In the process of growth, we notice first the blade, then the ear, then the full corn in the ear. And after the crop is matured and harvested, it is not found to be every year alike. The same amount and kind of labour does not always produce the same results. Yet, except when God's hand is spread abroad in wrath, as in the time of famine, every sowing ensures a reaping time, be the harvest scant or bountiful. We have the promise that there shall be " seed time and harvest." And so it is with the sowing of the seed of life—eternal life—in the uncongenial soil of the hearts of sinful men. Often there is a great amount of preparation necessary before the seed will take root, but if the workman will only persevere, and carefully plant and water in God's name, He who has promised, " My word shall not return unto me void; but shall accomplish the thing whereunto I have sent it;" and also, " My presence shall go with you," He, I repeat, will *surely* give the increase. " In due time ye shall reap if ye faint not."

Other results follow the true conversion of the people to God.

No genuine revival of pure religion has ever taken place in any quarter of the globe but what has materially benefited the nation as well as the Church. Christianity civilizes the peoples of the earth, that truly embrace it, as well as saves them. It should, however, be borne in mind, that all is not fruit which appears like it. Many a field which has seemed to promise a plentiful crop of wheat has at harvest yielded a very large proportion of chaff—perfectly worthless stuff. And similarly many a revival, which has seemed to promise well, has yielded little or no permanent good results. Care should be taken to distinguish fanaticism from zeal; and also true awakening from mere animal excitement. During the revival they may be mistaken for each other—indeed often are—but when the fruit is looked for it does not stand the test. Then many, both ministers and church members, are disheartened at the result; and some draw back from God and the Church altogether.

But looking over the whole field cultivated, and taking into account the entire results of the period of labor, removes much of the discouragement which one bad crop might occasion. And so the workmen who have "studied to show themselves approved unto God" need not be either discouraged or ashamed in view of the results of their toil.

What hath not the Gospel wrought through the faithful preaching of the Word? Behold the millions of redeemed souls now being converted to God, almost everywhere on this green earth! Christianity is not now confined to Britain and America; China and Japan, India and Africa, and the islands of the sea as well, are being blessed by the beneficent rays of the Sun of Righteousness.

But there is yet another result of the faithful preaching of the Gospel, which more nearly concerns the preacher himself. When all the toils of life are done, then the workman, who has thus studied to be approved, will not be ashamed to appear before the Master among the other reapers, as they gather in the golden sheaves, and join with them in singing the glorious "Harvest Home" of the redeemed.

They may, in the prosecution of their work, like Timothy, and Paul, and Christ, have had to endure the frowns of sinful men; they may have been subjected to contumely and scorn, or have had to suffer fierce persecution. But it is all over now. The final result is a CROWN OF GLORY. Oh what a company of crowned saints will meet around the throne of God! With angels and archangels, redeemed ministers, and redeemed people innumerable will take up the glad anthems of praise which ever rise and swell there; and the gracious promise will be fully verified; "And God shall wipe away all tears from their eyes: and there shall be no more death, neither sorrow nor crying, neither shall there be any more pain: for the former things are passed away."

> "Forever with the Lord;
> Amen so let it be,
> Life from the dead is in that word,
> 'Tis immortality."

PAUL'S EXPERIENCE AND PROSPECTS.

By the Rev. George Miller,

of Oshawa, Ont.

"Brethren, I count not myself to have apprehended; but this one thing I do, forgetting those things which are behind, and reaching forth unto those things which are before, I press toward the mark for the prize of the high calling of God in Christ Jesus."—Phil. iii. 13 and 14.

It is one of the chief glories of the religion of Christ, that it enables its possessor to rejoice in the most adverse circumstances of life, and fills his soul with undying hope, while earthly prospects are failing all around him.

In reading the epistle from which our text is taken, and noticing its joyful tone and triumphant utterance, we would suppose its author was surrounded with the most pleasant circumstances this world could afford, and cheered with the fairest prospects of life. Whereas we find it was written by St. Paul in a gloomy prison in the City of Rome, its writer not knowing what day he was to be led out and suffer death for the cause of Christ.

It is really strengthening to our faith to hear this noble man of God rising superior to his dismal surroundings, assert his continued adherence to the cause he had espoused, and for which he had suffered so much and laboured so incessantly, and tell of the blissful anticipations that cheered his heart in those times of darkness and trial.

No doubt he felt what the poet long afterwards expressed :—

> "That prisons would palaces prove,
> If Jesus would dwell with me there."

In the former part of the chapter, from which the text is taken, he refers to some things he possessed in early life that raised him in the estimation of his fellows, and would have secured to him many advantages in this world; but these things "he counted loss for Christ," and, contrasting them with his present position and prospects, declares they are but as the refuse we cast from our sight.

In the text and connected verses he seems to open his heart and allow us to look in and view the thoughts and feelings which stir that mighty soul. There we read the experience, not so much of the great apostle, as of the sincere and humble Christian.

We feel we are holding communion with one who has tasted the ills and joys of life out of the same cup of which we have been partakers, with one who has felt the same temptations that have assailed us, and had to contend against the same storms that have so frequently buffetted us in the voyage of life, with one, too, that held with a firm grasp to the same Saviour that we tremblingly cling to, and whose heart was lightened by the same prospects that have borne us up in times of darkness and suffering.

Let us now attend to his words. We notice his view of his life's work.

"It is the high calling of God in Christ Jesus."

Every word here is emphatic.

First, it is a calling.

Religion, with the apostle, was not something to be enjoyed merely; but a work; and not a work to be laid aside at convenience; but a life-work—a calling This was his understanding of it when arrested, by the power of God, on his way to Damascus. For when he learned who Jesus was and His claims upon him, the first question he asked was, "Lord, what wilt thou have me to do?"

And this idea is in strict accordance with our Saviour's teaching. He speaks of a burden to be borne; a yoke to wear; of talents to be improved upon; of a vineyard in which to labour; and most faithfully does He warn His disciples against slothfulness or neglect of duty in His service.

The unwearied diligence of the Apostle Paul, in the cause of his Master, is a continued illustration of the true spirit of Christianity, and a clear evidence of the constraining love of Christ. Religion is not to be regarded as an insurance policy, which, when obtained, is to be laid carefully away as a safeguard against future danger or harm, but an earnest life-work in the service of Christ.

It is true we have not all the same work to do nor the same positions to fill. In the great enterprise that Christ commissioned His Church to carry on, to its glorious consummation, a vast variety of duty and talent is required, and we believe God never converts a soul but there is a position for that one to fill, and a work to do, and woe to that man who turns aside from his work or neglects his duty, for to him the Saviour will say when He comes, "Thou wicked and slothful servant." May we be found, like the apostle, fulfilling our calling faithfully, that when death approaches we may like him be enabled joyfully to exclaim, "I have fought the good fight, I have finished my course, I have kept the faith." And then when the Master shall come to take account of His servants He will say to each of us, " Well done, good and faithful servant, enter thou into the joy of thy Lord."

Again, he says it is a high calling. The apostle regarded the service of God as of no ordinary work.

To his mind, it was indeed a high calling. He magnified his office, and sometimes in his allusions to it he seems astonished, that he who had been a "persecutor and injurious" should have had such mercy shown him and such an honour conferred upon him as to have been "called to be an Apostle, and separated unto the Gospel of the Son of God." It is true all the Church cannot be apostles, or even ordinary ministers of the Word, and many cannot occupy any official position in the visible church, but as in an army, while it is an excellent thing there to have good officers, yet it is the soldiers in the ranks that do the execution. So in the Church the officers should be men fearing God and full of courage, for theirs is a work of great responsibility; yet the real burden must always rest on the membership, and the most obscure member occupies a place, and if he or she is a child of God, it is a place of honour, and requires to be well filled if the Church is to move successfully forward in taking the world for Christ; and I think we may safely affirm, that the lowest position we can occupy in the house of God, or the most common duties we can perform for Christ, may appropriately be termed a " high calling." This will be clearly seen when we look at the change which it supposes to have taken place in our position, and the work wrought in our hearts.

From being enemies, we have to become the friends of God; from being the children of the wicked one and heirs of death we shall have been adopted into the family of heaven, made heirs of God and joint heirs with Jesus Christ. Its appropriateness will also be evident as we observe the beneficial results which flow to the world from Christianity. Paul once said that he was sent to the Gentiles, to open their eyes, to turn them from darkness to light, and from the power of Satan unto God, that they might receive forgiveness of sins and an inheritance among them who are sanctified by the faith that was in Him. To have any part in a work which has for its object the uplifting of humanity from the ruins of the Fall, scattering the light of truth over the benighted regions of earth, opening the prison doors and emancipating man from the thraldom of Satan. To do what philosophy and moral reform have always failed to accomplish, to ease the burdened conscience and give satisfactory joy to the troubled soul. Surely this is an important work, especially when we remember that the humblest effort put forth sincerely and in Christ's name may tell favourable on the eternal destiny of some precious soul. I do not know, however, that the apostle ever uttered a sentiment which magnified this high calling more than when he said, we were workers together with God; let no one suppose then that he degrades himself by becoming a servant of God or stoops any in accepting Christ and His cause.

The apostle also says "it is a high calling of God." He here asserts its divine authority. In all the writings of Paul he keeps this idea constantly before the minds of his readers. It was that which formed the basis of his noted declaration to the Romans, "I am not ashamed of the Gospel of Christ for it is the power of God unto salvation." He felt he was not trusting his eternal destiny to an arm less mighty than that of Omnipotence. Christ crucified to the Jew a stumbling block and to the Greek foolishness, he realized to be the "power of God and the wisdom of God." He always recognized the hand of God in his conversion, and felt he had received his commission from the same source. It was a consciousness of this divine authority that sustained him in his arduous work, and rendered him so courageous in his conflicts with the powers of darkness, and unswerving in stemming the opposition of the world. Now, just in proportion, as we realize the Gospel to be the power of God, will be our confidence in that Gospel to save;— and just as we feel we are serving God and not man, while engaged in christian work, will be our constancy in that work, in the midst of discouragements and trials. Then the apostle does not forget to add, " high calling of God in Christ Jesus." To him there was no name so dear as that of Jesus. And he is sure to intwine that name some way with every remembrance of his salvation.

The idea that he here brings out, is that, while it was God who had saved him and called him, yet it was God in Christ Jesus. That was a phrase almost peculiar to Paul, but to him it had a wonderful significance. It brings before the mind, the Father and Son working in harmony for the salvation of man. God the Father, moved by infinite love, giving His Son, and God the Son, actuated by the same love, giving Himself to the work. We see this harmony beautifully illustrated in the life of Christ, twice we hear the voice of the Father proclaiming in the hearing of the world, "This is My beloved Son in whom I am well pleased, hear ye Him." Paul saw in the twofold nature of Christ just the being to meet the wants of man. A God with an arm sufficiently strong to conquer all our foes, and a man with a heart so tender that He could be touched with feeling for all our infirmities.

He asserts that God without Christ is a "consuming fire;" but in Christ he beholds mercy blended with justice and offering unto man a way of escape from the fierceness of the wrath of God.

He sees in Christ the author and finisher of our faith, and the great captain of our salvation, leading on the hosts of Zion from victory to victory. Let us never forget that while we are called of God and working for Him, it is for God in Christ Jesus.

We pass now to notice his determination, and, first, concerning the past, "forgetting those things which are behind." By this he did not mean to forget the mercies of God, he always cherished the most grateful memory of those things, and frequently speaks of them; but no doubt he meant he would forget the past as the only ground of hope.

There are but few who have been favoured with so bright a conversion as that of Saul of Tarsus, but he even felt the necessity of keeping his body under, lest after having preached to others he himself should become a castaway.

As the competitor in the Grecian games, to which he alludes in these verses, would not feel his success secured by his having commenced well, but would realize the necessity of pressing on to the end of the race, so Paul felt that his conversion, however bright, would not necessarily secure his entrance into Heaven.

His hope was founded on his continued clinging to Christ with an ever living faith. His experience was in the present tense; "Nevertheless," he says, "at one time I live, yet not I, but Christ *liveth* in me the hope of glory." It is the privilege of every Christian to know that he has been converted to God; and it is a source of real joy to be able to call up the very time and place when that work was wrought in the soul. But, after all, the true foundation of hope is a present consciousness of an indwelling Christ, and an entire consecration to his service. He also forgot the past in the sense of resting content with past attainments. Paul enjoyed a deep and rich experience and knew much of that love which passeth knowledge.

There was no doubt in his mind relative to his religion, "He knew whom he believed." His feet were firmly fixed upon the rock.

His faith was so strong, he lived and walked by it. "The love of God which is in Christ Jesus our Lord" he felt, was so firmly fixed in his soul, that he was persuaded that neither death, nor life, nor angels, nor principalities, nor powers, nor things present, nor things to come, nor height, nor depth, nor any other creature would be able to separate him from it. This hope was so bright that he realized for him to be "absent from the body was to be present with the Lord." Yet after all he was not satisfied with his present attainments.

From the height to which he had ascended he could see the path of light stretching out far before him, and he wanted to tread that path.

This leads us to his determination for the present and the future. Keeping still in view the Grecian runner, he uses two expressions which to the Phillipians would be very familiar and full of meaning, "Reaching forth unto those things which are before and pressing toward the mark." We notice here concentration of effort. We can imagine we see the ancient competitor bending his body to the race with his eye fixed upon the prize before him.

The multitudes around may be variously occupied, but he heeds them not. The scenery through which he passes may be very attractive, but it does not draw away his attention.

Intent upon the one thing before him, his mind is not divided. This is the figure Paul wishes to place before us, as showing his determination in the Christian course.

See how strongly he puts it, "this one thing I do." This reminds us of the Psalmist's expression, "One thing have I desired of the Lord, that will I seek after," and also of his prayer, "Unite my heart to fear thy name." There is an intensity of meaning in those words, "reaching forth," and "pressing toward," which indicates energy of manner, and of which we can find no better illustration in human history than the life of this apostle.

Among the lessons we should learn, from the life and writings of Paul, there are not many more conducive to our stability and success in the service of God, than the one under present consideration. In this short life where there are so many conflicting attractions we must make religion our chief business, even weaving it into our ordinary avocation, and making all things subservient to the interests of the soul. And in the service of God untiring energy is needed. The world manifests no sign of laying down its weapons and ceasing its opposition to Christ, and there never was a time when greater vigilance on the part of the Church was demanded than at the present. He whom Paul represents as having sat down at the right hand of God, expecting, until all enemies become His footstool, is no careless spectator of the conflicts going on in this earth, between His Church and the powers of darkness, and in these conflicts He expects every soldier of

His to do his duty. There is nothing can be accomplished of much worth in this world without earnestness and energy, and especially is this the case with regard to the cause of Christ, and no where is idleness more inconsistent than in the house of God. In matters of religion it is well for us to remember the advice of the wise man, "Whatsoever thy hand findeth to do, do it with thy might."

We notice finally the prize the apostle had in view, which he mentions in brief in the eighth verse, "that I may win Christ." This he explains more in detail in the succeeding verses to which we now direct our attention.

First, to be found in Christ, as by nature he was in Adam as the federal head of the race, and subjected to sin and death through his fall, so he desired to be found in Christ as the federal head of God's spiritual race, consisting of all who have become the children of God by being born again. He felt he was now in Christ as the branches are in the vine, or as the members are in the body, and he wanted that union continued and the ties drawn more closely, that when the great day of reckoning should come he might be found not "having his own righteousness, which is of the law," to depend upon; "but upon that righteousness he had obtained through this intimate union with Christ, and by faith in His name."

Then he also wanted to know Christ. Paul had enjoyed eminent advantages in learning Christ. He had been privileged to see Him, and had conversed with many who had been familiar with Him while on earth. Then he had a higher source of knowledge for he says that, "God who commanded the light to shine, out of darkness, hath shined in our hearts, to give unto us the light of the knowledge of the Glory of

God in the face of Jesus Christ. Besides this Paul had lived near the cross and studied this subject for many years, and yet he realized there were "heights and depths, lengths and breadths in the love of Christ," he had not yet explored. This was one of the things in which he was not yet perfect; but he was "reaching forth and pressing toward the mark," expecting soon, in the undimmed light of Heaven, to pursue this study more rapidly, and drink in knowledge as it flows pure from the fount of infinite wisdom.

Then he wanted to have fellowship with the sufferings of Christ, and be made conformable to His death. To the sufferings and death of Christ, the attention of at least two worlds have been directed for centuries. The cause of those sufferings, their intensity, and the result of them, and of His death, have been studied by the wisest of men, and have taxed the mightiest intellects of angels.

Paul wanted not only to know these things, but to have "fellowship with those sufferings and to be made conformable to his death," by which he no doubt means that he wanted to find in his soul a response to those feelings which actuated the Son of God in taking the bitter cup and drinking it to its very dregs; and he also wanted his whole being to be made so conformable to Christ's death, with all its depths of meaning, that there would not be one discordant note; but as he now felt he was crucified with Christ, so he would be willing to suffer even martyrdom for His sake.

He also wanted to realize the power of His resurrection. To the Apostles and first preachers of Christianity, the resurrection of Jesus Christ from the grave was a subject of intense interest. It formed one chief theme of their preaching. Around it clustered their brightest hopes. And in it there was a power which was felt in their experience, and through which they looked for a general resurrection of the dead. And Paul wanted to realize fully the rich harvest of which this was the first fruits.

Paul says he desired that if by any means he might attain unto the resurrection from the dead. There were two words, both of which have been translated resurrection. The one means simply that the dead body be raised to life again. In this sense he knew he would share in common with humanity; but the other word, which means raised to eternal life and glory, is the one which the Apostle here uses; it was to this resurrection he aspired and for it he sought. And well he might. It was that lofty aspiration that kindled Job's heart of old, and which he wanted so deeply engraven in the rock that coming ages might read it. It is this hope that spans the grave, with a halo of light, and shines through the tears of the mother as she lays her darling one in its silent resting-place.

The last particular in this prize, which we shall notice, is thus stated that he might apprehend that for which he was apprehended in Christ Jesus. To apprehend means either to understand or to lay hold of. In the first sense Christ apprehends every man, understanding even the most secret recesses of the soul. Paul knew this, and acknowledges that all things are naked and open to the eyes of him with whom he "had" to do. Christ knew him much better than he knew himself. In the other sense he was first apprehended of Christ, when on the road to Damascus. And in all the vicissitudes of his subsequent life, in the changing courses through which duty led him, he ever seemed to realize that it was the Saviour leading and directing him through scenes of sorrow as well as joy, in times of want as well as time of abounding. Some of these things were very mysterious to him. He was "seeing through a glass darkly." This was also one of those things in which he was not yet perfect; but in the midst of all this he was "reaching forth and pressing toward the mark" expecting soon, in the regions of unclouded day, to review life's pathway; and then he trusted the glass would be removed, and he would understand all Christ's dealings with him here, and apprehend that for which he had been apprehended of Christ. He would see as he was now seen and know as he was now known. Not long after this Paul did suffer martyrdom for the cause for which he had so long laboured. He finished his course and reached the mark. May we follow him as he followed Christ. Pressing on, even should darkness surround, rejoicing like him in tribulation, and in everything giving thanks, keeping our eye on the mark of the prize of our high calling in Christ Jesus, may we finally reach those realms of light where God will be his own interpreter and all mysteries will be solved, and where "faith will end in sight and hope in full fruition die."

CERTAINTY IN CHRIST AND CHRISTIANITY.

Delivered at the dedication of the M. E. Tabernacle, in the City of Belleville, January 20th, 1878.

BY REV. S. CARD,

of Ingersoll, Ont.

"Worthy is the Lamb that was slain to receive power, and riches, and wisdom, and strength, and honour, and glory, and blessing." –Revelation, v. 12.

THE universe is a great volume in which the matchless glories of Jehovah are inscribed. On its ample pages you will find lessons of His wisdom, power and goodness, over which the wisest and best of all ages and nations, have lingered with delight. The daisy on the lea; the sea in its calmest flowings or mightiest thunderings; the mountains that stand like solemn sentinels lifting their brawny shoulders into the skies; the silent stars beyond them, "yon bright and burning blazonry of God," all, all proclaim the wisdom, power and majesty of the Lord. The sun, throned in the centre of the solar system, imparts life and light to every shining world within its charge. Beyond our system are the fixed stars. Were we to undertake an excursion to one of these and were we to travel a million and a half miles a day, it would take more time than has elapsed since the world was made to reach the nearest one ; and even then we would only be upon the boundary line of that immense universe that would still stretch upward, outward and onward forever. Truly these are immeasurable distances. But there is more glory, more of God in the salvation of one soul than is displayed in the whole material universe.

> " These lower works that swell Thy praise,
> High as our thoughts can tower,
> Are but a portion of Thy ways,
> The hiding of Thy power."

Astronomy is a grand study but redemption is a grander. It was not into the wonders of the physical universe, but into the mysteries of redemption the angels desired to look. The high priests of science can tell you nothing of salvation, or of life beyond the grave. With Professor Tyndall, the best hope it has to offer humanity is that " you and I, like streaks of morning clouds, shall melt into the infinite azure of the past." Ask them what you must do to be saved, and their bewildered oracles are dumb. The telescope of the astronomer has swept the heavens without catching even a glimpse of " the land of pure delight, where saints immortal reign." We must consult the Divine Word, the work of inspiration poured through human channels,—written by human hands divinely moved. We must give ears to messengers divinely sent to proclaim to us the great salvation. We must accept the testimony of the thousands of believers who know that Christ can save. Yes we must feel, we must realize in our own hearts the rich experiences of salvation from the power, from the pollution, and penalty, and even the presence of sin. Then we understand what science has never discovered, that

God is love. Catching the inspiring strains of Wesley, we sing in rapturous strains,—

> "*Jesus!* the name *high over all!*
> In *hell*, on *earth* or *sky*,
> Angels and men before it fall,
> And devils fear, and fly,"

There are many lines of thought in this exhaustless theme, but we invite attention to the following proposition, viz,—*I. Jesus Christ died for our sins.*

The real essence of the Christian religion, the foundation truth upon which our hearts and hopes rest, the only basis upon which faith can stand and claim eternal life, is, that Christ died for our sins. I have no sympathy with that bastard theology that teaches that Christ's death was only that of a good man, and that it is His life that is to inspire us, and in some incomprehensible manner, save us. We admit freely, that His life is an example and an inspiration to save men. But His moral character furnishes no gospel that can save sinners from sin and from sinning. The Apostle Paul, in the fifteenth Chapter of First Corinthians, effectually disposes of this question, and settles, we should suppose forever, the fact of the *vicarious nature* of Christ's atonement. Mark each sentence, " Brethren, I declare unto you *the Gospel* which *I preached* unto you, *which* also ye *have received*, wherein ye *stand*, by which also *ye are saved*. For I delivered unto you *first* of *all*, that which I also received, *how that Christ died for our sins, according to the Scriptures*. And that He was buried and that He rose again the third day according to the Scriptures." Now this, Paul declares to be *the Gospel* he preached to them—that Christ died for their sins. They received it. They believed it, and they were saved, Paul says, by believing it. Moreover he declares that he did not invent the statement, that Christ died for our sins, but that he also received it .And finally, to settle the matter, he puts the whole Bible underneath and behind this ever glorious fact that "Christ died for sins,"—for he declares it to be "according to the Scriptures." Therefore it must be true. This is the Gospel. It is the Gospel that saved Paul, that saved the Christians at Corinth. It is the only Gospel under heaven, that has ever saved a soul.

This doctrine is an absolute necessity. What is sin? The transgression of the law. Then there is law. But who ever heard of a law without a penalty? Here then is a divine law, with a divine penalty attached. Here too are transgressors. So that the case is clear. The penalty for sin must be executed, or the law is at once reduced to a nullity. Now that Christ died to satisfy the claims of God's law against a world of transgressors, in other words that "He died for our sins," meets the case provided His atonement is accepted. That His atonement was sufficient His resurrection attests. Had there been the least defect in the character of the Substitute, or in His sacrifice, the offering would have been inadequate; and being inadequate, the claims of justice, of law, would not have been met; and their claims not being met, there would have been no release of the Substitute from the dominion of death; and there being no release, He could have had no resurrection; and there being no resurrection from the dead, there could be no salvation. But thank God He arose from the dead. The best news that ever broke on mortal ears was that which the angels made known to the women at the sepulchre, "Why seek ye the living among the dead? He is not here but risen." His triumphant resurrection from the dead, is the best possible evidence that he was able to redeem and strong to deliver, and that his atonement for sin and sinners was finished and accepted. That Christ died for our sins, and that He rose from the dead the third day, is the Gospel that is to take the world.

Go tell a penitent sinner, burdened with a sense of enormous gilt, that Christ's life is to inspire him to holiness, and lift him to heaven. How can he live a pure life, with an impure sinful heart? How is he to get rid of that awful burden of guilt? What is he to do with that mountain of sin? Preach to him the Gospel that Paul preached to the Corinthians. Tell him that Christ died for his sins, and it will save him. It saves him now! Behold him rise while a new unutterable joy surges through every avenue of his being. Hear him exclaim,—

> "Jesus comes, He fills my soul!
> Perfected in him I am;
> I am every whit made whole!
> Glory! Glory to the Lamb!"

The blood that streams from the wounded side of Jesus, is atoning blood. Its power reacts upon every generation back to the very first of our race. Its power is felt to day in millions of hearts, and will be felt down the centuries and among future generations to the end of time. Yea, and on through the cycles of eternity, "We're washed in the blood of the Lamb," will be the chorus of glorified millions forever. "Worthy is the Lamb that was slain" will roll in glowing pentameters through the streets and mansions and chapels of the heavenly city evermore.

"Christ died for our sins!" this is the gospel, this the faith that was once delivered to the saints, and we have need in this sceptical age, to contend earnestly for it. Infidelity is making bold and vigorous attacks upon the Christian religion. So let it be. Thank God Christianity needs no underpinning. A few here and there, as in the case of Dean Stanley, yielding to sceptics, and Canon Farrar and his purgatory of Roman Catholicism, may compromise with the materialistic scepticism of the age. But the fortress of Christian doctrine will stand like the lighthouse on the coast of the roaring surging seas, when the forces of infidelity shall have retreated in hopeless dismay.

Dean Stanley informs us, that the Church will have to give up the supernatural in religion because the future will demand it. In formulating the creed of the Church of the future, he eliminates Christ and His redemptive work, the office and work of the Holy Spirit, sin, regeneration, &c. What the Church is to hold as essential is the unity of God, the brotherhood of man, the identity of morality and religion, universal charity and universal purity. Now this is not Christianity at all. It is absolutely Deism. To eliminate Christ and the Holy Ghost from the Christian religion is to eliminate religion itself, for there can be no Christianity without Christ. It is well to enquire just here, what is the divine testimony in the sacred volume, concerning the perpetuity of Christianity. "Upon this rock"— the Christ—"will I build my Church, and the gates of hell shall not prevail against it." " Other foundation can no man lay than that is laid which is Jesus Christ." "Wherefore God also hath highly exalted Him, and given Him a name which is above every name. That at the *name* of *Jesus*, every knee should bow, of things in heaven, and things in earth, and things under the earth, and that every tongue should confess that Jesus Christ is Lord, to the glory of God the Father— " " His dominion is an everlasting dominion, which shall not pass away, and His kingdom that which shall not be destroyed". This does not sound like the overthrow of Christ and Christianity, and the enthronement of Deism and natural religion in the world.

Now there arises at this point, necessarily, the question.

II. Was Christ Jesus *Divine*, as well as *Human?*

He was either a human being simply, or else He was divine as well as human. But there are attributes, works, and worship, ascribed to Christ that belong to God alone : therefore He must be divine, as well as human.

The proper solution of this problem lies in the application of human and divine tests to Jesus Christ.

1. The existence of a human being begins at a certain time, before which he had no existence. If Christ were simply a human being then His existence had its beginning at Bethlehem eighteen centuries ago. But He claimed to have had an existence before Abraham. And in His prayer for His disciples He puts up this petition, "And now, O Father, glorify Thou Me with Thine own self; with the glory which I had with Thee before the world was." Then He was more than a human being, than a created being, and beyond created beings there is no stopping place but Deity.

2. No human being, not even an angel, can be in more than one place at one time. Christ is omnipresent. He is with His people, with all His people, "always, even unto the end of the world." And furthermore, "Wheresoever two or three are gathered together in My name, there am I in the midst of them." Through all earth's continents, in all its zones, and o'er all its waters, everywhere that God's people are, there is Christ in the fulness of His saving power dispensing the joy of His great salvation.

3. Human beings are but weak at best, and the

utmost limit of their strength is soon reached. But Christ declares that all power in heaven and in earth is committed unto Him. How utterly absurd for any human or created being to lay claim to all the power there is in heaven. He must be divine. Any other conclusion impales us upon the horns of a dilemma from which relief is impossible. If He is not Divine, then to make the claims He does so frequently to the possession of attributes, and to the exercise of functions that belong alone to God, He must be either insane or an impostor. But the Apostles sustain His claims, and the Scriptures freely and fully endorse them. Paul comes forward and testifies, "For by Him were all things created that are in heaven and that are in earth, visible and invisible, whether they be thrones, or dominions, or principalities, or powers: *all things* were created *by Him and for Him.*" It is enough! With Thomas we exclaim, "*My Lord and my God!*" Help is laid upon One that is mighty. "He is able to save unto the uttermost." Oh what a circumference is here?

For six thousand years believers have been entering into heaven, washed in the blood of the Lamb. Trusting in His almighty name, they have routed the devil, vanquished death and conquered hell. Through the all sufficiency of Christ and Christianity, they have marched triumphantly to their graves shouting "Victory" all the way.

If there is certainty anywhere under these heavens it is in Christ and in Christianity. What is Certainty? Full assurance of mind and exemption from doubt. Then the millions of saved on earth possess a certainty. If a religion that has perfectly satisfied every person on earth or in heaven that has laid hold of it, is sufficient, then the religion of Christ is suffi-

P

cient. If a religion that makes bad men good and good men better, that has saved thousands and millions from the power and practice, and penalty of sin, constitutes a sufficient ground of certainty, then Christ and Christianity fully meet the case. They furnish to mortals of every clime, and colour and condition, a source of happiness as unfailing as the spring upon the mountain side, that the winter's frost cannot congeal or the summer's sun dry up. The joy that they supply is deepest and purest, when every other dependence is swept away by floods of trial. They put into the heart and upon the lips of every believer in Christ the plan of a grander victory than that of Wellington at Waterloo, enabling its possessor to exclaim, "We are more than conquerors through Him that loved us. Neither death nor life, nor angels, nor principalities, nor powers, nor things present nor things to come, nor height, nor depth, nor any other creature shall be able to separate us from the love of God, which is in Christ Jesus our Lord." A more sublime, victorious, transporting certainty, it is impossible to conceive of, and this certainty is the birth-right of every child of God.

You may carry the question, "What must I do to be saved?" to the ends of the earth. You may try every other system of religion in the world; you may knock at the door of every scientist and interrogate every infidel, and return at last with your problem unsolved. The stolid ignorant-trustfulness of heathens is not certainty. It is the paralysis of the human spirit. With feeble instincts of danger, ignorant of duty or of destiny, certainty is impossible. Certainty in regard to truth and human destiny must have an intelligent basis, and must rest upon divine foundations, yea must be divinely given. The Mohammedanism of

Turkey, the Buddhism and Brahmanism of India, the Confucianism of China and the Heathenism of Africa are enormous impositions.

If Christ and Christianity can make *one* man *pure*, and happy, and triumphant, if they can do the same thing for a thousand, for a million, as facts prove they do, then they can also for the twelve hundred millions of the world's population.

> " Oh that the *world* might *taste* and *see*
> The riches of His grace;
> The arm of love that compass me,
> Would all mankind embrace."

In view of the foregoing doctrine, two or three reflections naturally arise.

1. A word to the careless sinner. There is life in a look at the Crucified One. But Oh! a persistent refusal to look to Jesus, and you shall perish without God and without hope. The terrible spectres of wasted opportunities, the horrid demons of despair will prey upon thy unsaved wretched soul forever. Notwithstanding the utterances of erratic and weak-kneed theologians, you will prove to your sorrow, if you die unsaved, that God is not guilty of duplicity, but that the *threatenings* of the Bible are as *real* as its *promises*. There is no logic under these heavens that can eliminate the word everlasting from the Bible without destroying eternal happiness as well as eternal punishment. If God is not sincere in His threatenings, who can rely with any certainty upon His promises?

It is true, eternally and awfully true, that "he that believeth not shall be damned"—Oh the terrible reflection will haunt you through all the cycles of eternity, " I might have been saved but I would not." Conscience, like the eternal thunders of the deep, will repeat the fearful wail of thy lost and hopeless soul. Oh be persuaded to repent, and turn, and live.

2. Do I address any who are saying, "I have often thought of it. I ought to do it. I would like to be a Christian." Oh decide! choose to day! "Him that cometh unto me," says Jesus the Saviour of sinners, "I will in no wise cast out." The Church through all its wondrous history cannot furnish an example of one sinner that has failed in his prayer for mercy. Up dying sinner to His cross.

> "Thy mistakes His free grace will cover,
> Thy sins He will wash away;
> And the feet that shrink and falter,
> Shall walk through the gates of day."

Oh I rejoice to believe that Christ Jesus shall reign from the river to the ends of the earth. I believe in the future, and in the Church of the future. I believe there is a day not very far distant, when from the watch-towers of Europe, that for centuries has been the battle ground of the nations, from the watch-towers of China, that land of superstition and intellectual imbecility, from the watch-towers of India, a land beautiful enough to be the home of angels, from the watch-towers of long neglected Africa, and from the watch-towers of our own heaven-blessed America, there shall roll forth in rapturous hosannas, the world's doxology; while the myriad tongued choir of heaven shall catch the swelling chorus, and shout back responsive, "Worthy is the Lamb that was slain, to receive power, and riches, and wisdom, and strength, and honour, and glory, and blessing."

Let us trust ever, with increasing confidence, in Christ and Christianity, and, ere long, with our Father and those who shall come after us, we will go up with shoutings to the Kingdom of God.

WINNING SOULS.

A Sermon delivered at the Bay of Quinté Conference, Prescott, Ont., May, 1878.

BY REV. A. D. TRAVELLER, P.E.,

of the Kingston District.

"The fruit of the righteous is a tree of life; and he that winneth souls is wise."—Proverbs xi. 30.

NATURALLY enough as the year drew to a close the question presented itself to my mind, What is the line of thought you purpose pursuing in that Conference Sermon you are expected to deliver. To say that only one subject presented itself for investigation would be to assert what is untrue, for I confess I have had a little difficulty in making a selection; and finally concluded that soul-saving would be the most profitable theme to engage our attention; as this is a departure from our general usage, and introduces a new item in our minutes I made up my mind it would be necessary at least to have a proper subject, whether it got properly handled or not. Although we have not had that extensive experience that some of these aged fathers enjoy, and have not been cognizant of many of the difficulties through which they have passed, yet we think we are safe in saying that, taking our history into consideration, the men and means at our disposal, we will compare grandly with any Christian Church in this or any other country. And notwithstanding all this we are forced to the conclusion that as labourers together with God we have not been as fruitful in soul-saving as we might reasonably have expected. Gratifying instances of this kind have not been wanting; but their recurrences have neither been as frequent nor as extensive as the wants of the Church demand and the resources at our command justify.

Why is it, dear brethren, that ours, the grandest of human missions, has been a comparative failure? Why is it that our Sabbath services have been prosecuted on a scale of remuneration so painfully disproportionate? Why is it that while men of Cyprus and Cyrene shake old Antioch with their preaching and turn multitudes to Christ; we, prosecuting the same mission, placed in communication with the same power, and authorized to expect the same signs following, have occasion to exclaim despondingly: "Who hath believed our report, and to whom is the arm of the Lord revealed?" Brethren, if we have the same Christ seated upon His Mediatorial throne, the merit of the same blood to plead, and God has the residue of the Holy Ghost with Him, and is waiting, yea, anxious to bestow Him upon us, why not expect hundreds of sinners converted on every charge every year?

Would it not be well for us to stop right here and enquire, and if possible find out the reason why we have not been more successful?

First allow me to suggest the possibility of a defect in our personal piety. How many of us wear continuously the white robe of holiness? How many of us can in our own consciousness testify clearly and practically that the blood of Jesus Christ His Son cleanseth from all sin ? Upon whose forehead shines this jewel of sacred brilliancy ? Our opinion is that our piety should be of a much loftier character than that exhibited by the generality of Christians around us. The teacher should stand on a higher spiritual platform than the taught. This, no doubt, is the case with some, while others stand only on an equality with the people to whom they minister ; and is it supposable that any one of us is lower in tone of spirituality than those over whom the Holy Ghost hath made us overseers, and to whom the command is given, "feed the flock of God" which He hath purchased with His own blood. If so, no wonder we cry out, "O, my leanness." If we are desirous of learning the grand secret of evangelical power let us read the inspired biographer touching the character of Barnabas. "He was a good man, and full of faith and of the Holy Ghost, and much people were added unto the Lord."

Secondly,—perhaps our pulpit unfruitfulness arises from a want of earnest, persevering prayer. O what mighty exhibitions of the power of importunate prayer does the history of the Church afford? Did we as ministers, members of the Bay of Quinté Conference of the Methodist Episcopal Church in Canada, pray as importunately as did the old patriarch Abram for Sodom, it would not be long until this entire Dominion would be shaken with the mighty power of God. Step after step does the patriarch rise in his humble and disinterested importunities for that old city, and step after step does divine tenderness promptly follow the suppliant. First he comes with fifty, then forty-five, then forty, then thirty, then twenty, and even ten when Jehovah God responds to the final peradventure *ten*. It was when Moses in the Spirit groaned that God cried out, "Let me alone." Oh, brethren, how many of us have wrestled, Jacob-like, until the break of day for victory? If we had there would have been more of us that would have had power with God and prevailed. Or had we, Daniel-like, spent three weeks in fasting and prayer, *surely* God would have given us greater skill and understanding in winning souls. These cold, brief, ordinary prayers have not been the instruments or weapons the Almighty has made use of in sending consternation through the ranks of hell, and causing victory to perch on the banners of Israel. If it were necessary for our Divine Lord to spend all night in supplication; if in Gethsemane's garden, "so deep were His sorrows, so fervent His prayers, that down o'er His bosom rolled blood, sweat and tears," where is there room for coldness or indifference on your part or mine. The devoted John Livingstone having preached a sermon full of power, at the close of which five hundred were converted to God, says that there are only two sermons that he would care to see again in writing, and these were on Communion occasions, and in both these instances he spent the previous nights in conference and prayer with some Christians. Who was it that on every charge where he laboured witnessed the live touch of Apostolic revival from one end of the year to the other? It was William Bramwell, of whom it was reported that he spent six hours out of twenty-four on his knees. My dear brethren, let us rouse ourselves. Let every sluggish feeling and dormant power be stirred up to take hold on God.

> What though our shrinking flesh complain,
>   And murmur to contend so long?
> We rise superior to our pain;
>   When we are weak then we are strong,
> And when our all of strength shall fail,
>   We shall with the God-man prevail.

Again a want of directness in our pulpits is another source of weakness and our non-success. If we preached for souls, souls would be converted. Our desires and purposes are in a measure prophetical of what we are capable of accomplishing, making use of the multiplied facilities at our command. We need some of that holy enthusiasm that inflamed the soul of the Rev. Dr. Duff, the returned missionary from India, in connection with the Presbyterian Church in Scotland. Once while delivering a missionary speech he fainted; they carried him out; and when aroused, said he, "I was speaking for India, was I not?" They said, "yes," "Then," said he, "carry me back that I may finish my speech." They took him back. "Is it true, Mr. Moderator," said he "that Scotland has no more sons to give to the Lord Jesus? If it is true, then I am off to-morrow, and (although I have lost my health) shall there on the shore of the Ganges be a witness for Christ."

The immortal dreamer (Bunyan) said, "I could not be satisfied unless some fruit appeared in my work." Doddridge, in writing to a friend, says, "I long for the conversion of souls more sensibly than anything else." Daniel Brainard could say of himself on more occasions than one, "I cared not how or where I lived or what I went through so that I could but gain souls for Christ." "While I was asleep," said he, "I dreamed of these things, and when I awoke the first thing I thought of was this great work." John Smith once said, "Give me souls or I die;" and if we desire a stronger incentive to labour hear it from the lips of the Divine Lord, "Herein is my Father glorified that ye bear much fruit." To what extent, dear brethren, do these Christ-like yearnings touch the cords of sympathy within us? The palpable want of visible and continuous results supply an answer sufficiently and unhappily conclusive. Possibly you can boast of punctuality in attending to your appointments, and that you are more than ordinarily acceptable. Yea, the people are unwilling to part with you after your three years have expired, and possibly recommendations are in your possession or your Presiding Elder's for your return for the fourth year. Yes, and you preach a full, free and present salvation, and the people are pleased, instructed and even profited. But what of all this if men are not saved from sin, and death and hell? I am aware that some people comfort themselves and endeavour to ease their consciences by applying the flattering unction that they are not called to reap. Their business is to instruct and take care of the harvest after it is gathered. The command of the Master is, "Pray ye therefore the Lord of the harvest that he would send forth more labourers unto His vineyard." And to my mind these are about the only kind of ministers needed in the nineteenth century.

The cry of every minister should be

> Thrust in the sharpened sickle,
> And gather in the grain;
> Shall sheaves lie here ungathered,
> And waste upon the plain?

My dear brethren, let us stir each other up to the indispensable necessity of anxiety for fruit. I believe we have no conception of what force this singleness of aim would give to our character, and what irresistible power it would infuse into our ministrations. There is something awful to my mind in making preaching an *end* and not a means; in passing through the same customary routine of sermonizing, and exhibiting no eagerness for visible results; being perfectly complacent if the services have been performed with propriety, and the congregation have been tolerably gratified with the performance. Oh, it is this damnable Laodicean formalism that troubles the Church, in the ministry and laity; and if the devil can persuade us to respectably leave the purchase of Christ's blood in his hands, it is all he desires. May the Lord help us to choose our texts and preach our sermons with one sole object in view, viz., the salvation of souls. With mighty prayer may we clothe ourselves with the power of Pentecost; and, with Apostolic singleness of purpose, say, *this one thing I do.* Every effort shall then result in victory. Good men shall then glorify God in your behalf, and wicked men shall shake and tremble beneath your breathig thoughts and burning words. Christ will be glorified in the trophies of your toil. There are motives that should press upon us the importance of this mighty work.

First.—The conversion of souls will shed a lustre upon the Church we represent, which it can attain in no other way. I care not what our numbers may be, our financial, social, or political influence; what the attractions of our ministry; what the grandeur of our ceremonies; what the perfection of our order; the Church that does not lead sinners to Christ is a dishonour to God, a blight in the universe of Jesus, a misnomer, as useless and offensive among the trees in God's vineyard as a blasted, withered and rotten oak in a living forest of freshness and beauty. On the contrary, no matter how unpretending a Church may be, if it seek to lead souls to Christ, open the eyes of the blind, heal the sick, make lame men to walk, and wretched men happy, that Church bears its own credentials, the heraldry of heaven floats upon its blood-washed ensign, and the diadem of Him on whose head are many crowns sparkles on its brow. The true way to success is to devise means, adopt measures, and preach sermons that will take hold of the champions of the devil, and transform them into angels of light. You remember the day before Pentecost, the disciples were not very much known; very unpopular and very much despised; but the conversion of three thousand souls, fifteen or eighteen hours later, carried the names of these fishermen to the ends of the Roman Empire.

A Moody might have sold boots and shoes in the city of Chicago until the day of his death, and never been known much outside of his school on the North side; but, having consecrated his entire time, the noblest purposes of his life, the choicest affections of his heart, and the almightiness of the human will, to the service of God, his name, reputation, influence, and popularity leap the seas, and stretch across both continents. Lords, dukes, nobles, and divines sit at his feet, and hear the simple story of the cross.

Second.—The conversion of a soul in itself ought to furnish a sufficient motive. The words of Jesus come to us with peculiar force: "What shall it profit a man if he gain the whole world, and lose his own soul?" Death will soon kill the body; but the soul shall "flourish in immortal youth, unhurt amid the war of elements, the wreck of matter, and the crash of worlds."

I sometimes wonder how it is that the soul's value is a subject of so little thought. Surely the price paid to redeem it bespeaks its immense worth. "For heaven's inexhaustible, exhausted fund poured forth the price all price beyond." When we think of a life of love, and contrast it with a life of hate; when we think of a death of peace, and contrast it with a death of anguish; when our eyes glance into the dimness and bitterness of eternal storm; when we feast on the ravishing melodies of Eden, and catch a glimpse of the holy and happy ones that wander amid flowers that are always fresh and fair; when we read of God becoming incarnate; of Gethsemane's agonies and Calvary's shame; why is it that, in view of all these, we do not rush out to our appointments with cries and entreaties, and pluck men from the jaws of the destroyer. If this Bible be true, it is *tremendously true*, and it declares that the " wicked shall be turned into hell, with all the nations that forget God." Methinks if Christ were fully formed in us, we would think as He thought, weep as He wept; do as He did; and, if need be, to save men, even our enemies, die as He died.

Finally.—Our future reward is closely connected with this work. They that be wise shall shine as the brightness of the firmament, and they that turn many to righteousness as the stars for ever and ever. It seldom happens that the man who is extensively useful in the Church has full justice done him in his glorious work. The simple piety of the truly good, and the better judgment of sinners appreciate him; but some who should be his helpers don't seem to understand him; others do not seem to relish his plans; others look upon his success with feelings of envy; while some who have a disrelish for a living, holy, earnest religion, despise him, and pass by on the other side. The man who will take hold of heavy trench work for God, outside of the ordinary course of labour in Church enterprises, revivals, or work for Christ of any kind, has to take the shot and shell of the devil; and if this were all it would not be so bad; but even some of his professed brethren in the ranks of the ministry bend their bows and shoot their arrows, even bitter words. But, glory to Christ, like his blessed Master, the common people hear him gladly, while lovers of formality, respectability and rigid order stand coolly and stiffly aloof. But, tardy as the Church and the world are to acknowledge the merit of a true man of God while he lives, yet almost every one, sinner and saint, writes victor on his shield when he falls. The names of earnest Christian workers never die. Their deeds of holy Christian chivalry are handed down to future generations. While names of mere mental power and ministerial talent have passed from the pages of memory by the ravages of time, the names of those who have turned many to righteousness shall be as familiar as household words, and will become increasingly fragrant until the end of time. And, whatever may be the judgment of the world and the awards of earth respecting the faithful servant, one thing is certain, Christ will do ample justice. There will be enough reward in the final " Well done, good and faithful servant; enter thou into the joy of thy Lord." One class is to shine as the brightness of the firmament; their individual lustre will not be so apparent, but, blended one with the other, they will present, as it were, a luminous field, a magnificent milky way of light and glory. The other class are to shine as the stars for ever and ever, that is, as I understand their individual glory will be perfectly cognizable. They will strike and rivet the gaze in a moment; and high amid the universe of stars will these glow and burn. Such will be the reward of those who turn many to righteousness.

The spirit of the true Gospel ministry is that souls *must* be saved. Our appointments must not be considered in the light of composing and delivering so many sermons; but as so many glorious opportunities of winning souls for Christ. Our efforts must not be looked upon as so many human compositions; but, as channels of life-giving energy. We ought to be grieved if our labour produces no sheaves for the blessed Master. Let us, in the spirit of that poetic effusion from the pen of the gifted author, go forth and

> Seek those of evil behaviour;
>   Bid them their lives to amend :
> Go, point the lost ones to the Saviour,
>   And be to the friendless a friend.
> Still be the lone heart of anguish
>   Soothed by the pity of thine;
> By waysides if wounded ones languish,
>   Go, pour in the oil and the wine.
>
> Work, though the enemies' laughter
>   Over the valley may sweep;
> For God's patient workers hereafter
>   Shall laugh when their enemies weep.
> Ever on Jesus reliant,
>   Press on your chivalrous way;
> The mightiest Philistine giant
>   His Davids are chartered to slay.
>
> Then offer thy life on the altar;
>   In the high purpose be strong;
> And if the tired spirit should falter,
>   Then sweeten thy labour with song.
> What if the poor heart complaineth;
>   Soon will its wailings be o'er;
> For there, in the rest that remaineth,
>   It shall grieve and be weary no more."

There is no need for discouragement on the part of God's servants; they are protected and safe. As Whittier, in his famous poem on God's goodness, exclaims :—

> I know not where His islands lift
>   Their fronded palms in air;
> I only know I cannot drift
>   Beyond His love and care.
> And so, beside the silent sea,
>   I wait the muffled oar;
> No harm from Him can come to me,
>   On ocean or on shore.

THE NECESSITY AND SUFFIENCY OF THE ATONEMENT.

By the Rev. E. Lounsbury,

Of Strathroy, Ont.

"This is a faithful saying and worthy of all acceptation, that Christ Jesus came into the world to save sinners."—Tim. i. 15.

THE monuments of human grandeur perish. Earthly thrones crumble into dust. The gilded sceptre of the proud monarch falls at the feet of the invincible warrior, and the magnificent temples of human glory yield in succession their colossal forms to the destroying elements of time. Where is proud Babylon and Nineveh, and the ancient kingdoms of Persia, Greece and Rome and their renowned heroes! Alas! these, together with their systems of philosophy and of government, have long since perished. The proudest productions of human genius have each in turn measurably, if not altogether, lost their interest, and Time has written, as with an iron pen, the departure of their glories. A persistent familiarity with earthly objects often renders them powerless, at least so far as we are concerned, and they cease to excite our interest or command our admiration, much less to satisfy the cravings of our minds. Hence, in the conviction of our hearts, we adopt the language of Solomon and say, All is vanity. Such has been the experience of men in every age. But such, however, is not the fact, nor can it ever be in relation to the grand doctrine of the Atonement of Jesus.

As the natural heavens, by the aid of the most powerful magnifying-glass, develop with increasing interest their glories to the eye of the astronomical observer, so these grand old doctrines of the Gospel develop to the man of faith with increasing grandeur the imperishable honours of the cross of our Lord Jesus Christ.

And though centuries have come and gone since Paul the Aged gave expression to the sentiment of my text, yet all along the ages it has sounded out with increasing power and interest, and, at this hour, it touches every cord in our emotional nature, and our hearts respond: It is a truth worthy of all acceptation that Christ Jesus came into the world to save sinners.

In the contemplation of this text I invite you to consider,

I.—THE NECESSITY FOR THE ATONEMENT.

This arose from the fact that man had transgressed the law of God, and by this act of rebellion had fallen from original righteousness, and exposed himself to the divine displeasure. It is not my purpose, however, in this instance to detain you with any arguments upon human depravity. The point of interest with us now is, the necessity of an atonement for the offence.

The depravity and rebellion of man, taken in connection with the rectitude of the divine character, rendered it absolutely necessary that an atonement should be made before God could consistently save the offenders. We lay it down as an undoubtable truth that God cannot in any instance act contrary to any one of His moral attributes or unworthy of Himself. And to save the sinner without satisfaction being offered to His justice would be to act contrary to that atttibute, and, consequently, unworthy of Himself. Satisfaction, therefore, must be made or the sinner must be lost. The truth of this proposition may be shown from reason as well as Scripture.

Were we to suppose the Deity capable of one deviation from the rectitude of His character, either in disposition or in conduct, on the same principle we may suppose Him capable of deviation in every possible case. Hence He may wholly change His character, and, therefore, cease to be that God of holiness which all who admit His existence allow and the Scriptures declare Him to be. This, however, is placed beyond all successful contradiction by an express declaration of holy Writ in which it is said God cannot lie. And why? Because truth is a property of His nature. Hence, to destroy truth in God would be to destroy the divine existence. Therefore, satisfaction must be supposed to be made or the sinner must necessarily be lost. But again it has been said, could not God by the exercise of mere prerogative, as moral governor of the universe, have extended pardon to the sinner without any condition whatever? We answer, No. True, He might have done so if He had been destitute of character and regardless of moral principle. A little reflection will shew that such a course would have been at war with both the character and government of God. First, God had positively pronounced the penalty, "In the day thou eatest thereof thou shalt surely die." Now, had no regard been paid to this after man had transgressed, we ask again, where would have been the divine character for truthfulness, and what kind of lesson on the subject of veracity would have been taught His moral universe? The facts are, confidence in God would have been destroyed, and the whole system of faith in the divine word would have been overthrown.

Secondly, upon this principle, as has already been intimated, where would have been the justice of God? Had not the threatened penalty been a just and righteous one it never would have been affixed to the divine law. And if so, is it not equally clear that the same immutable principle of rectitude would require its execution upon the offender. And, further, if it be in accordance with justice to inflict the penalty, then is it not equally clear that it would be contrary to justice not to do it. Again, it is easy to see that pardon on the ground of prerogative without satisfaction would be in direct opposition to the divine goodness. The object of all good government is the security and peace of the subject, and the object of the divine Lawgiver is unquestionably the security, order and peace of His intelligent universe. Therefore, He could not justify the guilty without positive injury to the innocent, for it is absolutely essential to the interest of all that the divine government be maintained; for, as you will observe, the Deity has seen fit to connect His own glory and man's best interest for both worlds with His moral government established among men. Hence, it follows that trangression of the divine law is not only opposition to the divine will, but is certain destruction to all human happiness for time and eternity. Therefore, reconciliation must be effected or the offender must be cut off. To make this more simple, let us suppose a case. An individual enters your house and murders a member of your family. The penalty annexed to this crime in our civil law is death. We will suppose him to be arrested by the proper officer, brought before the proper tribunal, fairly tried before an honest jury of his own countrymen, and a verdict of guilty rendered. Can we see it consistent or even possible for the administrator to maintain the majesty of the law, secure the right of its subjects, and at the same time acquit and justify the criminal? Certainly not. Hence, said Mr. Watson, how sin may be forgiven without leading to such misconceptions of the divine character as would encourage disobedience, and thereby weaken the influence of the divine government, remains a problem of very difficult solution. A government that administered no forgiveness would sink the guilty to despair. A government that never punishes an offence is a contradiction—it cannot exist. Not to punish the guilty is to dissolve authority. To punish without mercy is to destroy. And where all are guilty it is to make the destruction universal. Therefore, I repeat, satisfaction must be supposed to be made, or the whole world of mankind must be lost. Finally, the Scriptures place this question beyond dispute, Luke xxiv. 46: "Thus it is written and thus it behoved Christ to suffer, &c."

II.—Notice how infinite Justice unites with Divine Compassion in the perfected character of Christ as a Saviour, and is exemplified in the execution of His work.

We have seen that when man had trangressed the divine law, justice demanded satisfaction at his hand, but man was utterly unable to meet the demand. Still justice, stern and inflexible, calls for satisfaction at his hand. But man cannot expiate his own guilt. Divine compassion comes to his relief. The Word was made flesh, or took up His abode in flesh. Christ became very man. He took our nature with all its weakness and infirmities, Hebrews ii. 14: "Forasmuch then as the children are partakers of flesh and blood, He also Himself likewise took part of the same; that through death He might destroy him that had the power of death, &c." As our poet hath said—

> He took the dying traitor's place,
> And suffered in his stead;
> For sinful man—O, wondrous grace!—
> For sinful man He bled.

Thus Christ became the substitute for sinners. But humanity alone, however pure in itself, could not meet the demand of justice and secure salvation to man. First, because of the magnitude of the offence. The transgression was committed against a Being who is infinite. I do not mean by this that sin is infinite in the fullest sense of that term, for no finite act can bear any proportion to infinity. Still in point of moral turpitude, sin is infinite in degree. In estimating the magnitude of an offence it is proper to take into account the dignity of the offended. According to this rule for me to employ certain words and maintain an improper course of conduct against a high ruler, either in church or state, would be accounted more guilty, and, therefore, I might expect a greater degree of punishment than in a case where an inferior or an equal is concerned. In the application of this principle how great must be an offence against Him whose being and dignity is infinite, and whose relation to man is so sacred. Hence, it will be seen that no mere created being could have atoned for the sins of the world. True the poet Milton makes such a supposition, which may pass for poetry, but not for sound theology. He supposes the divine Being to be making inquiry among the angelic host to know who among their number would go to earth and redeem man.

> "Say, heavenly powers, where shall we find such love,
> Which of ye will be mortal to redeem
> Man's mortal crime, the just, the unjust to save?
> Dwells in all heaven charity so dear?
> He asked, but all the heavenly choir stood mute,
> And silence was in heaven."

What, then, did the poet Milton imagine that if Gabriel had said, "Lo, here am I, send me. I am willing for the sake of man to assume his nature, to live and suffer and die, 'the just the unjust to save!'" did he imagine that the death of Gabriel in a human body would have been a sufficient offering to save the world? The thing would have been impossible. Nothing short of God incarnate could meet the demand of justice and secure salvation to man. Hence, Paul said God was in Christ reconciling the world unto Himself. Therefore, to redeem man the Godhead and humanity were mysteriously united, that, as man, Christ could offer Himself in sacrifice for man, while, as God, He could extend pardon to the offender. And thus by offering up His humanity upon the altar of His Divinity the sacrifice was rendered sufficiently meritorious to expiate human guilt. Therefore, a belief in the doctrine that Jesus Christ was truly and properly God, as well as man, becomes essential to our faith in the sufficiency of His sacrifice for the sins of the world. True, this doctrine involves a great mystery, but the existence of the mystery only strengthens our faith in its divinity.

THIS SALVATION IS ALL OF GOD!

The fact of both His Divinity and humanity was sufficiently exemplified during His life and in the exercise of His personal ministry. As a man, He was weary and hungry—as a God, He multiplied the loaves and fishes and fed the thousands in the desert. As a man, He endured reproach—as a God, He awed the multitude so that they were astonished at His doctrine. As a man, He drank the deep cup of grief and was tempted and buffeted by the evil one—as a God, He was transfigured on the mount and performed miracles of the highest grandeur, expelled demons, stilled the tempest and raised the dead. As a man, He was betrayed and arrested by the rude soldiers—as a God, He overwhelmed them by His voice, and when He said, " Whom seek ye?" they went backward and fell as dead men at His feet. As a man, you see Him suffering on the cross—while as a God, His Deity is attested by the darkening of the sun, the rending of the temple's veil, the shaking of the earth, and the opening of the graves. As a man, His mangled remains rested in the gloomy sepulchre—as a God, He dismantled Himself of His grave clothes, burst the bars of death and came forth triumphing over the grave. As a man, we see Him now conversing and eating with His disciples—as a God, He ascends amid the shouts of angels in the clouds of heaven, where He will exercise His reign until His enemies become His footstool. Here pause and reflect upon the perfections of His character as the Redeemer and Mediator for the world. Think, were He only man you dare not trust in Him for " cursed is man that trusteth in man and maketh flesh his arm ;" were He only God you dare not approach Him, for God out of the Mediator is a consuming fire. But, combining, as He does, all that is awful in the Godhead with all that is attractive in the man, we have all that is powerful to save with all that is sympathetic to feel. Such are the perfections of the character of Him who came to save sinners. And now behold Him on the cross, while His soul is made an offering for sin. He appears at once the dying Victim, and the immortal Victor as

He cries, "It is finished." In Him all the ends of the divine government are answered. No license is given to sin. The moral law stands unrepealed. Future and eternal punishments still display their awful sanctions. A marvellous exhibition of the awful purity of the divine justice is afforded. And yet pardon is offered to all who seek it, and the whole world may be saved.

> O Lord, what heavenly wonders dwell
> In thine atoning blood!
> By this are sinners saved from hell,
> And rebels brought to God.

III.—Observe the grand truth and faithfulness of the doctrine of my text—

CHRIST JESUS CAME INTO THE WORLD TO SAVE SINNERS

Skeptics have said that Jesus died simply to confirm the truth of the doctrines He had taught, and not as an atonement for sin. But we affirm that His doctrines needed no confirmation aside from the moral influences they carried, and the stupendous miracles by which they were attested. Behold Him stilling the tempest, opening the eyes of the blind, healing the sick, and raising the dead. And what further proof is required for the divinity of His mission, or of the truthfulness of His doctrines. The fact is, whenever we think of the sufferings of Christ, we are immediately reminded of the sin and rebellion of man. Christ died for our sins: 1st Cor. xv. 3. He suffered once for sin, --the just for the unjust, that He might bring us to God. Who, his own self bare our sins in His own body on the tree. He came into the world to save sinners. And will He save sinners? Has He saved sinners? Does He save sinners? Do you ask me for facts to prove that Jesus saves sinners? I refer you to the thief on the cross, who in that awful moment under a conscious crushing sense of guilt, cried "Lord remember me when thou comest into thy kingdom." And with the grasp of His omnipotence He wrests the sinner from the very brink of ruin, carries him up to the foot of the throne of God, that angels may rejoice over him as a trophy of His redeeming power. Do you ask me for further facts? I may refer you to a Mary Magdalene, out of whom Jesus cast seven devils, and invite you to look upon the character of Saul, who became Paul, the author of my text. You know there was a time when he was a most iron-hearted sinner, an inveterate hater of Jesus and of His religion; but he is arrested by the power of Christ; and at the mention of the name of Jesus, his invincible spirit is broken, and he cries "Lord what wilt Thou have me to do?" He now comes forth Paul the redeemed and saved sinner—the bold defender of the faith he had sought to destroy. And to-day he lives to testify before the throne of God in heaven, that it is a faithful saying, that Christ came into the world to save sinners. But I need not detain you with more scriptural evidences and facts. Are you not present who have felt and even now feel the power of Christ to save, and were it not for disturbing the order of this assembly, could rise and say, I know that the blood of Jesus cleanseth me from all sin. And, O brethren, bear with me a little further while, in conclusion, I say to the unconverted in my congregation, sinner you may be saved, yes, even at this hour, and in this service. O, look to the crucified One, though eighteen hundred years have gone since Jesus bled for you, yet even now, from the deep heart of infinite Love, there is a melting voice coming down through the agonies of the cross crying, Come and be saved!

DIVINE COMPANIONSHIP.

By the Rev. Wm. Service,

Of Farmersville, Ont.

"Yea, though I walk through the valley of the shadow of death, I will fear no evil : for thou art with me ; thy rod and thy staff they comfort me." Ps. XXIII. 4.

THIS beautiful psalm is doubtless from the pen of the "sweet singer of Israel." Though attributed by some to others, its spirit, composition, and subject place its authorship with David. David spent his youthful days as a shepherd. His mind had early been impressed, and associated with the dangers, hardships, cares, and anxieties of the shepherd's life, tending the flocks amid the perils of the wilderness. These early scenes and experiences made a lasting impression on his mind, which was manifested in all his future experience. The impressions of youth are always the strongest and most enduring ; time or distance can never efface them from the memory. And there is no doubt that all through David's eventful life he never forgot the days when he was a shepherd boy tending his father's flocks, and when, from the exuberance of his youthful heart, he daily broke the stillness of the wilderness with his joyous song, before he had become entangled in the cares and responsibilities which rested upon him in after life. And I doubt not, that from the eminence of his throne surrounded with all the glory of his kingly position, he looked back to the sheep cotes of Jesse, and longed to be back again free from those cares and burdens that brought from his heart this plaintive strain, "Oh that I had wings like a dove, for then would I fly away and be at rest. Lo, then would I wander far off, and *remain* in the wilderness, I would hasten my escape from the windy storm and tempest." And how forcibly this language expresses the longings of many a burdened heart! Yea all at some period of life,

"When cares like a wild deluge come
And storms of sorrow fall."

have looked back to childhood's sunny hours, and felt a longing desire to be back and live them over again. David's religious experience, all through, was very similar to our own. He had his joys and sorrows, his dark and lucid hours; he sang his songs and shed his tears; and, in reading his sublime psalms, which always speak his heart's experience, we find boundless comfort whether we are on Pisgah's top or down in the dark valley.

But let us now proceed to the consideration of some thoughts more immediately connected with our text.

Though we have no data given upon which we can fully decide at what stage of David's life this psalm was written, or precisely what circumstance suggested it, we must, however, consider the Psalmist as having arrived at mid-age, and from that point viewing life, in its past, present and future bearings. His past history had doubtless been passing in review before his mind; he had thought of how the Lord had mysteriously led him, and opened up his way, had guarded, and kept him while a fugitive in the wilderness, delivered him from the persecutions of Saul, and exalted him to be King over Israel. Then turning his meditations upon the future, as is indicated in the closing verse of the psalm, " Surely goodness and mercy shall follow me all the days of my life, and I will dwell in the house of the Lord forever; " and as he thus takes in the whole scope of life, and considers the goodness, longsuffering, and loving-kindness of the Lord, from life's beginning to its end, providing for all life's necessities, protecting from all its dangers, soothing all its sorrows, alleviating all its pangs, and gladdening the heart with rich promises, his mind seems to have become enravished with the sublime reverie, and he gives expression to the ecstacied emotions, which could no longer be pent up in silence, in the language of this delightful psalm. These, we think, were the reflections which awakened in the mind of Israel's sweet singer, this the sublimest of all his sacred songs.

It was doubtless under such inspiration that David, from the fulness of his heart sang in rapturous strains, " The Lord is my shepherd I shall not want ; He maketh me to lie down in green pastures, He leadeth me beside the still waters. Yea though I walk through the valley of the shadow of death, I will fear no evil : for thou art with me, thy rod, and thy staff they comfort me." To my mind, there was nothing more natural than for David, who was once a shepherd himself to express his loftiest ideal of God's tender compassion, and care for His children in the idea of a faithful shepherd caring tenderly and constantly for his flock. He remembered his own anxious solicitude for his father's flock among the hills and green pastures of Judea, how he had led them to the verdant pastures, and when thirsty, by the still waters, and how he had carried the lambs in his bosom ; and when the bear and the lion came among them to devour them how he, regardless of his own safety, had rushed upon them and rescued the lambs; how he had folded them at nightfall, counting them carefully to see if any were missing, and if even one of the youngest lambs were missing, how he penned the flock, and went away among the rocks and hills to seek the one which was lost. And when it occurred to his mind that the Lord was the "good shepherd" of his scattered flock, and that he was one of the sheep of His pasture, he rejoiced exceedingly amid all his troubles and said "I will fear no evil; for thou art with me," for thou hast "made thy own people to go forth like sheep and guarded them in the wilderness like a flock, and led them on safely, so they feared not, but the sea overwhelmed their enemies."

The Lord is frequently represented in both the Old and the New Testament as a shepherd, and His people as a flock. Jesus said to His disciples, "I am the Good Shepherd, and know my sheep." And who is not familiar with that inimitable parable of the shepherd who left his ninety and nine safely folded, and went away to seek the lost sheep, and finding it returned with joy. And Isaiah, in prophetic vision beholding Him as a shepherd, says: "He shall feed his flock like a shepherd, he shall gather the lambs with his arms, and carry them in his bosom, and shall gently lead those that are with young." Yes, we may each say, "The Lord is my shepherd," He careth for me. What care parents feel for their children, and how by the impulses of parental affection they cheerfully toil, and sacrifice for their good. And yet, God declares that a mother may forget her child, yet will I not forget thee. As a shepherd knows the defenceless condition of his flock, so our Good Shepherd understood our defencelessness. " And as a father pitieth his children so the Lord pitieth them that fear Him, for He knoweth our frame, He remembereth that we are dust," and He says, I will guide thee by my counsels, and afterward receive you to glory—

> "Lord, I would clasp thy hand in mine,
> Nor ever murmur or repine,
> Content, whatever lot I see,
> Since 'tis my God that leadeth me!"

Yea, though I walk through the Valley.

This beautiful passage is very generally misconstrued so as to mar its value, being understood by many to refer only to the hour of death when the Christian is passing over the " swellings of Jordan." But the text is rendered infinitely more precious to the child of God, when he considers it as taking in the whole of the present pilgrimage from earth to heaven; when he can apply the precious assurances therein contained, of the divine presence and help, to his present life, and feel that the great Shepherd is with him daily and that His rod and staff do now comfort him. And this is certainly the proper view to take of this delightful passage. This valley of the shadow of death is unquestionably the same as that spoken of by the prophet Isaiah, and repeated by St. Mathew, " The people that walked in darkness have seen great light, they that dwell in the land of the shadow of death, upon them hath the light shined." This passage is a presentation of the condition of the people of this world who sat in the region and shadow of death, and a prophetic reference to Christ, whose light appeared among them, to dispel the eternal darkness which had settled down upon this world, which is called the land or region of the shadow of death. Therefore when we enter upon this life we enter the vale of death, where death sways his sceptre over every living creature, and we continue to walk under the shadow of his grim visage until translated to the region of life eternal beyond the grave.

The true idea of dying is, that when we commence to live, we commence to die. Death at once begins his work, and never ceases until he has loosed the silver cord, and broken the golden bowl, and broken the pitcher at the fountain, and the wheel at the cistern, and sent the dust back again to dust, and the spirit to God who gave it, and caused the bereaved mourners to go about the streets. That which we call death is more properly escaping from death, for when death finishes his work he but drives the spirit from the house of clay far away into realms of life, whither he can not follow, and whose peaceful domains he can never invade. We associate with death the pains and groans and terrors of the last conflict, but these very frequently begin at a very early stage of what we call life, and come to an end at that dreaded hour that we call death; therefore we are passing through the dreaded ordeal of dying years before we reach the hour of final conflict. We all have our troubles, pains, and conflicts while yet living and passing through death's vale, but when death overcomes life he brings a sweet release to both body and soul. So death is not so much to be dreaded as what we call living. Death is the quivering point we finally reach, from which the soul takes her flight from the region of the shadow of death into the refulgent glories of heaven. Death is the exit from death. We are all passing through the valley *now*. We are under the shadow of death to-day. We may baffle him awhile but will sooner or later bow to his sceptre, and pass away. The poet has beautifully described the relentless monarch of the vale of death in these words:

> "Deep in a murky lair's recess,
> Laved by oblivion's listless stream,
> And fenced by shelving rocks
> And intermingling horrors of yew and cypress shade,
> From all obtrusion of busy noontide beam,
> The Monarch sits, in unsubstantial majesty."

"Surely in the midst of life we are in death."

> "Whate'er we do, where'er we be
> We're travelling to the grave."

But what boundless consolation to reflect upon the many assurances we have of the presence and care of the "Good Shepherd," and be able to say, confidently with David, "Yea, though I do walk through the valley of death, I will fear no evil: for thou art with me; thy rod and thy staff they comfort *me*." We are but walking through the shadow, the harmless shadow falls across our path but the substance is not there—only the shadow. Death, though not disarmed, has had the sting taken from him; the poison has been washed out of his arrows by the blood of his mighty Conqueror; his darkness has been turned into light in the presence of the world's Saviour, "and to them which sat in the region and shadow of death light has sprung up." Jesus, the "light of the world," has lighted up the vale, and His children walk in the light as He is in the light. As when the Hebrews were passing over the wilderness to the promised land, God was in the pillar of fire to give them light, He is still in the midst of His people, "a lamp unto their feet and a light unto their path." A shadow is caused by some object intervening between the sun or moon and the earth, and when we see a shadow upon the earth, it is an evidence to us that there is light beyond, for where there is no light beyond there can be no shadow. Therefore the fact that we are in the shadow now is proof that there must be light beyond. Death's dark form for a while intervenes between our world and the land of light beyond, and intercepts the light that streams through the bright portals of glory, causing a shadow to fall on us here, but when we pass from under death's dark shade the glorious light of heaven will fall full on the soul, as the light of the sun falls full on us when the cloud passes over. It is not improbable that when David wrote this part of the psalm that his mind was directed to those dark, dangerous mountain defiles through which, in many places, the road leads in travelling the hill-country of Palestine, and with which David was very familiar. These narrow passes are even to this day extremely dangerous to travel on account of ferocious beasts that inhabit the rocks, ready to pounce upon the passer-by and devour him. These were also the rendezvous of numerous banditti which infest that country, frequently assaulting travellers, robbing and killing them as they pass through these ways; consequently it becomes necessary for travellers to procure an escort to protect and guide them safely through, and with these guides they feel comparatively safe, but it is presumption for any one to undertake the journey alone, such an attempt being almost sure to result in death. So along life's journey,

"Death rides on every passing breeze
And lurks in every flower,"

as we pass o'er life's rugged ways, and devious wilds

"Dangers stand thick through all the ground
To push us to the tomb,"

R

and snares are laid for our feet by the arch enemy, and plans and devices formed for our destruction; deep dark pitfalls, there are into which the enemy would lead us, and plunge us into the abyss of eternal night and misery. Therefore they who would walk in safety along this road, and through these dangerous defiles, must secure the Guide, who alone is sufficient to guide us safely through life's dangerous paths. He who has passed over the whole way, and entered into all its dark defiles, and vanquished every enemy, can bring us victoriously through, but the journey will prove fatal to all who undertake it alone. Do not presume, therefore to walk alone through the vale of death; but secure the guidance and presence of Him who has said, "I will guide thee with mine eye," and let the prayer of Moses be your constant prayer, "If thy presence go not with me, carry me not up hence."

"Thy Rod and Thy Staff They Comfort Me."

There is something very significant and suggestive in the rod. It is an emblem of God's power. He is said to rule with a rod of iron. The Psalmist says, "Thou shalt break them (his enemies) with a rod of iron." His power is as the strength of iron, and that power is vouchsafed to every one who puts his trust in Him. And not so long as there is power in the divine arm, or love in the great Shepherd's heart, can any of His sheep or lambs be devoured by the prowling beasts that seek to destroy them. As the strength of the omnipotent God is the strength of His weakest child, who humbly and implicitly puts his trust in Him, so not until His own almighty power is exhausted, will He allow one of His children to be overpowered by the enemy. Man might as well think of dethroning the Almighty as to think of destroying one of His children, so long as he puts his trust in Him. Hear what Jesus said to His disciples " My sheep hear my voice, and I know them, and they follow me, and I give unto them eternal life, and they shall never perish, neither shall any pluck them out of my hand. My Father which gave them me is greater than all, and no man is able to pluck them out of my Father's hand." Therefore, we need not fear " though an host encamp against us."

> "Thus, strong in his Redeemer's strength,
> Sin, death and hell, he tramples down ;
> Fights the good fight, and wins at length,
> Through mercy, an immortal crown."

The rod is also an emblem of Christ. Isaiah says in speaking of Christ, "And there shall come forth a rod out of the stem of Jesse, and a branch shall grow out of his roots; and the spirit of the Lord shall rest upon him, the spirit of wisdom and understanding, the spirit of counsel and might, the spirit of knowledge, and of the fear of the Lord." Therefore Christ who is our great deliverer, mighty to save, being signified in the rod, we need not fear, for He hath said, " I will never leave thee nor forsake thee." " Lo, I am with thee always even to the end of the world," and " he that believeth on him shall not be confounded."

The rod of Moses was the symbol of God's presence, in the deliverance of his oppressed people from the cruel bondage of Pharaoh. Moses, who was a type of Christ, wrought all his wonderful works through the divine presence and power manifested in the rod. The rod in Moses' hand was the divine present with the human in working out the deliverance of Israel, which was a foreshadowing of the great deliverance of the world from the bondage and thraldom of sin, by the man

Christ Jesus in whom were mysteriously united the divine and human. The divine in the nature of Christ was the rod in the hands of the humanity of Christ by which the man Christ Jesus did the mighty works of Him who sent Him to redeem the world. Thus Moses' typical character was made complete when He had the rod of God placed in his hand, and when he went forth accompanied with that emblem of the divine presence to do the work God sent him to do in the deliverance of the Hebrews. We understand then by the rod, the divine presence vouchsafed to man to qualify him for any work that may be assigned him by God. It was neither the human in Moses or in Christ, which did the mighty works manifested in and through them, but the divine associated with them, in Moses manifested in the rod, and in Christ manifested in the flesh: God in Moses (the type) delivering the Hebrews from the Egyptian bondage, and God in Christ the Antetype reconciling the world to Himself. And that same rod of divine presence and power is given to every child of grace to qualify him for the work God may assign him whether it be great or small. When God sends any man or out to do a special work He puts a rod in his hand, as he did in the hand of Moses, by the power of which he can accomplish any thing, and say with the apostle "I can do all things through Christ which strengtheneth me:" And whether our commission involves duties beyond the power of the human to accomplish or otherwise it makes no difference, the rod placed in our hand enables us through Divine power to accomplish our work as in the case of Moses. Any one going out without the rod is powerless, but with it is mighty through God to the pulling down of strongholds. A man is invincible with the rod of God in his hand. What we want to impress upon your mind is this fact that divine power is given to every child of God to accomplish his work; we are "co-workers with Christ." Human weakness is no consideration with the child of God, for "It is not by might or by power but by my spirit saith the Lord." Moses pleaded his inability but God put the rod in his hand and sent him forth, and see what he accomplished through it: brought the plagues upon Egypt, opened a path through the Red Sea, brought water from Horeb's rock.

It was the principal agency in the deliverance of God's oppressed people. Christ taught the disciples this great truth. "Believest thou not that I am in the Father and the Father in me; the words that I speak unto you I speak not of myself, but the Father that dwelleth in me, He doeth the works. Verily, verily, I say unto you, he that believeth in me, the works that I do he shall do also, and greater works than these shall he do, because I go unto my Father." Therefore, the same divine power that Moses had, and the same divine power that Christ had, is vouchsafed to every one of God's servants. Moses is not the only servant of God that has had the rod; David had it. All the Prophets had it. Christ and all his Disciples and Apostles had it. Luther had it. Wesley had it. All good and faithful servants of God from Adam, have had it, and by it have done many wonderful works that have astonished the world. *We* have it, and let us use it, and the Almighty will manifest himself mightily through *us*. "My presence shall go with thee and I will give thee rest," is God's promise to Moses and to us. Therefore, what comfort we derive from this assurance that the rod of God is with us, withersoever we go.

And Thy Staff.

The staff also has a varied signification, and suggests to my mind, many precious considerations. The common, and probably primary idea of a staff is, its use as a help to the traveller, and especially as a support for the aged and infirm, whose limbs are too feeble to bear the weight of the body; these find the staff a very great comfort and support. The application is easy, God's truth is the Christian's staff; upon His promises can the Christian lean through all the journey of life, with great comfort and delight, especially when feeling the feebleness and infirmities of the flesh. When passing through deep waters, and under dark clouds, he can, with Jacob, worship leaning on the top of his staff, and in sweet resignation, say:

> " Let sickness blast, let death devour,
> If heaven must recompense our pains;
> Perish the grass and fade the flower,
> If firm the word of God remains."

Again, this staff of divine truth is a weapon of defence to the Christian pilgrim. The Psalmist says: "His truth shall be thy shield." Jesus discomfited Satan, by hurling at him the missiles of God's truth; and the Apostles used the same mighty weapon against their enemies, and their errors. This is the weapon that will prevail. Human argument however skilful, may be met with human argument, human wisdom by human wisdom, but nothing can stand before the mighty truth of God. It will cut its way through all error, and demolish every one of the enemy's strongholds; and, if *we* would prove victorious, we must wield the mighty truth of God. A "Thus saith the Lord," or, a "Thus it is written," will do more to defend the child of God, and his doctrines, and vanquish his enemies, than all the combined wisdom of man. It is sharper than any two-edged sword; not carnal, but mighty, through God.

There is one more comforting thought we would present before leaving this part of the subject. The staff means an escort, a suite of attendants; and this we are promised in Paul to the Hebrews; "Are they not all ministering spirits sent forth to minister for them who shall be heirs of salvation?" And it is possible, and, to my mind very probable, that prominent among this heavenly suite of attendants sent to us, are loved ones who have walked by our side in life, and who still, even among the glories in heaven, have not lost their interest in us, but frequently speed their way down to the abodes of friends who still linger on earth and struggle with its difficulties. That the angels are our attendants is certain. "He shall give his angels charge over thee to keep thee in all thy ways." And "The angel of the Lord encampeth round about them that fear him, and delivereth them." And, that the departed are employed in like missions to earth is both possible and probable, for God could as easily employ these as angels, in His mission of mercy to the children of men, and these having so many strong ties binding their affections to earth, and so well acquainted by personal experience with all the varied phases of mortal life would be the best qualified for such work and most likely to be employed as messengers to earth. The glorious personage sent to conduct St. John through his vision was one who had been a sojourner here below, for he said, when John fell at his feet to worship him, "see thou do it not for I am thy fellow servant, and of thy brethren." He seemed still to be engaged in the same work that John was engaged in for he adds, "that have the testimony of Jesus." It would seem that though gone from earth, he was still charged with the same commission. The testimony of Jesus, and some way or other connected with the work of Jesus on earth. By these texts we understand that not only angels but glorified spirits are commissioned to guard and guide us through the region of the shadow of death. Therefore will we fear no evil for thou, Oh God, the Good Shepherd art with us, and

> "Well appointed angels keep,
> Their watchful stations round our path,"

while

> "Sainted friends on pinions bright
> Fly to our help with eager haste."

We are told there is joy in heaven in the presence of the angels over one sinner that repenteth. What intense interest the inhabitants of the bright realms of glory feel for the inhabitants of earth that we may join in their songs and share their joys when life's pilgrimage is over. Then as we journey through the vale let this be our triumphant song:—

> "I will not fear though armed throngs
> Surround my steps in all their wrath,
> Salvation to the Lord belongs
> His presence guards His people's path."

> "Though in the paths of death I tread
> With gloomy horrors overspread,
> My steadfast heart shall fear no ill,
> For thou, O Lord, art with me still;
> Thy friendly crook shall give me aid,
> And guide me through the dreadful shade."

Just a word in conclusion to the unsaved. There is a thought in this text for you, The words "Though I walk" are full of meaning; they forcibly suggest the fact that we are going, that we are on the move, not standing, not sitting, but walking, travelling toward the end of our journey. We begin when we enter life to move toward eternity and never cease our onward march until the end is reached and death calls us to a halt. Day and night, whether in the broad or narrow way, on, on, onward we go—

> "What'er we do. Where'er we be
> We'er travelling to the grave."

Oh think before you farther go. Your days will soon be numbered. You are borne on time's most rapid wing. "Be ye also ready, for in such an hour as ye think not the Son of man cometh. Then will it be said to them who are ready, Come; but to them who are not, Depart.

MAN AND THE DAYSMAN.

By Rev. E. I. Badgley, B.D., LL.D.,

Professor of Metaphysics and Oriental Languages, Albert College.

"To the Unknown God."—Paul.
"Neither is there any Daysman betwixt us that might lay his hand upon us both."—Job.

THE nature of inanimate matter is determined by its properties, and upon these data is based its classification.

The vegetable world is divided into genera and subdivided into species upon certain differences and agreements that characterize this part of the material universe. Ascending higher, where we have not only life but also locomotion, the same principles are followed by students in this department of study. In this way man becomes classed anatomically with the higher orders of the ape family. To this we do not object; but when that classification presumes to venture beyond its legitimate sphere, and adopts and teaches a theory that makes man but the gradual evolution of some unknown and indefinite starting point, and will allow him finally to evolve into something which we nor they know not, we decidedly object; and we do so, we think, upon good and sufficient grounds.

It is plainly an open but most subtle attack upon the inspiration and authority of the Scriptures. It strikes at the foundation of man's spiritual hopes, and closes to him for ever the fountains of divine communion, at once his highest joy and greatest treasure. With one fell stroke, it annihilates and scorns that grand metaphysical truth intuitive in the mind of every human being, child or adult: effect implies cause, design implies a designer. It scatters fundamental truth to the four winds of heaven. It leaves the world, with its teeming millions, without any First Cause, and writes the creed of atheism upon the forehead of the universe.

For these and many other reasons, we object to that "science falsely so called," that robs man of his noblest attributes, and the universe of its first and highest Intelligence. We court a philosophy that leaves unshaken the foundations of the temple of truth, and bows before the authoritative declarations of man's most divine faculty—reason. We prefer plain Scripture to the multiplied contradictions of an incipient science.

Were a classification of the animal kingdom to be made upon the basis of a religious consciousness calculated from the religious manifestations, man is the only one that would find a place in such classification. This individualizes him as a distinct and separate creation, and not as the more perfect development of some lower organization. No development on evolution principles has yet been able to carry man from the purely animal into the higher realm of intelligence, and the yet higher sphere of conscience and the religious life. Like the noise of many waters blended into one grand harmony, the shout goes up from the universal race: "God hath made of one blood all nations of men to dwell on all the face of the earth."

A distinct creation does away with the absurdity of the mortal generating the immortal, the finite producing the infinite, nothing bringing into existence all things, imperfection begetting and perfecting in time the full-orbed attributes of an eternal God.

The original of the first chapter of Genesis and 27th verse, if accepted as written by an inspired penman, is all the proof we need ask that man has not, by any process of evolution, crossed the line that separates the intellectual from the non-intellectual world. "So God created man in His own image, after His own likeness; in the image of God made He him." The verb translated "created" in this verse, is used in the same form, and always with the same signification, about thirty-five times in the Hebrew Scriptures. In not a single instance is it applied to any act performed by man. Inspiration appears to give it a place peculiarly its own, and to imply that it would be an act unhallowed to use it in describing the operations of natural laws, or results brought about by human instrumentality.

Says a celebrated commentator on this passage: "This verb, as used here, means always 'to create,' and is applied only to a divine creation, the production of that which had no existence before. It is used for the creation of man and everything new which God created, whether in the kingdom of nature or of grace." But that organized clay, fresh from the hands of the Great Architect, is not yet man in the highest, noblest sense. The Divine has yet to impart His own nature, to breathe into man's nostrils the breath of life, and make him a living soul. And as the streams, if followed, carry us to their fountains, and the scattered rays that light up the globe point to the Sun as the dispenser of light and heat, so the shattered forces of man's moral constitution, and the infinite and immortal aspirations of that imparted life, declare with their invincible logic the everlasting rock whence he was hewn.

"Man is the image of God by virtue of his spiritual nature, of the breath of God by which the being formed from the dust of the earth became a living soul. This breath is the seal and pledge of our relation to God, of our God-like dignity; and man possessed a creaturely copy of the holiness and blessedness of the divine life. This concrete essense of the divine life was shattered by sin," and the whole history of the human race, through all the centuries of its existence, is a sad yet pleasing picture of man's seeking to recover the brightness of the divine glory. Reason, analogy, history—sacred and profane—all unite in declaring that man, instead of beginning his career far below his present position, began far above it, and that his evolution has been, and still is, a hard-fought struggle to gain the vantage ground from which he fell, striving to gain it, too, not wholly of himself, but by the aid of divine power.

We purpose, therefore, treating our subject under two divisions:—

I. MAN HAS A RELIGIOUS NATURE.

II. THAT NATURE HAS EVER BEEN LOOKING FOR A MEDIATOR, A DAYSMAN.

I. MAN HAS A RELIGIOUS NATURE.

For six thousand years the human race has been recording its history. Volume after volume has appeared, each with a different title, but marked with characteristics common to them all. Every passion has found expression, and left its imprint too legibly written to be misapprehended. Deeds of heroic physical daring, and tales of bloodshed and cruelty have left traces of having been enacted by those who have met upon the arena of conflict in the interest of their country's honour, or have given unbridled license to the baser passions, to satisfy their own cruel and selfish disposition. The heroic age, the age of chivalry, the periods of the political struggles of individuals and of nations, the gladiatorial contests between science and religion, have all found a chronicler to record their defeat or sing their pæan of victory. The early poems of Grecian and Roman mythology have given existence, life and personality to the various passions, appetites and desires of the human heart. Thus we have given expression to one side of our nature.

But our history has not all been written from this standpoint. Great moral conflicts, resulting in the noblest moral victories, have been waged against opposing powers and influences, and shewn that while man has a nature that in one sense connects him with a lower creation, there is in him a redeeming faculty that elevates him to a higher and nobler sphere. Into this higher life man alone of earthly inhabitants enters. He has taken a step that no inferior creature can imitate, because it lacks the nature that gives existence to this moral faculty. His is a long march from irresponsibility towards the Infinite and Eternal. It points out the path man should follow in order to perfect his development. It indicates that beyond and above his present attainments, and with this moral faculty still unchanged as to its fundamental characteristics, there is an ever-evolving future that will declare man's greatness, and mark his individuality among the innumerable occupants of earth.

We do not wonder that Germany's greatest thinker

could posit the Divine existence on the sole declaration of our moral nature. Responsibility means a throne of power somewhere, and a righteous administrator seated thereon. Linked by the invisible, yet omnipotent authority of conscience to the infinite God, man stands in a relation to absolute law that utterly refuses the perpetual fellowship and society of the irrational life around him. He intuitively feels that, standing in relation to a higher law, his higher nature subject to that law must have an existence bounded only by the eternity to which that law extends. By the free consent of God, moral law shapes His own divine character, and there is more than an intimation of our immortality and God-like origin in our relation to that same law as published to His creatures, and claiming the full consent and service of heart and soul. Our moral life is an unexplained and unexplainable factor in the history of our consciousness, if we have not to do with a future beyond the tomb.

Our moral nature is not the necessary outgrowth of our intelligence. Here is a gap in the evolution theory that can never be filled. The difficulties have been acknowledged and hypothetically accounted for; but hypotheses are not science. To-day, as ever, they prove its curse. No satisfactory account of its origin has been or can be given except on the admission of our relation to a personal Creator and futurity of existence. When the law of right has been violated, and we seek by a purely intellectual effort to calm the storm thus raised within our own bosom, conscience, as though speaking from the depths of its own eternity, scorns apology, refuses all recognition of the uprightness of the deed, and would fain wash its hands in innocency, and write its declaration of uncompromising war against the violation of the principles of eternal order, right and truth.

But man's moral life, connecting him thus intimately with God and immortality, is not the only phase of his many-sided nature. The moral consciousness can be understood only in the light of the religious consciousness upon which it always rests. As the centuries have rolled by, man's religious nature, as read in the temples he has erected, and the homage he has always and everywhere rendered to some being he believed divine, prove that he is of God, and that he shall return to the source whence he came. Altars and temples and all the paraphernalia of religious worship are found erected and associated everywhere. The nation or people, however rude, uncivilized, or degraded—with very few unimportant exceptions—has yet to be discovered that does not worship. So strong is this disposition, that men deify and worship each other. They believe the spirit of the immortal gods to have dwelt in those who figured most prominently in the world's history. Every nation has had its heroes, and those that have not been under the influence of Christianity have invariably run into hero worship. Christianity, too, clothed in the sacred vestments of the sanctuary, assuming priestly functions, and professedly acting under the authority of the divine word, has not unfrequently made use of this principle of man's nature to turn the adoration of the worshipper from the Creator to the creature, from God to man.

"In China, sixty thousand animals are yearly offered upon the altars of fifteen hundred and sixty temples dedicated to Confucius." As it is in China, so is it everywhere. The world is feeling after God, if haply it might find Him. This searching, and feeling after, and struggling for Him can be nothing less than proof that within man there is a nature that can rest and be satisfied only as it rests in God. Without God, it is like the imprisoned bird when the season has come for a flight to sunnier skies. It manifests a disposition that is explainable only by referring its uneasiness to a ground or fundamental principle that tells us the bird must have a climate suited to the demands of its nature, and that its Creator has given it an instinct that leads it to seek the proper surroundings. The sceptic might laugh when he observes the quiet satisfaction of the caged bird during the bright days of summer, if we spoke of the nature that finds a manifestation only when the autumn leaves declare that the bright days of sunshine are ended; but he has only to watch and wait to be convinced that what is affirmed is true.

So it is with the sceptic and the religious nature that we claim as man's peculiar heritage. The summer days of prosperity have a tendency to make him forgetful of his dependence for everything on a higher power. This prosperity, if uninterrupted, will restrain and, perhaps, for a period, completely silence the religious consciousness. It is then infidelity laughs at the folly of the humble Christian, and multiplies its converts to a cause that is built upon a foundation of sand. The followers of Mammon wickedly mock the true worshippers of Jehovah who, amid adversity, are led to adore God in sincerity and with humility of spirit. But wait! These same advocates of their own self-sufficiency will yet give evidence that the religious nature "is not dead, but sleepeth." The moments are rapidly approaching when the sceptic, as well as the believer, always speaks the truth, and humanity gives its surest, most correct expression. The sceptic's prosperity is turned into adversity. Health has given way to sickness. The treasures accumulated in the service of Mammon are gone. The forked lightning and the deep roar of the approaching thunder seem sent as death's messengers from the armory of an angry God. The tornado howls for its prey, and with a voice that whispers 'doomed,' tells him the door of mercy is for ever closed. The storm is upon him, and death is in the storm. The soul is stirred to its depths. Every power of his being is intensely active; and what is the result? Where before he boasted loudly of his own greatness, his utter helplessness tells him of his folly; and where in prosperity he read the clearest proofs of atheism, everything about and within him cries out in agony of spirit, "Let us pray." And he does pray, and to a God, too, not created by his own fears, or from a nature the product of his terrors; but the man has returned to his normal condition, and "his heart and his flesh crieth out for the living God."

Atheism is a lie to the heart's core. It is foreign to man's nature. It grows out of the wish that it might be true, and is the unnatural effort to break wholly free from the restraints which Theism would involve. A belief in the Invisible, the Unsearchable, the Unseen, has, like the pillar of cloud and of fire with the Israelites, followed the track of man's history by day and by night since the date of his expulsion from Eden until now. In war and in peace, in luxury and in famine, in rain and in drought, the burning victim and the smoking incense, the oracle, the Urim and the Thummim, the priest clad in sacerdotal robes, and the wizard and the witch, have been alike consulted to reveal the hidden mysteries of an omnipotent, omnipresent, and invisible power.

"Down from the far, far ages, from the infancy of the world and of the human race comes a voice from the heart of humanity. Its utterances in the past are recorded by the iron pen of history; it thunders in our very ears in the present; it speaks of God. And we are asked to believe that the great heart of humanity lies, has always lied."

O, Atheism, how blind thou art! and added to all thy wickedness wilt thou finally, with an impious hand attempt to erase the deeply engraven and indelible characters of Divinity and Immortality written upon the tablets of the human heart. If immortality pertains to the soul, must it be sent widowed and orphaned upon the pathless journeys of an unknown and untraversed eternity, with no Sun of Righteousness to warm it with His beams and reveal the source whence it drew its immortal breath? Must our intellectual life expire when we have but begun to tread the outer courts of the temple of knowledge and eternal truth, and have caught but the faintest idea of the glory of the inner sanctuary as it reflects the omnipotence and omniscience of the Infinite God? Must the numberless worlds studding the highway of immensity be unexplored and untravelled solitudes in the eternity to come? Can it be that blind, unintelligent Force has decked the heavens with grandeur, clothed them in robes of everlasting light, and beautified its throne with the diamond jewelry of the skies? Can their daily benedictions and their nightly vigils to earth's way-worn pilgrims be the silent and majestic mockery of the "original star dust" that sports as if in fiendish triumph with the highest aspirations of its last and noblest born? Must the sublime mysteries of Redemption, and the depths of divine love that gave us an Incarnate God be mere chimeras upon the historian's page or problems forever baffling every effort for their solution?

The universal heart of humanity cannot thus be mocked by the declarations of its own immortality and of its intimate relationship to God. A Being of justice and truth cannot thus trifle with our nature. Falsehood cannot underlie these religious manifestations. God has surely breathed into our spirits the breath of an immortal life. Humanity has within itself the prophecy of eternal truths, and their record has been written because they are true, and must be fulfilled.

Says Bulwer: "I cannot believe that earth is man's abiding place. It cannot be that our life is cast up by the ocean of eternity to float a moment upon its waves, and then sink into nothingness. Else why is it that the glorious aspirations which leap like angels from the temple of the human heart are forever wandering about unsatisfied? Why is it the rainbow and the clouds come over us with a beauty that is not of earth, and then pass off and leave us to muse upon their favored loveliness? Why is it that the stars who hold their festival around the midnight throne, are set above the grasp of our limited faculties, forever mocking us with their unapproachable glory? And, finally, why is it that bright forms of human beauty are presented to our view and then taken from us, leaving the thousand streams of our affections to flow back in Alpine torrents upon our hearts? We are born for a higher destiny than that of earth. There is a realm where the rainbow never fades, where the stars will be spread before us like islands that slumber on the ocean, and where the beings that pass before us like shadows will stay in our presence forever."

II. Man's Religious Nature has ever been looking for a Mediator, a Daysman.

Says Job: "For he is not a man, as I am, that I should answer him, and we should come together in judgment; neither is there any daysman betwixt us that might lay his hand upon us both." And again: "O that one might plead for a man with God, as a man pleadeth for his neighbour."

I never open the book of Job but with peculiar feelings. Believing it to be the earliest written of the books that compose the volume of revelation, and that the person whose history it records, was an earnest searcher after truth and God, I am always anxious to know his views and experience upon the great subjects that have since been explained in the clear light of the New Testament revelation. The poem relates the position and prosperity of Job; the sad disasters that befell him, and the visit of three friends, apparently to comfort him, but who, in reality, are a temptation and a snare. The visit of these men and their conversation give us additional information concerning the search after God and its results.

Says J. Baldwin Brown: "This book touches the depths—the depth of man, the depth of God. Its writer had the longest plummet-line which the men of olden time were able to drop into the abyss of the divine counsels. He gauged the mystery though he could not solve it; the key was not with him, though he could instruct us to look for it in the Daysman, who should explain and justify the dark and far-reaching methods of the fatherly discipline of God."

The affliction and adversity of Job have been made the subject of conversation between him and his three friends. If Job's life has been pure they are unable to account for these sad visitations. Seven days and as many nights of silent grief spent in sympathy with the sufferer, with mantles rent and dust upon their heads, have not revealed to them the solemn fact in religious experience, that whomsoever the Lord loveth he chasteneth, and scourgeth every son whom he receiveth. Alas! it is but the morning time of revelation, and this book contains the first faint streaks of twilight that brighten the oriental sky, and tell the world that the darkness of midnight is gone forever, and that the Sun of Righteousness is rising with healing in his wings.

Unable to bring any charge against Job which they can substantiate, they accuse him of private sin. We will hear what the speakers themselves have to say:

Job is the first to break the painful silence, and bitterly complains of his sad lot. Then Eliphaz the Temanite answered and said: "If we assay to commune with thee, wilt thou be grieved? But who can withhold himself from speaking? Behold, thou hast instructed many, and thou hast strengthened the weak hands. Thy words have upholden him that was falling, and thou hast strengthened the feeble knees. But now, it is come upon thee, and thou faintest; it toucheth thee, and thou art troubled. Is not this thy fear, thy confidence, thy hope, and the uprightness of thy ways? Remember, I pray thee, whoever perished, being innocent, or where were the righteous cut off? Even as I have seen, they that plough iniquity, and sow wickedness, reap the same. By the blast of God they perish, and by the breath of His nostrils are they consumed. Now, a thing was secretly brought to me, and mine ear received a little thereof. In thoughts from the visions of the night, when deep sleep falleth on men, fear came upon me, and trembling which made all my bones to shake. Then a spirit passed before my face; the hair of my flesh stood up; it stood still, but I could not discern the form thereof; an image was before mine eyes, there was silence, and I heard a voice, saying: 'Shall mortal man be more just than God? Shall a man be more pure than his maker? Behold, he put no trust in His servants; and His angels He charged with folly; how much less in them that dwell in houses of clay, whose foundation is in the dust?'"

His charge against Job is a weighty one, and the more so because of its being untrue. He gives some consolation in the same speech, when he says: "Happy is the man whom God correcteth, therefore, despise not thou the chastening of the Almighty." But he has more than hinted at Job's unrighteousness. He has charged him with ploughing iniquity and sowing wickedness, and now he must expect to reap the same. He accuses him of claiming a purity and holiness equal to that of God Himself.

Conscious of his integrity, and stung to the quick by this unwarrantable censure from one who enjoyed his confidence, Job replies: "To him that is afflicted, pity should be shown from his friend; but he forsaketh the fear of the Almighty." He stands up in vindication of his integrity. Did I say, "bring unto me or give a reward for me of your substance? Or, deliver me from the enemy's hand? Or, redeem me from the hand of the mighty? Teach me, and I will hold my tongue; and cause me to understand wherein I have erred. How forcible are right words, but what doth your arguing reprove?"

Bildad the Shuhite follows, and cruelly repeats the accusation of Eliphaz, and closes with an implied declaration of Job's guilt, and an encouragement to still hope in his sorrow: "Behold, God will not cast away a perfect man, neither will he help the evil doers: till he fill thy mouth with laughing, and thy lips with rejoicing."

"I know it so of a truth" replies Job, "but how should man be just with God? If he will contend with him, he cannot answer him one of a thousand. . . . For he is not a man as I am that I should answer Him, and we should come together in judgment. Neither is there any Daysman betwixt us that might lay his hand upon us both."

Job has reached the crisis in his effort to get to God, and argue his cause before Him. It is humanity struggling upon the bank of the river it cannot ford. It is a fearful moment. The march has been continued all along the track of human history, until the whole company is obliged to halt unable to proceed. The rapid current swollen of God's wrath and man's rebellion, defies every human effort. O that some person, both human and divine, but stood in the midst of the fearful stream, and with one hand upon man and the other upon God would thus bridge its awful depths, and bring the parties at disagreement into a relation by which the divine government should be upheld, and yet pardon granted and peace secured. "Neither is there any Daysman betwixt us that might lay his hand upon us both." It is the wail of an orphaned race. It is lost humanity struggling for life. "O that one might plead for a man with God, as a man pleadeth for his neighbour." It sounds the call for the oppressed and wearied sons of Adam to struggle for an entrance into their Father's house, and for a seat around that Father's board. Home, home, home to God, is the cry that breaks from every lip, and finds a response in every human heart. Job is here the world's pioneer, the people's representative.

Says Brown, before quoted: "I regard the cry for a mediator, with which the book of Job seems to me to be charged as one of the chief of those spiritual things in the Old Testament, which, be these difficulties what they may, make the Old Testament one book with the New. We do not find it simply in an isolated passage in this ancient drama of sorrow; it runs through the whole of it, and is, in some sort, its key. Eliphaz, Bildad, Zophar, the sages charged with the wisdom of the past, the young and brilliant Elihu, full, even to distention of the new wine of genius, and freighted with the eloquent wisdom of the present, offer themselves successively as God's expositors. But the sufferer will not hear them. His cry is for God, for the living God; and this is the real essence of the book. On this, as the spinal column, the whole form depends, for books may be vertebrate as well as men. The cry grows more earnest as the pitiless mongers of orthodox platitudes are successively silenced, and it is answered at length by the appearing of the Lord Himself. He came with lightning and tempest, and out of the whirlwind the awful challenge broke. But still He came. The cry was heard; the Daysman appeared; the passionate appeal of this agonized soul was not stifled but answered, and a prophecy of the incarnation was given to the world."

From the book of Job we turn to the heathen races. Humanity here meets us in every phase. The æsthetic Greek, the military Roman, the ancient metaphysical nations of Asia, the degraded Bushmen of Africa and Australia, and the aborgines of America, all present themselves as instructors upon this question. If humanity is an unit, the same testimony will be borne by all;

if not, we may look for creeds as various, and in as striking contrast as are the nations themselves. It is a solemn fact that all these various peoples have or had their altars and divinities. The history of each and of all bears testimony to the carefulness of humanity in matters of religion. Altars to the Unknown God are erected everywhere, and the world like ancient Athens is wholly given to idolatry. Temples of the most exquisite finish; statues of the gods so exactly planned and so delicately executed, as though formed and fashioned in the studio of heaven, and nature's wealth lavished in richest profusion in the imposing ceremonies at the altar, all declare how deeply inwrought in man's intellectual and moral constitution is the belief in a Divine personality, and his righteous claims upon the service and homage of the human heart.

How frequently do we hear lamentations concerning the heathen, not so much that they do not serve God, as that they worship idols. Better a thousand fold that they adore idols than nothing. It seems to me that one of the most encouraging thoughts that can fire the breast, and urge to action a mission society or missionary labourer, is the fact that those in whose interest they are engaged are already worshippers, and that all that is needed is to turn that religious nature in the right direction, and they are immediately won to the cause of Christ. How dark would be the prospect if they were like the beasts of the field, manifesting no religious consciousness whatever. This very idolatry is itself a pledge and proof of the unity of the race; that "God hath made of one blood, all nations of men to dwell on all the face of the earth." Converse with an intelligent idolater, and you will learn that he is not an idolater after all. He will inform you that his worship is not directed to the dumb idol, but to God through the idol as mediator. The Persian worshipper of the Sun considered its rays but the dim and feeble representatives of Him who dwelleth in light unapproachable. It is true, the great majority of heathens know no God beyond their idol, but we must remember there are ignorant heathens as well as ignorant christians, and just here our "charity can cover a multitude of sins."

Man, as shown under our former proposition, is always striving to get back to God, but the distance intervening is so great that he instinctively feels he must make an effort to have it filled, and hence idolatry. Mediation is an idea that we exercise instinctively. It is drawing between ourselves and danger a third party. The little child gives an illustration of it, when it turns from the reproof of one parent for sympathy and help from the other. The attorney pleading for the prisoner at the bar, is a mediator between him and the stern sentence of the law, and how confidently does the accused commit his cause to his advocate's skill and care. How natural, then, for man to seek such help in spiritual things. There is something divinely human in the thought that Christ, our great High Priest, hath ascended on high, where "He ever liveth to make intercession for us." "This search for God, and for one to stand between God and man, which is consistent with religious being and feeling, is the knocking at every gate and passage-way, and the trying of every door leading to the halls of truth. It is the soul of man prying into every crevice where a ray of light appears. It is a peering into every nook and corner which is thought to hold invaluable treasures. It is a shout to the keeper to deliver up the treasures or let the seeker in."

"O wretched man that I am, who shall deliver me from the body of this death?" is the cry that goes up from crushed and bleeding hearts everywhere. Plato, the philosophical John the Baptist of Christianity said: "We must wait patiently until some one, either a God or some inspired man, teach us our moral and religious duties, and, as Pallas in Homer did to Diomede, remove the darkness from our eyes." The heathen Stoic, Seneca, realizing in his own experience how terribly sin had taken hold of the human heart, and seeing how fearfully it had wrought ruin in society, utters his plaintive cry for help: "No man is able to clear himself, let some one give him a hand, let some one lead him out." Had Christ been then presented to him, this noble Roman might not have popularized suicide as the most convenient and praiseworthy way to end a life of wretchedness. Everywhere the agonized spirit of humanity is waiting, watching, and weeping for the coming of the Deliverer, and knocking at the door of life and demanding an answer to its call. "O that I knew where I might find Him," is the prayer that forms the web and woof of sixty centuries of earthly sorrow as men have reaped the terrible harvest

> "Of man's first disobedience, and the fruit
> Of that forbidden tree."

When any substance has been repeatedly tried under every test that chemical analysis or experiment can subject it to, and always gives the same results, scientists very justly give it a classification, and legitimately formulate their theories concerning it. We claim for ourselves the same right in the province of theology. No larger collection of facts under so diversified circumstances, no wider range of experience, no more uniform results upon any question can be collected and presented than are recorded in the six thousand years of man's history, as written upon the temples and altars, the monuments and obelisks he has erected, and as woven into the poetry and prose of the mythic, the barbarous, and the enlightened ages of literature, by every people of every color and of every clime. These facts are our sufficient vindication. With these arranged for our defence, we fear not the "push and pull" of a Tyndall, the "protoplosm" of a Huxley, or the "evolution" of a Darwin to banish the religious element from the race, or do away with the belief of a living, personal God. We simply ask, that Huxley and those of kindred views practise his own manly and philosophical sentiment that "Logical consequences are the scare-crows of fools and the beacons of wise men."

Everywhere we find the world looking and waiting for the Deliverer. The Magi coming from the distant East to Jerusalem are humanity's deputation seeking "the desire of the nations." Balaam, a heathen soothsayer, had, fifteen centuries earlier, declared his coming, and pointed to him as the Star that should arise out of Jacob. Virgil, a Roman poet, forty years before the Christian era, utters with a sublimity almost equal to that of the Hebrew prophet, the approaching birth of a Virgin's son who should introduce a reign of peace and bring back the innocence and happiness of the golden age. The modern Hindoo asks to-day, "When will the Helper come? when will the Deliverer appear?" History declares that since before the days of Confucius, the Chinese have been expecting a Mediator. "We expect this divine man" say they, "and he is to come after three thousand years. The people long for his coming as the dry grass longs for the clouds and the rainbow."

Historical illustrations from the Peruvians, the Mexicans, and the Aborigines from our own locality might be indefinitely multiplied, but we forbear.

Can we believe that man is thus made the sport of the Almighty, deluded by vain phantoms and imaginations? I cannot believe that God will thus deal with the human spirit, deceiving it with these immortal aspirations only to blast its fondest, most natural, most cherished hopes forever. Everywhere in sacred and profane history, the world is stretching out its hands for God.. The prophecy of Isaiah is the prophecy of humanity: "Behold a king shall reign in righteousness, and princes shall rule in judgment, and a *MAN* shall be as an hiding-place from the wind and a covert from the tempest; as rivers of water in a dry place, as the shadow of a great rock in a weary land."

Is Christ "the one that should come, or look we for another?" We believe the Daysman of the Gospels is the Deliverer promised in Eden, predicted by the prophets, typified in the temple service, and expected by the nations; and "For this cause I bow my knees unto the Father of our Lord Jesus Christ, of whom the whole family in heaven and earth is named, that he would grant you, according to the riches of his glory, to be strengthened with might by his Spirit in the inner man; that Christ may dwell in your hearts by faith: that ye, being rooted and grounded in love, may be able to comprehend with all saints what is the breadth, and length, and depth, and height; and to know the love of Christ, which passeth knowledge, that ye might be filled with all the fulness of God."

Now unto Him that is able to do exceeding abundantly above all that we ask or think, according to the power that worketh in us, unto Him be glory in the Church by Christ Jesus throughout all ages, world without end. Amen.

THE PRAISES OF THE LORD.

By Rev. James Gardiner, P.E.,

Of the Erie District.

Preached at the Dedication of the M. E. Church, Trenton, Ont.

1. Praise ye the Lord. Praise ye the name of the Lord; praise Him O ye servants of the Lord. 2. Ye that stand in the house of the Lord, in the courts of the house of God, 3. Praise the Lord; for the Lord is good; sing praises unto His name; for it is pleasant. 4. For the Lord hath chosen Jacob unto himself, and Israel for his peculiar treasure. 5. For I know that the Lord is great, and that our Lord is above all gods. —Ps. cxxxv. 1-5.

THINGS are pleasant which are not good, and good things are not always pleasant; but it is good, pleasant, and acceptable, to praise Almighty God. It is decent, comely, and proper, that every intelligent creature should praise the name of the Lord. Let everything that hath breath—natural, spiritual, or eternal life—engage in this blessed exercise: because of Jehovah's mercy, essence, wondrous works, profundity of counsel and sublimity of glory. The Scriptures are interspersed with praises.

To stimulate *us*, we may consider or recall *Israel* in captivity at Babylon, carried from the place of her nativity in a strange land; stripped of every comfort, weeping, harps unstrung; restless and unhappy when remembering Zion. They were as travellers lost, exiles in reproach and sorrow. Sick without the hope of healing. Wrecked mariners, yet preserved. What vast and oppressive changes, since a flourishing people assembled in their own land. What ecstacy when God resided among them, and dwelt in the temple at Jerusalem. The rulers and the people were called to join in sacred festivities; the honored memorials of wonders wrought by Omnipotence, as at the Passover or Pentecost.

So we to-day can unite with music and speech, having our hearts attuned to hallowed lays, to celebrate the praises of the Lord, who descended from heaven to deliver our souls, and now appears in His Church to bless her. As wants prompt men to pray, a revealed view of gracious ability, which declares Jesus able and willing to save; leads us to prepare our hearts as a habitation for the God of Jacob. Then we may join to celebrate a greater triumph, a spiritual salvation, an eternal redemption, in "the sanctuary."

How delightful when that people restored, again assemble to dedicate the second Temple. The great joy of that event was intensified by offering *twelve* goats for a sin offering *for all Israel*, "one for each tribe, a decisive proof that the returned children of the captivity regarded themselves as the representatives of all Israel." He who rescued the seed of Abraham so often, designs that we may be delivered from all our ghostly enemies, and made like Him, by receiving His grace to purify the heart. This is the work of His power, by the laws of redemption, to reproduce "the lost image," and cleanse the soul from corruption. The Creator makes earth verdant and fruitful to yield us nutriment for life; He also provides for the spirit's wants. In the intellectual and moral world "*He is King*" Supreme. By greatness that removes obstacles, souls are saved, and He moves upon the minds of men. It is therefore fitting that angels, elders and worshippers, should join to praise the name of the Lord, who is "worthy to receive glory, and honour and power." The Church of God is a necessity—and her edifices are loved and honoured. Outward observances are valuable even when no spiritual benefit results. Piety and virtue are the strength and glory of a nation, or a people. In maintaining and diffusing revealed religion—always the basis of Jewish prosperity, as it is of all true greatness and excellence—God gives prominence to chosen agents.

By direction Moses built a *tabernacle* for the Divine glory. Here the Shechinah appeared and rested in Shiloh. At the capture of the ark the glory departed. When recovered, David erected a *tent* on Mount Zion, with religious exultation. The Temple of which God was artificer followed. The nation in her best days united her prosperity, wealth and art to construct it. Solomon, king and priest, dedicated to God, this gorgeous, magnificent structure, for sacred uses as an example; but not for a select people. Its design is stated—"A house of prayer for *all* people."

At this opening by royalty, embellished with piety, the symbol of the presence of the personal Jehovah filled the house, assuring *all* that HE had chosen it, to dwell there. This occurred about five hundred years after the Exodus, and stood about five hundred years the glory of Jerusalem—the joy of the whole earth. Why was this costly, glorious temple, built by God's direction with such singular care and skill, destroyed? Was it the penalty for guilt, a certain consequence, the result of the sin of backsliding and transgression? If so, all men should learn "that true life consists in the discharge of duty from religious motives." Let no

T

man substitute a religious philosopher for a spiritual believer.

After the captivity of seventy years in Babylon, the exiles returned in colonies by appointment. Zerubbabel, Nehemiah, and Ezra were chief leaders. The first colony set up the "great altar," where adoring thousands often worshipped in Solomon's temple. Jehovah accepts their sacrifices, and renews His covenant with them. In religious order thus restored, they beheld the germ of the future nation and Church. In two years they laid the foundation of the second temple, and commenced to build. "The servants of the God of heaven and earth," by His direction, the teaching of the prophets, the labour of the elders, and the favour of the kings, united to erect the latter house. How wonderful that Cyrus should allow the captives to return to Jerusalem, and rebuild their city and temple; but he also sent them laden with good things, and under a most favourable decree. It provided that the expenses of the edifice should be paid from the royal treasury; but this was not done. The people contributed liberally of their own substance. "The riches and labour of the Gentiles did much, a type of their calling." Samaritan opposition, and other obstructions that delayed the work for twenty years were all overcome, and the faithful triumphed in complete success in the reign of Darius—twenty-one years from the decree of Cyrus, and the commencement of the building (B. C. 515).

Jacob's Bethel, Moses' Tabernacle, and Solomon's Temple, had each accomplished its design. The predicted "glory of this latter house," led Israel, priests, levites, singers and people to dedicate it with delight. The worshippers "purified together as one man in pious acts agree" to perpetuate devotion therein.

Although the Ark, the Mercy-seat, the tables of the law, the pot of manna, holy fire, Urim and Thummim, and the Shechinah, were all lost, never to adorn this temple, they resumed Divine worship, as revealed after the ordinance of David, and kept the Passover, observing the seven days of the unleavened bread.

The wisest and richest king, in a time of profound peace and greatest opulence, built the former temple. This one is by the returned captives now released, in the face of the most formidable, and desperate opposition. "They had to deal, not with malignant adversaries, but with the just authorities of a settled government."

The events by which God distinguishes His Church from the rest of the world, in leading men to serve, love and praise the Lord, recalls the happiness of earlier days when joyful worshippers came thrice in the year, to appear before God in Zion. Such celebrities "never leave God's work undone for want of a place in which to do it." Long encouraged, waiting in faith, they are now animated by the fulfilment of the promise, "I am returned unto Zion, and will dwell in the midst of Jerusalem: Behold I will save my people from the east country, and from the west, and I will bring them, and they shall dwell with me." Such successes, as fulfilment of prophecy and promise enable saints to sing:—

> "Happy is he that hath the God of Jacob for his help:
> Whose hope is in Jehovah his God."

The inspiration of the text, with its poet author, in those surroundings, furnishes this thrilling fervent exhortation to praise God in His temple. Other inspired odes crowd the memory and ask for utterance: "Lord I have loved the habitation of thy house. One thing have I desired of the Lord, that will I seek after, that I may dwell in the house of the Lord all the days of my life." "Praise ye the Lord." It is right as an act of devotion by which we confess and admire, in a becoming manner, His attributes—acknowledge His perfections, works and benefits. For His glorious acts of every kind, that regard us or others, and for His excellencies, let Him be praised: "His works praise Him." It is agreeable: "Praise is comely for the upright." Let no creature offend the Maker with faint praise. "Praise Him, all ye the seed of Jacob; and of Israel." "All the people"—as did Noah, Abraham, Moses, David, Daniel, the Apostles and disciples—are to praise Him. This reasonable service is due, because it is written: whoso offereth praise glorifieth Me. Men should "praise the Lord with singing. So will we sing and praise Thy power." "Let us offer the sacrifice of praise continually, that is the fruit of our lips. I will praise the Lord at all times. My mouth shall speak of thy praise all the day long." Thus ancient worshippers expressed their estimation of God the Lord.

This grandest theme gives greatest pleasure to God's servants in "the courts of the house of our God." He comes to us with rich sufficient grace: let us meet Him with ardent praise. He reveals the glorious Gospel; let us prize its worth, by attending to it, by accepting its gracious provisions. In it we may learn the value of souls, their need of grace, the blessedness of religion and the misery of being without it. For this sacred treasure, offered to all, given to believers, bestowed freely, renewing and saving the soul; let us offer grateful praise. Hear the saints of olden times —Bless the Lord, O my soul: and all that is within me bless His holy name. O Lord I will praise Thee.

Praise the Lord, proclaim his name. How genuine. Salvation prepared and given by the divine favour, designed to make us godly, wise and holy; imparting peace, love and power over sin; cancelling guilt, freeing from condemnation; reconciling us to God, and fitting us for heaven; demands a loving heart, an open mouth, and a liberal hand to show forth the praises of the Saviour and Lord. A plentiful effusion of saving grace, to convert, purify and establish the soul in perfect love, makes a holy life easy and delightful. It is proper to set forth our interest in so good a God, and thereby incite others to serve so honourable a Master. This is a worthy life-work: "As long as I live, I will praise thee." God always renews the exercise of mercy under the warm and genial act of praise, in which all creation unites. Praise God for his electing love, declared in the text: the Lord hath chosen Jacob unto himself, and Israel for his peculiar treasure. It is also written: "The Lord had a delight in thy fathers, and He chose their seed after them"—"I know whom I have chosen"—"out of the world"—chosen you to salvation through sanctification of the Spirit and belief of the truth." What blessedness in this new relation: "When a man's ways please the Lord, He maketh even his enemies to be at peace with him." How disinterested the choice on God's part! His glory and happiness perfect—goodness abused, justice injured, holiness insulted. Man is ruined by sin. Going to the grave, the pit, doomed to it. God in Christ interposed, deciding without passion, interest or prejudice; the verdict is right. Jesus took our nature, obeyed the law—died for us, ransoming us by His mercy and merit—His own precious blood, life and intercession, paying the ransom price. Let us accept such grace, with purest, highest, perpetual praise. This declared electing love is sincere: "As my father loved me." It is ancient, constant and honourable—a heritage, a memorial of glory and power. "Enter into his gates with thanksgiving, and into his courts with praise." On this important theme the saintly John Fletcher says: "In the smiling plains of primitive Christianity, you have God's election without Calvin's reprobation. Here Christ chooses the Jews without neglecting the Gentiles, and elects Peter, James, and John to the enjoyment of peculiar privileges, without reprobating Matthew, Thomas and Simon. Here nobody is damned for not doing impossibilities, or for doing what he could not possibly help. Here all that are saved enjoy rewards through the merits of Christ, according to the degrees of evangelical obedience which the Lord enables, not forces, them to perform. Here free wrath never appeared. Our damnation is of ourselves when 'we neglect so great salvation' by obstinately refusing to 'work it out with fear and trembling.'" But this is not all: here free grace does not rejoice over stocks, but over men who gladly confess that their salvation is all of God, who, for Christ's sake, rectifies their free agency, helps their infirmities, and "works in them to will and to do His good pleasure." Elect Christians flourish in the courts of our God: They shall still bring forth fruit in old age. In Luke ii. 36, there is a refreshing example recorded: "One Anna, a prophetess, of a great age," (perhaps 125 years) "who departed not from the temple, but served God night and day, and gave thanks likewise unto the Lord." This elect lady, in consort with the venerable Simeon, praising God for the incarnate Saviour, was a fitting companion in holy exercises. "Blessed is the man that heareth me, watching daily at my gates." To worship with elevated motives in this dispensation, we must honour God by public praise, in the assembly of the saints. In such services where men "hear the word of God and keep it," communion delights the soul, and gives it the earnest of endless felicity; as the disciple who exclaimed "My Lord and my God."

> "Salvation to Thy Name
> Eternal God, and co-eternal Lamb!!
> In power, in glory, and in essence, One!"

"Praise the Lord; for the Lord is good." The sentiment of infinite goodness is clearly proven, being repeated in many forms, but not exhausted in Scripture. Divine goodness is love to all in action. Men, though always slow to learn "the Lord is good to all," may see it in the cheering promises of the Messiah's coming—as the Desire of all nations—to honour the Second Temple with his personal presence. That act more than typifies, that the glorious spiritual temple, under the guidance of our living Head "shall stand forth on the heavenly Zion, an eternal monument of the grace of God bestowed on sinful man." Frequent and plain allusions to the work and mediation of the incarnate Son of God, and the glory of the Gospel Church are good. In descriptions of her beauty, stability, perpetuity and safety, there are forces to enliven devotion and illume the mind. The great doctrines of grace are exhibited in her trials, deliverances, and triumphs. To which may be added the rich profound lessons of experience to quicken the heart, and increase our faith, in agreement with the teachings of the highest and nobles purposes. The wonderful alchemy of the grace of our good God changes tribulations into triumphs. Inspiration affords glowing and exact delineations of Jesus as the Christ of God, and of the momentous affairs of His gracious kingdom. The Psalms especially, yield a literary and spiritual Eden, in which an old author declares "was every tree that was pleasant to the sight or good for food, and in the midst thereof the tree of life." These sublime and sacred poems direct our hearts to David's Lord, the King of Zion descending from His glory—doing and suffering—then returning in His ascension to His palace to celebrate the victory. In the bright mirror of Scripture truth, the gift of our good Lord, we behold the glory of the person of the Only-begotten of the Father—His royalty and priesthood. By this view we are drawn to the Saviour, in the affections of the soul, the endearments of communion, and the purposes of life. As the decree of Cyrus, the workmen from Phœnicia, the people and High Priest, co-operated to bring cedars from Lebanon, and stones from afar, to erect a temple at Jerusalem: so the Lord Jesus engages, by Gospel agencies, to gather a multitude innumerable from the Gentiles—saved by His grace—to build up a spiritual house. He, by a sacrificial death, secures salvation for men who die unto sin, live by faith, and follow Him. The truth of God is a power that will press to destruction His enemies, as surely as it saves those who trust in Him. Herein is furnished a grand summary of revealed religion, doctrinal, practical and experimental, with its aggressive designs and capabilities. His all-sufficiency—as a boundless ocean—meets no want which he cannot supply. He proffers to believers present mercy, future grace, and eternal glory. The Gospel brings peace everywhere, and prosperity in every thing. A heart rich in love is happy, and may have eternal life, in the pleasant service of the good Lord. "The Lord is great; our Lord is above all gods." He who reigns in heaven's imperial palace—His throne the cherubim, His dominion the universe—reveals Himself, allows us to know Him. The great God who dried up the waters of Jordan as He did the Red Sea—"That all the people of the earth might know the hand of the Lord, that it is mighty"—declares that He will indeed dwell on the earth. "What God doeth shall be forever." He says, "there I will meet with the children of Israel, and they shall be sanctified by my glory"—at the tabernacle. The Incarnate, God manifest in the flesh, said, "whoso hath seen Me hath seen the Father." He dwells in believers and in His Church by His Spirit. He sends the Comforter that He may abide with us forever, even the Spirit of Truth. He dwelleth with you and shall be in you. The whole Trinity proclaims, "we will make our abode with him." This is true blessedness. He shall reign in universal dominion—the knowledge of God shall cover the earth. By displays of great grace and power, the Saviour paid the redemption price for a lost world, and exhibited the grand scheme of human salvation, at Calvary, Olivet, and Jerusalem. With majesty unparalleled, He comes not to observe or inspect, but to dwell with men. In infinite dignity, almighty merit and unbounded compassion, He dispenses the greatest blessing—a full, and free, and present salvation. It delivers from danger, guilt and misery—regenerates, sanctifies and glorifies body and soul. It is pleasant to rehearse His works of mercy, grace and judgment—in Egypt, the wilderness, Canaan: Athens, Corinth, Patmos, Asia, Europe, America. They unite to teach the love of His heart, the power of His arm, the perfections of His atonement, the prevalance of Christ's intercession, and above all, the excellence of His own eternal character. "O Lord my God, Thou art very great." By His presence at Jerusalem on the day of Pentecost, the highest civilization of the whole world is required to pay a tribute at the altar of piety. "The Lord is king, and

He shall reign forever. Praise ye the Lord, God of gods, Lord of lords, the God of heaven, the God of Jacob—even thy God O Zion."

The great king "our Lord" is a Rock, a Sun and Shield; His rule is equitable, pure and holy. He provides for His subjects, as a Father's gift, every good grace, glory, light, life, salvation. "The Lord taketh pleasure in His people," instructs them by His words, heals, protects, and keeps in safety, giving angels charge over them, He lays up an inheritance of glory, honour, immortality, eternal life, and will come to receive His own and welcome them to the mansions prepared for their home. By His operation in the original production of the materials, "all the primitive genera of things receive their forms, qualities and laws." The globe, planets, plants, animals and intelligent and spiritual beings, lead us to conceive the most awful ideas of His creative ability. "The voice of the Lord is full of majesty. In His temple doth every one speak of His glory." The eternity of God without beginning, end, or succession, and the glorious unity of the God-head in the Trinity of persons, with self-existing attributes in relation to the universe and to the Church, entitle Him to perfect praise. All things, past, present, and future are known by the Lord. "To Him all truths are but one idea, all places but one point, and all times but one moment." The glory of the incorruptible God, who is over all, blessed forever, exhibits in the Gospel kingdom a gracious indication of His triumphant reign over the Church, throughout all generations. The risen Saviour, our Lord, having all power in heaven and in earth, is worthy of all praise. Let His name and praise be heard from all the servants of the Lord, who stand in the house of the Lord. Let us pay our vows, present our offerings, and celebrate His praise with the voice of gladness, and the spirit of thanksgiving " in the courts of the house of our God."

Let all who know His name, worship and glorify with praise the Almighty. That men may learn to know His goodness, greatness, and love. " Praise ye the Lord," who can justify the penitent believer, the Sacrificer, Mediator, and Saviour of souls, the Deliverer, Comforter, and Keeper of His own, the Upholder of His saints, and the builder of His Church, the satisfying Portion of His people. Praise the Lord who will raise all the dead, and judge the whole world.

"Then shall He sit upon the throne of His glory: and before Him shall be gathered all nations." " O that men would praise the Lord." *Amen.*

SALVATION BY GRACE.

By Rev. S. G. Stone, D.D.,
Editor of the Canada Christian Advocate.

"Not by works of righteousness which we have done, but according to His mercy He saved us, by the washing of regeneration and renewing of the Holy Ghost."—Titus iii. 5.

THE Gospel of the grace of God is a blessed revelation of His method of salvation for a lost and ruined world. It describes a finished atonement for the sins of all men, the benefits of which it offers to all who will receive it on the simple condition of repentance toward God and faith in our Lord Jesus Christ. The law was called the ministration of death, not because it was not founded in love, "for love is the fulfilling of the law," but because it declared principles of eternal righteousness which man had violated, and made no provision for his deliverance from the penalties which his rebellion had brought upon him. It demanded love but could not produce it; it presented rules for a condition of being in vital harmony with God; but with which mankind dead in trespasses and sins could not comply. The Gospel is the ministration of life because it reveals Jesus Christ, the Mediator between God and man, as having "died the just for the unjust to bring us to God," He having borne our sins in His own body on the tree, and purchased to Himself the right to offer pardon, life, and salvation to man.

> Our sins on Christ were laid,
> He bore the mighty load;
> Our ransom price was fully paid,
> In groans, and tears, and blood.

The originating cause of our salvation, as set forth in the text, is the Mercy of God. He saw man, whom He had created in His own image, ruined by sin and helpless, and hopeless in its bondage; and in the fulness of time manifested that wondrous system of redemption, the advent of which was hailed by angel song as the harbinger of universal brotherhood among men, and the restoration of unity between God and His rebellious offspring.

The interposition of Divine mercy in the employment of supernatural power for the recovery of humanity, presupposes man's inability to save himself, and upon this fact the whole economy of grace is based.

For four thousand years the world groaned beneath its weight of guilt and corruption, but had found no deliverance. Philosophers and sages, from time to time, propounded systems for the enfranchisement of the race, but being founded upon the assumption of recuperative power in the moral qualities of the human heart, they failed. They turned upon the vices of men the deepest wells of cleansing which they could fathom, but the corruption became deeper, and the darkness of the moral understanding more profound. The arts and sciences flourished, but instead of elevating society to a higher place of moral purity, only refined its vices and multiplied its oppressions. So completely had the world's struggles ended in defeat, and so completely does truth seem to have perished, that the cultured governor of Judea curls his lip in scorn at the mere intimation that it had any place in the thoughts or convictions of his age, and so entirely had men forgotten

God, that the Saviour contemplating their wickedness and spiritual ignorance in the very land which had trembled at Jehovah's presence, cries out in the agony of his soul, "O righteous Father, the world hath not known Thee." The language of the Apostle Paul in the third chapter of Romans, quoted from the Psalms, and applied to his own generation as descriptive of the moral condition of all unbelievers, both Jew and Gentile, is a portraiture of the unregenerate heart in all ages. "Dead in trespasses and sins," is his description of the world. Upon such a condition of moral apostacy, the holiness of God could look with abhorrence only. Unjustified rebellion can claim no rights from the sovereign it has defied. Corruption is and must always be offensive to purity. Sin in its very nature is enmity to God, and every heart which it pollutes is infected with its hatred. It will not be denied that the moral agencies of the present times have no inconsiderable influence upon the manners and consciences of unbelievers, but the same enmity—though it may be more temperate—must ever dwell where sin is. It will also be admitted, that among those making no profession of experimental godliness, there are many who possess social qualities which command admiration, and endear them to all who know them, but like the young man whose social virtues won the special approbation of Christ, there is among them no exception to such a measure of divergence from submission to the Divine Government, as betrays a willingness to sacrifice their Lord and all promise of the life to come, rather than yield to His terms of acceptance. And does not a disposition to enter heaven by some other way than by the door—repentance toward God and faith in the Lord Jesus Christ—a disposition which, if it had the power, would rob God of His sovereignty, and change the fundamental laws of His moral government—sufficiently demonstrate their enmity to His rule.

If the portraiture which both sacred and profane history give of the moral aspect of human society, without God and Christ, were the result of indifference to truth and righteousness, it would be a sufficiently deplorable aspect, but mankind has not been indifferent. In all ages, and among all nations and tribes of men, some form of religion has proven the struggle against the bondage of sin. The light of God's spirit, which has never been completely extinguished, has given to all men, even the most barbarous, some perception of the difference between good and evil, and has borne sufficient testimony against sin to awaken a consciousness of guilt; for deliverance from which all men have had some remedy, but none have proved effective. "The whole creation continued to groan and travail together in pain." The moral law written upon the heart and conscience demands unqualified obedience, and once violated cannot, though subsequent submission were rendered, relinquish its claims. Hence, admitting the law to be obligatory, and at the same time perfect, one sin unatoned for must be followed by condemnation. But this is not all. The stream cannot rise above, and must be of the nature of the fountain, therefore the corrupt heart can only produce sin. The testimony of Scripture, and the experience of all men, if confessed, is that "the carnal mind is enmity toward God, is not subject to the law of God, neither, indeed, can be." If then there be none who can truthfully say they "have not sinned," and if there be no man who can say "he hath no sin," how can deliverance come by the merit of human works? If a perfect obedience only can meet the demands of the Divine law, there can be no reasonable hope of salvation by works, to one who has not lived without sin. Moreover, it is not sufficient that he hath done no wrong. There are positive as well as negative duties imposed by the law. If its condemnation rest upon the man who has done what it commanded him not to do, equal condemnation follows the neglect of the positive duties it enjoins. Upon this point the concluding verses of the twenty-fifth chapter of the Gospel by Matthew are sufficiently clear, and furthermore it is distinctly affirmed that final condemnation follows a refusal or neglect of the gracious overtures of the Saviour. Hence, whether we consider the prohibitions or requirements of the law, every mouth is stopped. "For all have sinned and come short of the glory of God." Therefore it is added, " By the deeds of the law shall no flesh be justified in His sight." Surveying the helplessness of humanity in its depravity and slavery, and the rigorous demands of eternal righteousness, the Apostle uttered the despairing wail of Jew and Gentile, when he cried out, as though oppressed by an eternity of anguish, "Oh, wretched man that I am, who shall deliver me from the body of this death?" Thanks be to the infinite mercy of God, He was able to send back over all the misery, despair and death of a world in condemnation, an answer of hope: I thank God through Jesus Christ our Lord.

What man could not accomplish for himself the mercy of God thus provided for him. If infinite holiness could not make allowance for sin, infinite love could and did compassionate the sinner. If infinite justice must impartially administer law, not enacted by the will of Omnipotence, simply because it was His will, but declarative of eternal principles of righteousness, and if a perfectly just law as such can make no provision for the pardon of sin, infinite love can and does pity the culprit convicted and condemned, and therefore, in the fulfilment of His eternal purpose of mercy, God's love found a ransom in His own Son, who loved us and gave Himself for us. Here is the fountain head from which spring the glorious provisions of the Gospel. " God so loved the world that he gave His only begotten Son that whosoever believeth in Him might not perish, but have everlasting life." He who in the beginning became our surety offered Himself without spot or blemish as an atonement for our sins. He became our ransom, and laid down His life for us. He took the handwriting which was against us and nailed it to the tree upon which He paid our debt to the uttermost farthing. We confess the mystery involved in the sacrifice of the innocent for the guilty; we bow with profound reverence over this mysterious abyss of love which angel eyes cannot fathom; but while we do this we rejoice in the glorious assurance that He hath purchased unto Himself as an inheritance our fallen race, and that He hath the prerogative to give unto all who believe in His name " power to become the sons of God," How vast is such mercy as this; vainly we traverse human history for its parallel. The best that humanity can do is to sacrifice itself on the altar of friendship; but God commendeth His love towards us in that while we were yet *sinners* Christ died for us. In vain we attempt to explore the illimitable resources of such mercy, but on, beyond all bounds, which ever way we turn our flight, it beams in such effulgence as passeth knowledge. *It is the glory of God.* Let us stand beneath the cross upon which its Offering hangs a bleeding sacrifice for the sins of the world, and while the heavens grow black in astonishment and the earth burst its trembling bosom as He breaks His heart for men who mock His sufferings and stain His thirsty lips with gall, let us realize that He has power to come down from the cross but does not; that He has authority to command the attendance of more than twelve legions of angels to His defence, but does not employ it; that He has power with a breath to sweep away the whole race of murderers and to create anew the world and inhabitants for it, yet, instead, His unfailing mercy holds Him to the cross, and with His expiring groan He prays for His enemies; and then, if we can, let us tell how much He loved. If human hearts are not subdued, if they open not wide to admit Him when contemplating Him in the supreme hour of His agony and yet of His divinest glory, if a sympathy for human need which bore Him on through poverty and desertion, insult and suffering, and finally culminated in such a violent death, and gave Him an experience which brings Him into companionship with all human suffering, and assures every troubled soul that He can and will deliver or sustain, win Him not the allegiance of the heart, then are its fountains sealed to all good and all hope; and yet all this is "according to His mercy." "According to His mercy." How we dishonour the ever blessed God when we imagine Him to take pleasure in human suffering or to be so indisposed to pardon that it is only by an agony of pleading that we can move His heart to tenderness. It is only sin that God hates; toward the sinner He is ever moved with compassion. It is not because Christ came that the Father loves us, but because He loved us He gave His son. Do we forget that love is His essence?—that love dwells in Him, not as a passion, but as a pure and holy principle; that it baptizes all His attributes, and determines all His purposes. It brings Him near to every troubled soul with His omnipotent helpfulness, and no wail of suffering hath ever risen from the lips of man, no tears of anguish have ever fallen from human eyes, no sigh of grief hath ever heaved the human breast, that touched not the Divine heart. If we would know the Fatherhood of God we must study the life of Christ, who manifested Him in the flesh, and, as we behold His compassion on the fainting multitudes whom the disciples would have sent away fasting, His tears as He stood by the grave of Lazarus with the bereaved orphan sisters, and His sympathy for the distressed and sorrowing who were the subjects of His merciful ministrations, and then follow on until on the Mount of Ascension we hear Him breathe His benediction upon a world that had denied Him shelter in His birth, and with fiendish malice had pursued Him to the death, and had done its best and worst to curse even His memory; let us learn that His tender mercies are over all His works, and that from His feet no broken and contrite heart will ever be turned away. It would be a great error to suppose that the ministry and sacrifice of Christ marked an epoch in the operations of God's love, or that it exhausted its fulness so that the fountain can no longer flow as freely and as graciously. Let us remember that Christ is the Lamb slain from the foundation of the world, that throughout all the ages of darkness and apostacy which intervened between Eden and Calvary, the purposes of Divine love never faltered, and that now at the right hand of the Father He is to every penitent and believing sinner the Lamb newly slain. The life and sufferings of Christ were remarkable manifestations of the Divine love and mercy, but remarkable only as manifestations. He saved us "*According to* His mercy," which is ever the same, hence the love of Calvary knew no depth of sympathy, no forgivingness, no forbearance, no pity which does not now dwell in the heart of our blessed Mediator. But the offering of a sacrifice and the proclamation of the remedial plan of salvation, though opening the doors of mercy, do not of themselves save men. Man is not only guilty, he is polluted, and Jesus Christ came into the world to save sinners, not in, but from their sins, to place man as a sinner in a new and hopeful relation to Divine Justice and holiness. He has not instituted a system of salvation, of power, founded on prerogative, for if salvation could have been accomplished thus He needed not to die, and moreover, if salvation by prerogative had been possible, the death on the cross would be more like a tragedy than an atonement. Whatever comfort those who indulge a hope of such a salvation may find in the speculation, there is certainly no intimation in the word of God that He ever has, or ever will save by such means. It is not such a salvation which my text declares, but a salvation provided by, or according to the mercy of God and applied by the Holy Ghost. Saved, according to His mercy " by the washing of regeneration and the renewing of the Holy Ghost." " Marvel not," said Christ to Nicodemus, " that I said unto thee ye must be born again." Sin did more for man than to involve him in guilt—it corrupted and slew him. Morally he became a lost being. Not about to be, not in danger of being, but already, and in so far as his own power of recovery was concerned, irretrievably lost. This is his condition as declared by the Holy Scriptures and as such the Son of Man came to seek and to save him, by stretching between him and eternal loss a bleeding hand which he might grasp and live. This doctrine of loss, it is true, is not agreeable to human pride. Few men, if any, are unwilling to admit some moral taint, some inward bias towards evil, some corruption of the affections, but to be told that "in the flesh dwelleth no good thing," is too humiliating to human pride. Yet this is the doctrine of the Gospel and therefore an essential principle in Christian ethics, and there can be no evangelical faith in the Lord Jesus without its recognition. Human loss, if it had not involved the loss of all spiritual life, would be a much less serious fact than it is as it would involve less serious consequences, for the loss of spiritual life implies the loss of that distinctive quality which constituted the image of God, and which being forfeited carried with it the loss of all good. The crime of treason, unlike any other, attaints estates, as well as persons, and imperils both lord and heritage. Man's fall was ruinous, because it began at the very centre of his being. He failed in the loyalty of his love when he suspected the goodness of his Creator and the wisdom and justice of the prohibition under which He had placed him, and love failing, its twin sister, trust, perished with it. Disobedience was a step further on. The breach had already been made. The plucking and eating of the forbidden fruit was its development. All that followed—the loss of Eden, and the heritage of sorrow, disease and death—were necessary consequences of the spiritual change which the transgression involved. Corruption followed death as its fountain and overspread both home and inhabitant, for when—

> " Forth reaching to the fruit, Eve plucked and ate;
> Earth felt the wound, and Nature from her seat,
> Sighing through all her works, gave signs of woe
> That all was lost."

The restoration of man can therefore be accomplished in no other way than by the regeneration of his moral nature, and in no other way can his lost heritage be recovered. The corrupt heart, the fountain of evil thoughts and evil deeds must be renewed or salvation is impossible. Nature teaches us that no healing is from without. The wounded surface cannot be healed by the application of salves or ointments. They may serve a useful purpose by excluding unfavourable external conditions but the healing forces are within. The heart, the fountain of physical life hears the appeal for help, and instantly along the mysterious highways which thread the entire physical structure, sends out her builders to repair the injury. So repentance of wrong and prayer and charitable deeds, and ordinances may and will do much to place the soul in conditions more favourable to the reception of the Lord Jesus as the Saviour of sinners, but if He be not admitted to His rightful throne in the heart, if the soul open not to His abiding presence all these shall become in us but sounding brass or tinkling cymbal. It is such a transformation that is wrought in the soul by the regenerating and renewing power of the Holy Ghost, not the mere forgiveness of sin, which in itself is a judicial act, and does not affect the moral nature, but simply places the sinner in a new relation to Divine Justice, nor the removal by pardon of the penalty attached to transgression ; for mere pardon, unless the conscience be dead, cannot give peace to the mind which is conscious of its guilt and that punishment has been escaped only through the interposition of mercy ; but the beginning of a new life begotten, " not of blood, nor of the will of the flesh, nor of the will of man, but of God." This new life springing up within the soul, being begotten of, and drawing its nourishment from the eternal spirit, is essentially a new creation, constituting, in all that pertains to the spiritual nature, a new man. "Old things have passed away and all things have become new." The enmity of the carnal mind is slain, the old man with his deeds is "put off," and the soul restored to its allegiance to God, and to fellowship with Him finds in Him its true portion. The current of its affections is turned away from self and things earthly and sensual, and flowing out toward God and all good, it enters upon a new existence of peace and "joy" which is "unspeakable and full of glory." That such is the nature of regeneration the Scriptures plainly teach. That such are its effects upon those who are its subjects the history of Christianity fully demonstrates. The mystery involved in this doctrine is no argument against it. Life in any form is mysterious, and except in its effects, inexplicable. What it is, philosophers and scientists have attempted to define, but the terms they employ signify nothing more than certain signs which distinguish its presence. It does not appear in the catalogue of Creation, is no finite substance which the laboratory can analyze or resolve into simpler form. Life hides itself in God with all those secrects which He only can explain. The mystery of this new birth was admitted by the Great Teacher who announced its possibility and necessity, and who disarmed the questionings of scepticism by an illustration which all may comprehend, "The wind bloweth where it listeth and thou hearest the sound thereof." In its fury it lashes the ocean into foam and bends to earth the forest monarch of a century; it drives the clouds like winged chariots through space and bears the tempest on its bosom; or, gentle as the breath of a mother over her sleeping babe, it quivers among forest leaves; we feel it kissing brow and cheek, and inhale the perfume of rose and violet with which it freights its wings, but cannot tell whence it cometh or whither it goeth. So is every one that is born of the spirit. Weighted down with the helplessness of sin, conscience-stricken and defiled, and dismayed at the hopelessness of his condition when contemplated in the presence of a holy law, in penitential sorrow the sinner prostrates himself before the cross, "faith lends its realizing light," the promises appear, the Spirit's intercessions move within him, he ventures all on Christ and cries

> "Just as I am without one plea,
> But that Thy blood was shed for me;
> And that Thou bid'st me come to Thee,
> Oh Lamb of God I come."

The golden link which binds his helpless soul to Jesus' all atoning merit, and the omnipotence of Divine Grace is fixed, and over the moral ruin which sin had wrought within him, as over the valley of dry bones from which sprang an army of living men, the Spirit breathes His living flame of love, and he who was dead in trespasses and sins is quickened into life. But how this miracle of grace is accomplished the believer cannot tell. He knows, however, by a conscious experience that a great moral change has been wrought in his soul, that love and peace and joy have taken the place of a tormenting fear and by these fruits of the spirit is assured that he is born of God, and he knows this as certainly as the blind man whose eyes Jesus opened knew that whereas he was once blind he then saw, and he knows it by as indubitable evidences.

It is thus that by the mercy of God and through the energy of the Holy Spirit we are saved, for to be saved from sin is to be saved from its consequences.

Firstly :—From condemnation. "There is therefore now no condemnation to them which are in Christ Jesus who walk not after the flesh but after the Spirit, for the law of the Spirit of Life in Christ Jesus hath made me free from the law of sin and death."

Secondly:—From the fear of death, there is a natural shrinking from the physical sufferings which are supposed to be inseparable from the dissolution of the body, which make it an object of dread, yet when the hour of trial comes from this as well as the fear of that something after death, which gives it sting, the believer is delivered. Death is to him a vanquished enemy.

> "No tyrant now but servant, whose chief task
>   Is to unbind
> The chains by which the children of the king
>   Are here confined.
> For since Christ's body rose from out the tomb
>   And sought the skies,
> To the whole race of man now joined to Him,
>   Like Him *must* rise.
> Oh! false, ungrateful words, to call the grave
>   Man's long last home!
> 'Tis but a lodging held from week to week
>   Till Christ shall come.
> It is a store, of which Christ keeps the key,
>   Where in each cell
> Are laid in hope the vestments of the souls
>   He loves so well.
> And when He comes upon His marriage morn,
>   In light arrayed,
> He will invest His own in the same forms
>   All glorious made."

Finally:—It is to be saved from the fear of Hell.

This is the fear that hath torment, a fear which is begotten by a consciousness of guilt in the eyes of a holy God and of moral unfitness to appear before His judgment bar. It is Sin which makes Hell what it is, and it is this fact which casts upon the condition of the finally impenitent a conviction of absolute hopelessness. If it could be conceived that guilt-suffering, the penalty of its own crimes, could atone for them, and that in such suffering there could be found a purifying element by which sin itself, of which transgression is the fruit, could be uprooted and destroyed, there might be some ground of encouragement to a hope that at some time in the future of the perdition of a lost soul escape would be possible, but there is no reasonable ground for such a speculation, neither in God's Word, nor in the nature of things. But he that is born of God, he upon whose soul the Holy Ghost hath exercised His regenerating and sanctifying power hath in him that perfect love which casteth out fear, "for ye have not received the spirit of bondage again to fear, but ye have received the spirit of adoption whereby we cry, 'Abba, Father.'" To the child of God heaven is assured by the fitness of his own character. There is no other possible destiny for one who bears the Divine image. His safety, his inward peace and final triumph are not questions of place or circumstance. Persecution may deprive him of liberty, may destroy his property and torture his person. Slander may cover his reputation with reproach, and Satan may pursue him as he did his Master with all the malice of which he is capable, but his character they cannot touch. There is a peculiar significance in the following words spoken by our Lord: "No man hath ascended up to heaven but he that came down from heaven, even the *Son of man*, which is in heaven." What is the meaning of the closing sentence of this quotation, if not that heaven instead of being that distant, cold intangible sphere which some suppose it, was in him, and he in heaven, and that such is the blessed state of all who are truly born of God and made children of the kingdom; not that the fulness of that final manifestation of the sons of God of which the Scriptures speak is experienced, but that the earnest of the inheritance is ours, even while we are yet in the Church militant. We are not yet admitted within the sacred walls of the Celestial City, but as we draw nigh unto them we pluck the precious fruits which cluster on the overhanging branches. This assurance is confirmed by the exceeding great and precious promises of the Scriptures. To the believer they pledge eternal life, a place at the right hand of the Father, eternal exemption from all sorrow, and eternal possession of all good. "Behold, the Tabernacle of God is with men, and he will dwell with them, and they shall be his people, and God himself shall be with them and be their God. And God shall wipe away all tears from their eyes; and there shall be no more death, neither sorrow nor crying, neither shall there be any more pain: for the former things are passed away."

INDEX.

SERMON I.
THE CHURCH OF GOD.
1 Tim. iii., 14, 15........*Bishop Carman, D.D.*................... 1

SERMON II.
STRENGTH THROUGH FAITH.
Hebrews xi., 34..........*Rev. J. R. Jaques, D.D., Ph.D.* 36

SERMON III.
THE WEALTH OF TRUE BELIEVERS.
1 Cor. ii., 9-12..........*Rev. Wm. Barnett* 56

SERMON IV.
THE LATER PROPHET.
Rev. i., 13 ....*Rev. C. S. Eastman*.................... 74

SERMON V.
THE CONFESSION OF SIN.
1 John i., 9..............*Elijah H. Pilcher, M.A., D.D.*.......... 92

SERMON VI.
SELF EXAMINATION.
2 Cor. xiii., 5............*Rev. Wm. Blair, B.A.* 109

SERMON VII.
GENUINE CHURCH PROSPERITY.

PAGE.

Acts ix., 31... .... Rev. James A. Campbell 119

SERMON VIII.
CALVARY.

Luke xxiii., 33.......... Rev. Geo. Abbs 135

SERMON IX.
THE PROFIT OF GODLINESS.

1 Tim. iv., 8 .... Rev. W. H. Graham.................. 149

SERMON X.
ABIDING IN CHRIST.

John xv., 4.............. Rev. R. E. Lund..................... 158

SERMON XI.
DAVID'S CHOICE.

2 Samuel xxiv., 14....... Rev. I. B. Aylsworth, M.A., LL.D., P.E. 165

SERMON XII.
SINNERS ADMONISHED.

Jer. vi., 16.............. Rev. A. T. Ferguson.................. 183

SERMON XIII.
THE GOSPEL MINISTRY.

2 Tim. ii., 15............ Rev. Thomas Webster, D.D. 190

SERMON XIV.
PAUL'S EXPERIENCE AND PROSPECTS.

Phil. iii., 13, 14 .... Rev. George Miller..................... 205

SERMON XV.
CERTAINTY IN CHRIST AND CHRISTIANITY.

Revelation v., 12........*Rev. S. Card*........................... 218

SERMON XVI.
WINNING SOULS.

Proverbs xi., 30. ....*Rev. A. D. Traveller, P.E.*............ 229

SERMON XVII.
THE NECESSITY AND SUFFICIENCY OF THE ATONEMENT.

Tim. 1., 15..............*Rev. E. Lounsbury*..................... 240

SERMON XVIII.
DIVINE COMPANIONSHIP.

Ps. xxiii., 4 ....*Rev. Wm. Service* 250

SERMON XIX.
MAN AND THE DAYSMAN.

Paul, Job.............. *Rev. E. I. Badgley, B.D., LL.D.* 266

SERMON XX.
THE PRAISES OF THE LORD.

Ps. cxxxv. 1-5 ....*Rev. James Gardiner, P.E.*............. 287

SERMON XXI.
SALVATION BY GRACE.

Titus iii., 5.............*Rev. G. S. Stone, D.D.*................ 300